The foundations
of
business organisation

to

Brook Street,

This book is du

Prepared in association with
the
Coventry Business School

Stanley Thornes (Publishers) Ltd

Text and original line illustrations © Tony Shafto 1990

First published in 1990 by:
Stanley Thornes (Publishers) Ltd
Ellenborough House
Wellington Street
CHELTENHAM GL50 1YW

97 98 99 00 01 / 10 9 8 7 6 5

British Library Cataloguing in Publication Data

Shafto, T. A. C. (Thomas Anthony Cheshire) 1929 –
    The foundations of business organisation.
    1. Business firms. Organisation
    I. Title   II. Coventry Business School
    658.11

ISBN 0-7487-0538-4

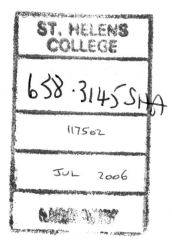

Printed and bound in Great Britain by
Scotprint Ltd, Musselburgh

Preface

The foundations of business organisation was originally planned to provide the core text in a multi-media, semi-distance foundation course for the first year of a B. A. (Business Administration) degree, offered by the Coventry Polytechnic in association with a number of partner colleges.

The course was then adopted by other degree schemes within the polytechnic where it was desired to provide a broad understanding of the essential elements of business organisation for students studying specialist and technical subjects such as computer science and engineering. Students are introduced to some of the pressures for business growth and the managerial complexities which result from successful expansion. They are also shown the contribution made by each of the major managerial functions of production, finance, personnel management, purchasing and marketing. Throughout, they are encouraged to observe and think about business practice and relate this to their own experience.

Clearly this course was meeting a widely felt need and it was modified for publication as a general text, independently from its original supporting material. This published version can be used either as a normal text book or as a course for self-study under the general guidance of the tutor.

When writing this text I recorded a series of interviews with practising business managers in a variety of business organisations and I would like to record my thanks to the following people and organisations for making these possible: A M Electronic Office Equipment; Mick King of Equity and Law; Robin Verso and John Jackson of the Coventry City Treasurer's Department; Simon Page of Flavel-Leisure Ltd and especially to Sir Peter Holmes, Chairman of The 'Shell' Transport and Trading Co. for his generous time and encouragement. This series of interviews is still planned to continue so perhaps I should give advance thanks to those who do not yet realise that they are intended victims.

Thanks are also due to the National Westminster and Barclays Banks for permission to reproduce material and particularly to Richard Gamble of Barclays Commercial Services Limited for making some valuable, constructive comments on part of unit 4.

For their invaluable assistance in turning a distance learning course into a working text book I must also thank Tania Hackett, freelance editor, Bill Boswell of the Teaching Resources Unit of Coventry Polytechnic and Brian Carvell, publishing director of Stanley Thornes.

Finally I would like to thank the management of the Coventry Business School for providing the time, resources and imaginative co-operation in this innovative project. The School, incidentally, will be happy to provide further advice and information concerning the support material used with this course.

Tony Shafto *Coventry Business School 1990*

Contents

1
Organisations in the modern economy

Organisations

What is an organisation?

Organisation is one of the many words which you may assume you understand but then find it difficult to define. Nevertheless, definition is important because you need to know what you are talking about and because it will contain elements which are likely to need further explanation and discussion. It is possible to build up a definition.

- Is it a group of people? Yes, it involves people and this is of fundamental importance but, if you look out of the window and see a group of people chatting in the street they clearly do not form an organisation. In a few minutes they disperse and go their separate ways.
- Is it a group of people coming together for a common purpose? This brings you closer. All the group members have something in common and are held together until the purpose has been fulfilled. But would a football crowd or a bus queue be an organisation? People are coming together to see the match or catch the bus but they are hardly organised. Something is still missing from the definition.
- Is it a group of people held together by an agreed structure involving the acceptance of agreed rules and a system of authority and seeking to pursue a specific objective or set of objectives? This much tighter definition eliminates the group in the street, the football crowd and the bus queue and it adds to the idea of people coming together the fact that they are pursuing definite objectives and are bound by a structure involving the acceptance of rules and authority.

You now have a definition which contains people, structure, rules and objectives. This covers a wide range of structures from the local sports club and its committees to Parliament and the Armed Forces.

The economic organisation

Notice that, at this stage, the term business organisation has been avoided in favour of the wider term 'economic organisation' in order to include both public and private sector organisations. It is necessary to understand these terms.

- **Private sector** organisations are those which are owned and controlled by groups of people acting in pursuit of their own, private, objectives.
- **Public sector** organisations are those which are formed under the authority of the State to pursue objectives established by the political machinery of the State.

The full significance of the term 'economic' will be examined later but at this point it is necessary to accept that it relates to the use or employment of scarce economic resources such as people and physical materials. The organisation brings these together to pursue a definite objective, involving the meeting of an expressed need of the community or people in that community.

The differences between public and private sector organisations, therefore, depends on ownership and control of resources and on who sets the organisational objectives.

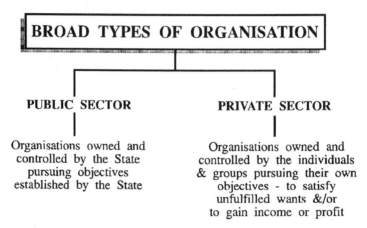

Figure 1.1

TEST YOUR UNDERSTANDING

1   How would you classify the following organisations?
    British Coal; ICI; The Motor Agents Association; Eton College; Coventry Polytechnic; The Department of Health and Social Security?
2   What do you think are the objectives of the bodies listed in Question 1?

Economic organisations

Organisational objectives

Why should a group of private individuals come together to form an organisation? Clearly they do so to pursue an objective or objectives shared by all members of the group. If the common objective is to play football then the group forms a football club and or team(s). To qualify as an economic organisation the group must be pursuing objectives which meet economic needs, i.e. to provide goods or services for which people in the community are prepared to sacrifice their own resources. The term business organisation also describes this type of group.

What motivates people in the group to come together? There are two possible reasons; either because they see this as a way

- to satisfy economic needs which otherwise would not be met, or
- to achieve their own personal economic objectives which, in modern society, usually means securing incomes or profits.

These two possibilities are important because they help to explain the emergence of such organisations as building societies, retail co-operatives, mutual life assurance societies and friendly societies, all of which would otherwise be difficult to explain but which are too important to ignore and they also help us to understand the driving force which has assisted in creating the modern, complex economic community.

Temporary and permanent business organisations

The earliest business organisations were usually temporary in that they were set up to achieve specific and limited objectives and when these were achieved they disbanded. In the UK. up to around the mid-nineteenth century, groups of merchants formed themselves in to 'companies' to finance specific voyages. They would purchase or more usually, hire a ship, equip it and buy goods to trade during the voyage. One of the group would be the master of the ship and he would be given written instructions as to where, what and roughly how long, he should trade. Any one merchant might be a member of several different 'companies' of this kind. The objective was to obtain goods that would sell in the home country and, of course, to provide profits for the merchants. Early building societies also had specific objectives. A group of people would come together to share their resources so that all could build a house. When the last member gained his house the society ceased to exist.

Early manufacturing organisations were also fairly fluid. Wool merchants obtained orders and arranged for the wool to be produced and made up into the garments they could sell. The merchants provided work for large numbers of spinners, weavers and other specialists but they did not combine them into a permanent organisation. As industry and trade developed these loose structures could not meet the demands for mass-produced, standardised goods and more permanent organisations developed, bringing workers more directly under the control of an authority structure of managers and supervisors. Increasing reliance on power-driven machinery, first water and then steam, brought a rapid movement towards the industrial organisation recognised today, with the owners controlling what is produced, how it is produced, providing the means of production (the buildings and equipment) and in return gaining the profits created by the organisation.

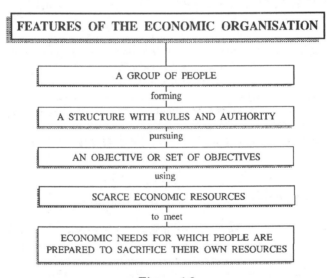

Figure 1.2

TEST YOUR UNDERSTANDING

3   How would you explain the existence of the following organisations:
    The Women's Institutes; St John's Ambulance Brigade; The Scout and Guide Associations?

4   In terms of the definitions used so far would you describe these as 'economic organisations'?

The significance of profit

It is a feature of the economic organisation that it is capable of adding value to the materials it uses. The farmer who picks, sorts, cleans and puts potatoes into weighed bags expects to sell the potato crop for more money than he or she paid for the seed, fertiliser and the labour involved in growing and packaging the crop. This value added by the activity of the organisation is, in broad terms, profit.

If you ignore the activities of the 'non-profit seeking organisations,' such as the building societies and others already mentioned, you will recognise that most business organisations in the private sector of the economy are formed by people who hope to enjoy a share of the profits created by successful business activity. Profit is an important incentive for inducing people to create business organisations. At the same time, if you regard the people employed by the organisation as part of it, then they too are largely motivated by their desire to earn income and to pursue their own personal objectives - which usually require an income for their fulfilment.

Profit is discussed later in more detail, but it is desirable at this stage to stress the importance of profit as a prime motivation of business activity. At the same time you must avoid the temptation of thinking that profit, or the desire to increase income, is the only incentive for people to work. If this were the case it would be difficult to explain the origins of the non-profit seeking societies, such as the co-operatives, building and mutual life assurance societies, and the many voluntary organisations which depend on the work of largely unpaid volunteers.

Organisations and objectives in the public sector

Earlier in this unit it was suggested that economic organisations in the private sector of the economy were formed when a group of people came together to meet needs or to achieve personal objectives. These objectives need to be examined more closely but before doing so it is necessary to pay some attention to organisations in the public sector.

Here the organisation is also set up to meet a need but the need is expressed, and the decision to meet it is made, through the political machinery of the State. The type or style of organisation is also decided through the same machinery. In the UK there are three main types of public sector organisations. They are:

1 Part of the machinery or structure of government

These organisations include the administrative departments of both central and local government, for example, the Department of Trade and Industry or the Export Credits Guarantee Department (central) and the various departments of local government such as environmental health, education, and the social services. They also include organisations which may operate with a limited degree of independence but which are financed by and directly responsible to central or local government and which must pursue objectives established by the machinery of government. Examples are schools, most non-commercial museums and art galleries, public libraries, police forces and regional health authorities. Although it is often convenient to distinguish between organisations controlled by central government and those controlled by local government authorities, in practice it is often difficult to do so convincingly. As central government has come to contribute a major share of the finance of local authorities it has tended to insist on having a significant say in control over how that finance is used and the organisations which use it. Schools, for example, are mostly under local authority control but central government has gained a significant degree of control over what is taught in schools and it also controls the payment structure of those who teach in them.

Notice the opportunities this form of dual responsibility provides for friction where, say, the educational objectives of the local and central government authorities differ. Some schools can even have a third controlling authority. Schools owing their origins to a Church must also recognise a limited degree of authority exercised by that Church which may appoint its own representatives to ensure that the Church's objectives are not ignored.

2 Established by legislative statute

In the UK this refers to organisations set up by Act of Parliament, and was the method by which the public corporations, were established in order to administer the national-ised industries. The objectives of these bodies are established by the statutory act which brought them into being but they can usually be changed, modified or interpreted in greater detail by a government minister acting under authority granted by the legislature, or in many countries by that country's constitution. For example, the original objectives set for most of the nationalised industries were rather vague, mainly because many of their financial and management problems were not foreseen at the time of nationalisation. These objectives were subsequently modified by a series of White Papers (documents setting out government policy), each imposing financial objectives which became increasingly specific. Each also tended to move a little further away from the original ideals of the people who brought the industries into the public sector. Objectives can thus change as, perhaps, they must do if the organisation is to survive in a changing economic, social and political environment.

3 Quasi autonomous national government organisations (Quangos)

These are bodies set up by the central government under the authority of the legislature (Parliament) with specific objectives and with a significant degree of independence in carrying out these objectives. Examples include the Monopolies and Mergers Commis-sion and the regulatory bodies established to represent the public interest and oversee the performance of certain privatised organisations, e.g. OFTEL (overseeing British Telecom). The degree of actual independence of the central government which quangos can enjoy is limited by their dependence on the government for finance and by the fact that most members with executive authority tend to be appointed on fairly short term contracts, with renewal in the hands of the government.

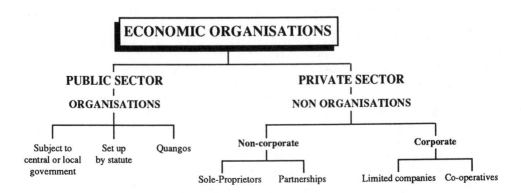

Figure 1.3

TEST YOUR UNDERSTANDING

5   One of the problems of the public corporations under State control was their inflexibility in the face of changing technological, social and political conditions. Taking an example such as British Coal suggest ways in which a public corporation might have adapted to change had it not been nationalised.

6   How are decisions about the use of scarce economic resources made in the public sector? Who makes these decisions? On what principles are these decisions made?

7   Suggest reasons for the transfer of power from the local government authorities to the central government that has taken place over much of the past half century.

8   Name two surviving nationalised industries. Suggest reasons why these have not been privatised. Is there a strong case for retaining these industries in the public sector?

Organisations and objectives in the private sector

The majority of economic organisations in the private sector are operating some form of business activity with a view to securing profit or income for the owners; these are referred to as business organisations. In the UK anyone can start a business provided that any special conditions relating to the activity are met, e.g. lawyers, medical doctors, passenger service vehicle operators and others claiming to have special skills - or with a special potentiality for harming the public - must have approved qualifications or be licensed by the State. Trading with a view to profit does not, in itself, form an organisation. The person who buys and sells antiques in his or her spare time is not an organisation. Only when that person starts to enter into a business relationship with others as an employer or partner does an organisation start to emerge. It is usually convenient to distinguish two main classes of organisation; those which are constituted as separate entities, legally distinct from the people setting them up or owning them and thus recognised to have corporate status, and those which do not have this degree of legal individuality.

Non-corporate organisations

- **Sole proprietors**
  Although there is a financial obligation for the owner to maintain a degree of separation between personal and business assets there is no strict legal distinction between the responsibilities and assets of the business owner and the business, particularly where the business is owned and controlled by one person only, as a sole proprietor. In this case, of course, the business objectives are simply those of the proprietor. The objectives can be as varied as the people who enter business life. One important objective must clearly be to make a profit. Unless the business generates profits it cannot continue to exist for more than a very limited period. Whether this is always the only, or even the most important, objective is less certain. Economic theory has traditionally assumed that profit is the reward for successful risk taking. The owner of a non-corporate business is certainly taking a risk. He or she has to accept unlimited responsibility for all the debts of the enterprise. The risk of losing virtually all one's possessions is certainly a real one, as many unsuccessful business proprietors have discovered. The lure of profit can be very powerful and can induce people to accept these risks, to work long hours and incur the many headaches inseparable from running an organisation.
  Nevertheless it must also be admitted that large numbers of business owners

continue in business even though their profits are relatively small - smaller perhaps than the incomes they could earn if they were employed by larger firms. On the other hand there are also business owners who continue to run their organisations even when they have accumulated sufficient wealth to provide very comfortable incomes without having to work at all.

This suggests that profit and income are not the only motives for running a business. Social psychologists frequently suggest other objectives and sources of work satisfaction that are not confined to business proprietors but also motivate workers. Some of these will be examined later, but at this stage it is sufficient to recognise that there are likely to be quite powerful non-economic motives both for working and for owning a business enterprise and any attempt to analyse business objectives on the assumption that the only objective is profit can lead to some false conclusions and predictions.

- **Partnerships**
Most of the comments made about sole proprietors apply also to business partners. When two or more people combine together in some form of business activity with a view to profit they form a partnership. They thus also form an organisation whose rules they determine for themselves, either expressly by making a partnership agreement, or by implication through the way they conduct their affairs over a period of time. In the comparatively rare cases where there is dispute or uncertainty and the terms of an agreement cannot be discovered then legal rules established by statutes and legal cases apply. In almost all cases partners have to accept full responsibility for the debts of their enterprise, even if that means personal financial disaster, whatever private agreement they may have reached among themselves. A partnership, therefore, rests on trust and integrity between the partners. If this does not exist it is far better - and safer - to dissolve the partnership.

It is essential to have agreement over the objectives of the partnership organisation and over the powers and responsibilities of each partner in the pursuit of these objectives. In human terms this can cause problems because the personal objectives of each partner can rarely be identical. Some may not be prepared to admit to themselves what their true motives are. The possibility of conflict is thus very real. Apart from the highly structured professional partnerships such as those of legal and accountancy firms which usually have a clear structure of control and authority, the casualty rate among business partnerships, including married teams, is fairly high, usually arising from lack or failure of trust or clash of objectives. This, however, should not obscure the fact that large numbers of business partnerships operate very successfully over long periods and that for most small business organisations, where large sums of money are not being risked, this is the most satisfactory and flexible form of organisation.

Legal business corporations - limited companies

- **Private companies**
The limited company is a device to enable business organisations to gain some important benefits from legal corporate status. One of the most important of these is the privilege of limited liability whereby the owners stand to lose only the amount of money that they agree to invest in the company - usually the amount paid for shares (see unit 8). Contrast this with the full responsibility, known as unlimited liability, that partners and sole owners have for the debts of their enterprises. Other benefits include the company's right to own property and sue and be sued in its own name. Most industrial countries have similar business organisations with this type of legal corporate status. The private company structure was devised to provide a framework for the small organisation where this needed to have limited liability but, while most are still small and many owned and controlled by two or three members of the same

family, it is now recognised that some very large organisations can retain private company status as long as they can obtain all the finance they need without having to advertise to the public to sell their shares or loan stock.

- **Public companies**
  The public company is able to advertise its shares and loan stocks for sale to the public and, in effect, this opens up the resources of the various capital markets centred on the London International Stock Exchange and, if the company's resources are sufficient, to the chain of other major stock exchanges throughout the world. There is thus no financial limit to the growth in size of the successful public company. There is a lower limit of capital of £50 000, of which a quarter must be actually paid for in full, known as paid up, but most public companies are much larger than this. Although the main *legal* distinction is between private and public companies the main practical distinction is between small and large companies; a number of important aspects of this are examined later. The formal overall objective of all companies is to operate in the interests of the shareholders who can be regarded as the legal owners of the organisation. The shareholder interest is considered to be profit. More precise objects relating to the activities that the company is authorised to undertake are contained in one of the compulsory documents of incorporation, the **Memorandum of Association**. However, this document is now usually worded very widely and normally contains a phrase or phrases giving discretion to extend or modify the objects, e.g. ' as the company may from time to time determine'. Consequently it becomes important for the controlling managerial body to establish company objectives and ensure that these are known and understood by all those involved in seeking to achieve them.

The non-profit seeking societies

These should not be entirely ignored. They include the building societies, mutual life assurance societies the Co-operatives and the Friendly societies. Their existence is evidence that profit is not the sole motivating force for the emergence and development of business organisations. Nevertheless it must also be admitted that, with the exception of the building societies, their numbers and influence has tended to decrease since around the middle of this century. More recently, with the flotation of the Abbey National building society as a public limited company (a move which seems likely to be followed by several others) these too seem to be reaching the logical conclusion of a long period during which financial return and operating efficiency have become increasingly important objectives. If these trends continue the societies could become simply part of the historical development of the industrial market economy and no longer a challenge to the belief that profit is the prime motivator of business enterprise.

TEST YOUR UNDERSTANDING

9   What are the basic differences between a legal corporation and a non-corporate business organisation?
10 Suggest reasons why many people seem to be content to run their own small businesses even though they could probably earn more working for another employer.
11 If profit is the main motivating force for engaging in business how do you account for the existence of the following: building societies, co-operative societies; the National Trust; The Red Cross?

Functions of economic organisations

Meeting objectives

For an economic organisation to survive it must fulfil the objectives of those who own and control it. To achieve this in the long run it must meet a need of the community, for which the community is prepared to sacrifice some of its resources. In the public sector this means that the organisation must fulfil the objectives which were established by the political machinery of the State. While, left to itself, the community might not fully approve of the resources devoted to it, actual hostility to the extent of undermining the stability of the established political machinery is likely to lead to the end of the organisation, a radical change of structure, or a transfer to the private sector. To survive in the private sector organisations must attract sufficient revenue to meet the costs incurred by the organisation with sufficient surplus to meet the profit objectives of the owners.

You might also wish to add that the organisation must meet the aspirations of the people who work in it, if it is to attract and retain workers with the skills and abilities to carry out the work necessary to meet the expectations of its customers. The higher the quality of the work performed the more important will this aspect become. An accountancy firm, for instance, is unlikely to survive very long if it cannot employ competent accountants. This is one reason why accountants valuable to their firms are frequently offered the prospect of becoming partners and hence part-owners of the enterprise. In fact all service organisations, whose survival in a competitive private sector market depends on customers being pleased with the service they receive, must pay particular attention to securing and retaining high quality workers. In a radio programme in 1989 the head of a major international hotel chain commented that he believed that the company needed to look after its staff and these, in turn, looked after the business. A manufacturing company, in which the majority workers never meet the actual buyers of the products they make, may consider that worker satisfaction is a matter of little importance. However, a car manufacturing company which gains a reputation for producing too high a proportion of 'Friday cars' starts to lose business, suffers losses and soon has to face the prospect of being taken over by a more successful company. A manufacturer of components whose products do not go direct to the final customer must meet delivery dates and ensure that the components do not give rise to quality problems, otherwise orders from the product manufacturer will be cancelled.

Ultimately all economic organisations must satisfy these three groups of people, those who own and control it, those who purchase or finance through taxation the final product and those whose skills and co-operation are necessary for continued, trouble free production and for producing a product of the necessary quality.

The organisation of production

It may seem superfluous to say so but one of the most important functions of any organisation is to organise! The economic organisation has to organise the resources it needs to produce its product in such a way that objectives can be satisfied as explained earlier.

Economists usually use the concept of **factors of production** to mean economic resources, i.e. those resources or elements which are combined in order to produce the articles and/ or services on whose provision the continued survival of the organisation depends. These production factors are usually classified in the following ways:

- **Land**

  This has a double meaning. Land is used in the sense of **space**. Everyone occupies some space whenever they do anything and the business organisation is no exception. The larger it is, the more space it occupies and acquiring land of the type and in the place required can often pose significant problems to the organisation.

  Land is also used in the sense of **basic resources** which must originate in some way in the land, sea or air. Basic minerals or gases are often, therefore, included as part of the factor 'land'.

- **Capital**

  This is also used in two senses. One relates to **physical capital**, i.e. the physical resources employed in the production process. Examples are factory buildings, machinery, office equipment, word processors and so on. It is difficult to imagine any form of economic production which does not involve the use of some physical capital. The hairdresser uses scissors, clippers and a chair at the very least. Financial services seem to be incapable of coherent operation without a telephone, including, today, fax facilities! Authors in the past had quill pens, most now have word processors.

  The second, and to most people the more familiar sense, is that of **financial capital**, i.e. the money used to acquire physical capital. The organisation must have capital before it can start to produce; those who control or manage the organisation must obtain the use of capital from their own or outside sources. The need to obtain capital in advance of production is a recurring problem facing organisational management. This also means that there is often a risk of loss of capital if the organisation fails to survive. This is more than just the loss of money. The images which lasted in the minds of those who lived through the Great Depression of the 1930s were those of idle cranes rusting in the shipyards, farm machinery rusting in the fields and a forest of 'To Let' signs outside suburban houses in the industrial cities. This was the physical sign of business failure. Side by side went the less obvious but just as real hardship of retired people whose incomes from past savings fell as share values declined or disappeared and dividends declined. Some even lost their pensions in the days before protected pension funds became essential, as firms failed and were unable to maintain pension payments.

- **Labour**

  Nothing produces itself. Human effort is always necessary. This includes both physical and mental effort and usually some mixture of both with an increasing emphasis on mental labour as production becomes increasingly complex and dependent on technology. The co-ordination of work effort has always been a primary function of the economic organisation. Pre-factory manufacturing depended on the organisational skills of merchants who purchased and delivered materials to the actual producers and then collected and marketed the finished product. Sometimes, for example in the manufacture of spurs in Walsall, the merchant acted as a kind of moving production line, collecting components and passing them to the next producer in the production process at the end of which the assembled, finished spur was collected and prepared for the market. The merchant, however, was not a manager of the actual production process though, of course, he could influence it by giving more work or higher payment rates to the producers whose product was felt to be superior and whose ability to deliver on time could be trusted.

  When the work was brought into the mill and the factory the merchant became an organiser and provider of both capital and labour and responsible for managing and co-ordinating both. Mills and factories in the eighteenth and early nineteenth centuries were mostly small and the majority of business owners organised their workforces after the pattern of extended families though with a clear, if not unbridgeable division between worker and family. Workers were expected to conform to the religious beliefs and ethical standards of the owners. As factories grew in size and as the owners moved their families to the new outer suburbs developing at the edge of newly industrialised areas the physical gap between owner and worker increased with the relationship declining to one based simply on the provision of labour in return for wages. The problems of managing labour tended to increase and became a specialised function of the organisation. Further aspects of this function are examined in more detail later in the course but at this stage you should also be aware that the first organisations of labour on a large scale were those formed for military purposes. A few British army regiments still bear the names of their founders - a reminder of the days when wealthy and powerful members of the landed aristocracy raised units of the armed forces for service under the Crown. This meant recruiting, clothing, equipping, training and organising a substantial body of men. Not surprisingly, when it became necessary to form large economic organisations of people to operate railways, the post office and the police, these were modelled on the armed forces and became uniformed services with codes of discipline not too remote from their models. These origins help to explain some of the organisational and management problems that were later experienced in the railways and post office.

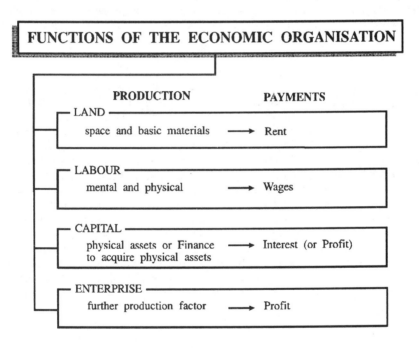

Figure 1.4

TEST YOUR UNDERSTANDING

12 Has the trend towards increasing use of capital in business made labour more, or less important to the business organisation?

13 The most common explanation of the reward to the production factor capital is that it receives 'interest'. Some economists argue that its reward is 'profit'. Discuss the implications of this difference in approach.

14 How did the relationship between employer and employee change as a result of the First Industrial Revolution of the eighteenth and nineteenth centuries? What changes, if any, do you think may be taking place in the current period?

Enterprise and profit

The concept of production factors was developed to explain how the earnings of the firm were apportioned. The owners of land received rent, the suppliers of capital received interest and labour received wages. These are general terms for the factor rewards, covering a range of payments by different names such as salaries, commission, royalties and so on. However, when all these payments had been made there remained, if the business was successful, a residue which was profit. It was felt that profit also was earned and could be seen as a payment to a further production factor, the one that organised and co-ordinated all the others, which took the risks of failure and losses and which could justly be rewarded if success was achieved. This fourth factor of production was described as enterprise and the person who supplied the enterprise and who received the profit was described as the **entrepreneur**.

Many economists and economics text books continue to adopt this approach and the term entrepreneur is often used to describe the initiator or owner, of any business organisation. On the other hand the concept of enterprise as a factor of production rewarded by profit, much as labour is rewarded by a wage, poses many problems, especially when it is applied to modern industrial economies.

Enterprise

The most common definitions of enterprise and entrepreneur stress the element of risk taking, probably on the grounds that a readiness to risk loss in the event of failure justifies the earning of profit when business activity results in success. However, the business manager who is frequently disposing of other people's money entrusted to the enterprise, has no brief to take risks with that money. Much of business management is concerned with reducing and avoiding risks. Awareness of the dangers of stressing risk taking has led some writers to stress instead the element of organisation, i.e. the ability to co-ordinate production factors successfully. This has the merit of recognising the part played by large scale business in the modern economy and consequently the importance of organisation to business success. Indeed some have gone further and described enterprise as a special aspect of managerial skill. It would be foolish to deny the importance of all these aspects of the art of running a business, but to use them to explain the disposal of profit comes up against the uncomfortable fact that, in modern large scale business, the people who possess and employ these attributes are not the ones who receive the profit.

Profit and the large public company

In the case of the limited company profit belongs to the shareholders. For small family companies this does not usually present major problems. The shareholders are likely to be the present, past or sometimes the future managers. These are the ones who take the risks and organise production in the way familiar to the earlier economists who developed the concept of production factors, including enterprise. It is when we come to the large public company which, today, is the dominant business organisation, that the reality begins to look rather different. In this case profit still legally belongs to the shareholders but it is purely a reward for the use of the shareholders' capital. Indeed the shareholders, as such, have no part in the management or decision making within the organisation. Few individual shareholders in large public companies have more than a vague general idea of what the company actually does and, in practice, the gain to the shareholder from owning shares in established companies arises from events outside the control of either the shareholder or the company manager, e.g. from the state of the economy, from movements in interest rates and the political fortunes of the government. Shareholders certainly take risks and have skill (or luck) if they are successful but the risks and skills are not those closely associated with the tasks of organising the activities undertaken by the companies in which they have a shareholding.

A further look at profit and enterprise

Enterprise in the context of the large public company is examined later. At this stage we look at enterprise and profit in more general terms. If we can separate the ideas of profit and enterprise and look at both in the context of modern business activity we may be able to gain some useful insights into the importance of each.

- **Enterprise and its rewards**
  It is common today to refer to entrepreneurial attitudes and to see these as an important attribute at all levels of business activity. The meaning is not so much willingness to risk money as to depart from rigid custom and practice, to detect opportunities and to be willing to seize them in ways that require some personal initiative and energy. It can apply to both the public and private sectors and be shown as much by the teacher who adopts a new approach to teaching a difficult class as by the manufacturer who develops a new consumer product. The reward is by no means always profit. It can be increased income in the form of personal career progress or development or it can simply be making a difficult job simple and satisfying. One of the problems of management in large organisations is that of stimulating and harnessing this quality without introducing organisational anarchy.

- **Profit and its origins**
  Profit can arise for a number of reasons, successful enterprise or organisational skill being only two possibilities. There is no direct, in mathematical terms, functional relationship between these and the amount of profit earned. This can be contrasted with wages and interest. If you work two hours you normally expect to earn twice as much at any given wage rate as you earn for working one hour. If you lend £2000 at a given interest rate you expect to earn twice as much as you would from lending £1000. However, even if you could devise a method of measuring enterprise, you could not guarantee that your profits would rise in direct proportion to the amount displayed. They could well fall!

  Profit is one of those deceptively simple concepts which appears more difficult the more you examine it. There has been much discussion as to how it can arise and the extent to which it can be used as a measure of efficiency. Clearly it can arise from a number of very different causes but the association with monopoly tends to be very strong. Monopoly can be achieved by the possession of a unique skill or quality, from innovation - being first in the field with a new idea or product - from the ruthless elimination of competitors or from chance, happening, say, to own land which suddenly becomes desirable when a new road link is planned.

  All these have implications when we come to look more closely at what is involved in business management and especially when we come to consider profit as a measure of business efficiency. By now, however, you should be ready to recognise that not only is profit an extremely important element in business but it is also quite complex and there is no simple formula to ensure that a particular activity or set of decision making techniques will guarantee a given profit return. There are no university degrees in profit making!

TEST YOUR UNDERSTANDING

15 In what ways is the enterprise-profit relationship different from the labour-wage relationship?
16 What justification can you suggest for seeing profit as a return to capital rather than to enterprise?

What is a small firm?

Enterprise and the small firm

Earlier in this unit you were invited to think about the meaning of enterprise and the idea of the entrepreneur. Most of the difficulties which arise when applying this idea in practice are associated with large firms, where it is often difficult to locate the source of enterprise and even more difficult to link risk taking directly with the receipt of profit.

These difficulties do not arise when we consider the small business which is owned and managed by one person or a small group of people, usually belonging to the same family. Here there is clearly risk taking as is shown all too often in the bankruptcy courts! The person or small group of people taking the risks are doing so largely in the hope of earning profits and although no one can say that any given input of enterprise will always be rewarded by an associated profit return, there is, nevertheless, an evident link between successful managerial enterprise and the achievement of profit.

Success in small scale business enterprise is also closely linked to skill in management. Making a desirable product of high quality or providing a high quality service are not, in themselves, guarantees that a business will be profitable. The business must be managed effectively so that earnings are greater than costs and there is continuing support from buyers of the product and suppliers of essential inputs of materials and services. What this involves is the ability to organise all the various activities that are necessary to maintain the firm as a continuing organisation. It is these activities that need to be explored at this stage.

Problems of definition

If the small firm is to be identified as a definite class of organisation some method of defining what is meant is needed. Clearly the most precise way to make this definition would be to set some form of quantity standard in terms of say, number of employees and/or the amount of capital employed by the firm.

There are two objections to this. In the first place different activities require different quantities of both labour and capital and a standard that would be fairly large in one might be very small in another. A farming organisation, for instance, that employed 100 workers would be considered large within the farming industry whereas a motor vehicle assembly plant employing only 100 workers would be thought very small indeed. A further objection arises out of changing technology. Machines relying on modern electronic advances make it possible for a small number of workers to produce at a level formerly only feasible if large numbers of people were employed. Computers and electronic, laser printing are making it possible for one or two people to produce work that would formerly have required a substantial number of people. At the same time the advances of microtechnology have been so swift and extensive that the cost of equipment is now very much less than in the early days of computers. It is becoming possible for a small organisation employing very few people and with a total capital employed of a relatively modest ratio to the average earnings of a skilled worker, to produce a volume of work that would have seemed far beyond the range of possibilities just a few decades earlier.

Given these conditions it is not too helpful to try and make a rigid definition based either on number of employees or on the value of capital employed although for some purposes this may be necessary. British employment legislation, for example, exempts firms employing fewer than twenty workers from some employment protection measures and industrial tribunals (bodies with special powers to enforce certain aspects of employment law) will also take into consideration the number of workers employed when deciding whether or not an employer's procedures for dismissing or making redundant a worker were fair and reasonable.

What really distinguishes a small from a large firm are the structures and attitudes of ownership, control and management.

The ownership of small firms

The small firm is essentially owned by one or two people or a small group of people, many of whom can be expected to belong to the same family or to a few families able to co-operate with each other. This will be the case whether the legal structure is that of sole proprietor, partnership or limited company. The limited company is a very flexible structure. In the case of small companies the main body of shares can be expected to be held by just a few people who will also be or have close links with the controlling directors and the senior, executive managers of the business. There will not, therefore, be any effective division between ownership and control of the enterprise. Although the legal responsibilities and functions of shareholders, directors and managers are different, the dominant people will normally hold all three positions. They may wear different hats for these different functions but the head underneath each hat is the same!

There is one fairly modern development that can affect the ownership and control of some firms. In order to acquire the equipment they need in order to start or extend production some companies whose future growth and profit potentialities look promising may obtain the support of merchant banks or other financial institutions able to provide risk (venture) capital. Whereas in the past such firms were often able to borrow the finance they needed at fixed rates of interest, experience of high inflation rates has made that less likely and the providers of venture capital are now more likely to want to hold a substantial proportion of the company's shares. Often they insist on owning at least 51 per cent in order to have legal control of the business. Having a controlling interest in the equity instead of being just lenders or debenture holders, offers the suppliers of capital some important advantages including:

- A proportional share of the increased profit made possible by the capital they have provided.
- The legal right to take control of the enterprise should it appear to be heading for disaster or suffering from mismanagement. As debenture holders or lenders they would have no rights until the company failed to pay interest due on the debt and then they would normally have no legal rights beyond insisting on the sale of any 'secured' property to repay the loan. This would usually finish the enterprise and cause losses for other 'unsecured' creditors, some of whom might be influential customers of the bank.
- The legal right to insist on changes in the board of directors and so secure changes in management style and structure, e.g. if the company was very successful and growing to a size where a changed style of management was essential to avoid organisational breakdown.
- Sufficient influence to be able to offer advice and ensure that this was taken seriously over matters felt to be important to the future profitability of the enterprise.

Clearly the acceptance of financial support in the form of equity share represents a substantial surrender of full independence on the part of the owners of a small company. As earlier noted the desire to be independent is a powerful motivating force accounting for many able entrepreneurs leaving large organisations to form their own businesses, so this tendency does represent something of a problem for many successful business owners.

One partial safeguard of independence is the ability, now provided by company law, to issue ordinary shares that the company can re-purchase in the future. Thus, if the company is successful and the owner-managers wish to regain legal control, perhaps to prevent take-over by a larger company or to maintain their own policies which they feel are not being sufficiently respected by the bankers, they can re-purchase sufficient shares to resume full effective control of the enterprise. Of course, if the company is not successful it will not generate the funds needed for this and the suppliers of capital retain the means of taking whatever action they believe necessary.

The control and management of small firms

It has already been suggested that the essential feature of a small firm is that ownership, control and management are effectively in the same hands. This is not difficult within the structure of the limited company. The dominant shareholders simply ensure that they, or their nominees, are appointed to be directors of the company and thus assume control of the enterprise. Often the principal shareholder is the managing director and as such, under the usual 'constitution' of the company (contained in a written set of rules known as the **Articles of Association**), has considerable executive powers to act in the name of the board. In the small company most of the directors are likely to be **working directors** and as such also have specific managerial roles within the company. Control and management are thus normally in the same hands.

This is another important feature of the small firm. The senior managers hold their positions because of their financial contributions to the enterprise or because of their possession of skills or knowledge believed to be essential to its success - or simply because of their position as a member of the controlling family or one of these families. This means that the **organisational structure has to be moulded around the presence of the people who are its managers**. The people dominate the structure which is shaped by their individual interests and abilities. Often the managing director is a dominant personality whose influence, attitudes and objectives pervade every aspect of the enterprise.

TEST YOUR UNDERSTANDING

17 Write down a single sentence definition of what you understand by the term 'a small firm'.
18 What are the benefits and risks of holding equity in a small firm as opposed to making a loan?
19 Suggest reasons why successive British governments have sought to encourage the development of small firms.

Strengths and weaknesses of management in small firms

Management strengths

The great strength of small firm management is the **personal identification of owner-managers with the firm**. After all, their wealth and careers are usually locked into the firm and depend on the success of the firm. The commitment of the successful and enterprising manager is usually far greater than is found in large organisations, as work for the firm is part of the owner's life.

The manager has to be a great deal more **flexible** than the large company specialist. The company is unlikely to be able to afford to employ a manager for each of the various specialised aspects of management, i.e. purchasing, production, marketing, finance and personnel. Consequently managerial functions have to cut across these specialist boundaries. The attitude that a person has to do whatever job is necessary and not stick to a particular function spreads down throughout the firm so that demarcation lines between tasks either don't exist or are far weaker than in large organisations. The range of a person's work is limited by time, ability and availability and not by artificial restrictions of past training or current trade union rules.

Flexibility also often extends to attitudes towards product and market development. This can be important in times of adversity. It is notable that areas containing a high proportion of small, owner-managed firms have suffered far less in periods of economic depression than those where employment is concentrated among a relatively few large organisations. Leicester is one example, and the resilience and speed with which the Birmingham area recovered from the steep decline of manufacturing, particularly motor manufacturing in the early 1980s, adapting to a changed economic environment contrasts with the long-term problems of some other regions of Britain. Both Leicester and Birmingham have a high proportion of small owner-managed firms. The reasons for this resilience are:

- Flexibility which gave them the ability to adapt quickly to new needs and opportunities instead of wasting resources on political pressures to preserve a departing past.
- Owner commitment which ensured that the owners stayed with their firms and made every effort to ensure adaptation and survival. Collapse of the firm would mean collapse of their own wealth and living standards as well as job losses for employees. Large firms were more ready to close small subsidiaries and make their managers and workers redundant.

Employee relations depend, of course, on the personal attitudes of managers but for the successful, established small firm they are usually good, otherwise success is difficult to achieve. It is difficult for owner-managers not to get to know their long-serving workers as individuals. They may get to know their families and recruitment to the firm is often made through personal connections with present or past employees. The alienation and indifference sometimes found in large organisations is rarely a feature of the small firm.

Management weaknesses

Some of the management strengths become weaknesses when the firm begins to grow. Managerial problems, and changes that become necessary with growth, are examined later but at this stage it is necessary to outline a number of important weaknesses.

- **Lack of specialist skills**
  This deficiency can weaken the whole structure of the workforce. It can for example lead to legal problems if managers are not aware of legal requirements relating to product design, employment, finance and other issues.

- **Failure to develop lines of responsibility**
  Senior managers may be aware that their work load has to be shared but they often fail to establish clear functions which can be fully transferred to an appropriately trained and experienced manager. Autocratic managing directors find it almost impossible to devolve responsibility and find it difficult to obtain suitable assistance.

This is often because they are looking for subservient mirror images of themselves - a clear impossibility. Senior managers sometimes fail to understand the nature of the specialised functions they have been undertaking and so find it impossible to establish a managerial structure which can exist without their own personal involvement. Consequently the more assistance they try to obtain the more their own work load increases until the structure collapses.

- **Failure to provide for the succession of key workers**
  These may be managers or workers on whose special skills the quality of the product or the loyalty of customers depends. If any of these leave, fall chronically ill or die the firm can be in serious trouble. Eventually, of course, age will also take its toll and firms can decline as the energy and enterprise of a once successful business leader decline. Loyalty to long serving managers and workers can even keep them employed when their work has become a burden to the firm.

  All these weaknesses, and others which can be as varied as the personalities involved, can be summed up as **failure to build an effective organisational and managerial structure**. This issue is examined more closely in the next unit

TEST YOUR UNDERSTANDING

20   Many people who have been trained in a large firm find it extremely difficult to adapt to conditions in a small firm. At the same time those who have spent some years in small firms find working in a large firm very frustrating. Suggest reasons for this.
21   How would you justify the view that flexibility is one of the greatest strengths of the small firm?
22   There is evidence to suggest that employer-employee relations are better in small firms than in large. Do you agree that this is the case? Explain why you agree or disagree.

NOTES TO QUESTIONS

Questions 1 and 2
British Coal is a public sector organisation with the objective of producing coal and meeting such financial objectives as may be set by the Government. ICI is a private sector business organisation with the general objective of making profits for its shareholders. The MAA is an organisation in the private sector but it is not a business. Its objective is to advance the interests of members - the Motor Agents (wholesale and retail distributors of motor vehicles). Eton College is an organisation in the private sector with the objective of providing an education to the standard expected by the fee paying parents. Coventry Polytechnic is an organisation in the public sector with the objective of providing higher education courses approved by the various educational regulation agencies established by the Government.; The DHSS is a department of the Government with the objective of administering the health and social security policies of the Government as approved and authorised by Parliament.

Questions 3 and 4
The Women's Institutes, St John's Ambulance Brigade and the Scout and Guide Associations are all voluntary organisations established to meet community needs not fully met by other State owned or business organisations. They were all founded by people who wished to influence attitudes and behaviour of people in the community and all have a common ideal of service to the community. They rely heavily on the services of unpaid volunteers. These (and the organisations listed in Question 1) would all fall within the definition so far provided of an 'economic organisation'. This is because they

all use resources such as people and finance in order to meet perceived community needs. They are not, of course, profit seeking organisations.

Question 5

One of the lessons of privatisation has been that it does give organisations greater flexibility in the use of resources. Associated British Ports and BAA for example have been able to make use of their land and property in ways that would not have been possible under nationalisation. On the other hand British Coal has been confined to the single activity of mining coal, thus tying it to a declining industry. Had it not been restricted in this way it is legitimate to wonder whether it might not have entered other sectors of the fuel industry, gas or oil production perhaps. It might also have been able to use its land in some areas to develop tourist properties. Generally it might have been able to develop and prosper without being tied so firmly to the single activity of coal mining.

Question 6

Almost all public sector organisations have to make decisions that are economic in the sense that they involve the use of scarce resources and thus have both resource and opportunity costs. These decisions, however, are made through the political machinery of the State usually for political or social reasons. Economic costs are often of secondary importance but they cannot be ignored and frequently they undermine the political and social objectives of the decisions.

The question of who makes the decisions is an interesting one which cannot always be easily answered if you want to look at the reality rather than just the apparent position. Officially all public sector decisions must be taken under some kind of legislative authority - ultimately authority given by Parliament which, however, may delegate a great many practical decisions to government ministers.

Elected representatives to Parliament or to Local Authorities cannot actually run organisations so that, in reality, it is the organisational managers in public sector bodies that make most of the decisions affecting the use of scarce resources. Elected representatives rarely have the specialised knowledge to challenge the 'experts' employed by public sector organisations. These all tend to claim that they are operating within clear rules and constraints established by law. Nevertheless it is they who interpret these rules and constraints and it is very evident that officials in different regional areas frequently interpret the same rules very differently. Decision making within the public sector does, in fact, present a great many problems.

Question 7

It is partly the lack of uniformity between similar bodies in different areas that has led to greater centralisation and the passing of power to central government. Perhaps, more important, however, has been the increased financial involvement of central government which has frequently found itself having to fund operations to which it has been committed by local authority decisions over which it has not been able to exercise effective control. This has led to changes made through Parliament, the general trend of change since the 1930s being to transfer power to the centre. Education, the last great area of local control, is now under considerable pressure to become more controlled by central government.

Question 8

In the summer of 1989 the main surviving nationalised industries were: British Rail, British Coal, the Post Office and British Nuclear Fuels. The Electricity Boards and Water Authorities were being prepared for early privatisation. Given the earlier privatisation of the other former transport and power industries (air, shipping, road and gas) there is no purely economic reason why either coal or the railways should remain in the public sector. If it is argued that British Rail, as a natural monopoly and thus, by nature, not a competitive market, should remain nationalised then these arguments would support the re-nationalisation of gas and telephones.

Again it is difficult to defend on economic grounds a position where telecommunications are in the private sector while letter post remains in the public sector. Logic would seem to suggest that both should be in the same sector.

Similarly, it is difficult to make an economic case for having a private sector oil industry with coal in the public sector. In fact, the reasons for the survival of coal, rail and the Post Office as public sector bodies are largely historical, political and practical. The coal industry is almost a symbol of the past social battles to achieve improved conditions and a degree of economic and social justice for ordinary workers. The railways also have a historical place in the labour movement while the Post Office has a long history of public service under the Crown. It is believed that the Monarch would be reluctant to see that traditional link finally broken.

Nuclear power is a special case. There is considerable public suspicion of nuclear power and any move to put under the control of a commercial enterprise would provoke widespread hostility with accusations that the safety of the planet was being sold for profit.

These are all interesting cases where economics is subordinate to wider considerations - in some cases almost to emotional feelings.

Question 9

A business 'corporation' enjoys the legal status of being an entity in its own right. A company has a legal existence quite apart from its shareholders or directors. This enables it to own property in its own name and to sue and be sued in its own name. In fact it has all the rights and obligations of a legal individual. This separate existence enables most companies to have the great privilege of limited liability which protects shareholders from risking their own private possessions when they become part owners of a business enterprise.

In contrast, sole proprietors and partners do not have this separate legal existence. They remain personally responsible for business actions taken in their names. The risks are, therefore, rather greater but they have more control over business decision making.

Question 10

No one disputes the fact that large numbers of business owners would apparently be better off financially if they sold their businesses and became employees of a larger enterprise. The fact that they remain in business suggests that they either do not realise this fact or they do realise it and they ignore it because being in business gives them other important, non-financial benefits. These might include independence, flexibility, self-esteem and, in some cases, the belief that one day they will substantially improve their financial returns. You may be aware of other reasons why so many people start their own business ventures each year.

Question 11

This question lists a number of bodies which were not established in order to make profits for their owners. Some do not have any legal owners. All were established to meet community needs not being met in other ways. All were established by people who had both practical and idealistic objectives.

Building societies started, literally, to build homes for groups of people who could not otherwise afford to acquire property. The first members were concerned to provide their own homes. In time they became specialised financial institutions.

The co-operative societies originated around the same time as the building societies. Their aim was to provide retail services to members in a period when many working people were being exploited by shops geared more to serving the interests of the better off, and when retailing was really in its infancy.

The National Trust is concerned to acquire and protect land and property on behalf of the nation. Without the Trust much land would be neglected or commercially exploited and much property would have disappeared. It controls the use of a significant proportion of the nation's land.

The Red Cross is an international movement founded for humanitarian reasons to try to protect individuals caught up in war and political conflict. Unlike the other organisations listed it has no major economic significance but socially its work is of immense importance.

The purpose of bringing these well known bodies to your attention was to suggest that, while accepting the very great importance of profit, this was not the only spur to human initiative and enterprise. The pursuit of an ideal can also be a powerful force.

Question 12

It is common to say that increased use of capital through the introduction of increasingly advanced machines is de-skilling a great deal of industrial work. To some extent this is true. Some skills which arose from long experience in a particular task in a particular industrial process have been replaced by machines. For example in the old steel making process much depended on the skills of the man who knew by the colour of the molten metal exactly when it was ready to be poured. Modern technology now defines the precise time more exactly and reliably. Years of experience in the cutting room of a clothing factory could produce a cutter able to cut garments with the minimum waste cloth. Computers now perform this task with even greater precision and reliability.

However, new skills have been created which have made firms even more reliant on workers. The people capable of designing, maintaining and repairing the advanced machines are extremely important. Even many apparently unskilled jobs are of great importance to firms. Automated machines can go wrong very swiftly and though many can detect or even correct faults there is always the possibility of an undetected breakdown which can be very expensive indeed. There is still a need for workers to monitor machines and to take speedy action when problems arise. The completely workerless factory or office does not exist nor is it likely to exist. Anyone who has left a computer printer alone for a time knows what can happen when fast moving equipment starts to go wrong!

It is notable that the more advanced industrial processes are becoming, the more frequently do we here complaints from employers that their business expansion is being delayed by shortages of essential workers.

Question 13

Is capital rewarded by interest or profit? This question has political as well as economic implications. Those who argue that capital receives profit usually also argue that the owners of capital are receiving created wealth that more properly belongs to labour. Nevertheless this remains an interesting question with important economic implications.

The shareholder in the public company receives dividends which are legally a division of the profits of the company. Nevertheless anyone making money available to another expects to receive a financial return and most shareholders of large companies look upon the dividend as a return to be expected for the use of their money. In most cases they receive a lower immediate return than they would from a building society deposit but hope that the return will increase in the future. This increase, however, will only take place if the company's profits grow - so we are back to profit.

It could be argued that the investor who wants interest only will buy debentures (loan stocks) and these are not dependent on profit. On the other hand, although the amount of interest does not depend on the amount of profit the company will only be able to afford to pay interest if it is able to make sound profits.

It seems that interest and profit are very closely linked and it is, perhaps, useful to recall that at one time paying and receiving interest was prohibited in Christian countries as 'usury' - an activity regarded with the kind of distaste that some socialist politicians now regard profit making. Interest is still banned in some Islamic countries.

Consequently many people in these countries with money to spare make it available to business firms in return for a share of profits!

Question 14

Before the First Industrial Revolution the employee was usually regarded as part of the employer's family. It was the employer's responsibility to feed, clothe and shelter the employee and to provide for him/her in sickness. Most employers also accepted responsibility for dependents following death in service. The master-servant relationship was a very close one with many rights and duties established by custom and practice and social expectation and, of course, it depended a great deal on mutual trust.

Such a relationship was clearly open to abuse on both sides but on the whole it probably worked quite well in the majority of cases until the increased pace of large-scale industry in the nineteenth century started to break it down. As the speed of industrial change quickened and as firms became increasingly vulnerable to the uncertainties of the market place, employers found it impossible to maintain the lifelong relationship that had been inherited from a much slower, dependable, agrarian economy. By the mid-20th century the relationship had become simply one of the employer hiring labour with responsibility limited to paying agreed wages and providing safe working conditions as defined and established in law.

Many of the old responsibilities were taken over by the State - the welfare state that has developed since 1945. However, in more recent times the State has recoiled from taking on the increasing burdens of social welfare and has sought to return at least some of the old responsibilities to the employer who now has to accept limited and clearly defined obligations for such matters as sickness payments and pension arrangements. It will be interesting to see if this trend continues and how it is going to be reconciled with modern economic uncertainties and the economic need for a reasonably mobile labour force.

Question 15

Wages and wage rates differ greatly but in all cases there is a direct relationship between either the length of time worked or the quantity of product produced and the amount of pay received. Thus, if you agree to work for £10 per hour you know that working for ten hours will bring twice the return obtained from working five hours. Similarly if you agree to a payment based on a rate per 1000 words written you know that writing 2000 words will bring in double the amount paid for 1000 words.

The important thing is that once the basis of payment and pay rate has been agreed there is a direct and predictable relationship between amount of work and amount of wage paid.

There is no relationship of this kind if we regard profit as a return to enterprise, still less if we think of enterprise in terms of risk-taking. Every poker player knows that taking risks in card playing is not the surest way of earning profits and it is much the same in business. There are always risks in business but success usually comes from a careful assessment of the risks and the choice of a strategy that minimises risk in order to ensure achievement of profits. Gamblers do not, on the whole, make good business managers. On the other hand neither do those people who lack imagination and the ability to look ahead and see what the situation is likely to be tomorrow and what important differences are going to arise between today and tomorrow.

Question 16

The discussion of the enterprise-profit issue often appears to imply that the only risks taken in business are the risks of losing money, so that the people who risk their money are the ones who are entitled to the profits from successful business activity. If we think in terms of the public company it is possible to suggest that the risk taken by the shareholder is often much less than that taken by the worker who risks an entire lifestyle and pattern of living on a career with a particular firm. The shareholder risks a fraction of savings. Few investors would put all their savings into the shares of just one company. Employers do not encourage workers to spread their risks by working for several firms!

Moreover shareholders have no rights as such to take part in the activities and decision making of the firm. Managers risk their reputations, careers and present jobs on some of the decisions they have to make. Nevertheless the legal position is that profits are the property of shareholders. It is not difficult to see that there is a case for suggesting that profit is the return paid to the owners of capital without any regard to enterprise or risk taking.

Recognition, at least in part, of this problem has led to increased interest in profit sharing schemes for managers and these are discussed later.

Question 17

A small firm is one that is capable of being owned, controlled and managed by an individual or small group of people, usually linked by family relationship.

If we attempt to give a more precise definition we face problems in that advances in technology are making it possible for individuals to control larger scale operations and to continue to replace workers by equipment. Inflation also erodes the value of capital so that what would have been accepted as being a large firm half a century ago may today appear to be relatively small. The essential feature of the small firm, however, is the existence of a personal style of management at the highest decision making levels.

Question 18

The ordinary (equity) shareholder, especially one with a controlling interest of more than 50 per cent of the shares, can enjoy the following benefits:

- Effective control over the business enterprise. A majority shareholder has many of the benefits of the sole proprietor but with the privilege of limited liability for debts (maximum liability the loss of the value of the shares) and with the further benefit of being able to control the use of other shareholders' funds.
- The returns from investment in small firms can be much greater than from investment in one of the major companies quoted on the normal stock exchange. If the firm prospers the value of the shares can increase significantly and the income from dividends can also grow.
- The shareholder can actually see the use made of the funds and if unhappy about any aspect of the business can become involved. As such the shareholder has no right to intervene in management but an influential shareholder will usually be in a position to become a director or appoint a representative and so become involved in the top layer of decision making.

At the same time the risks of investing in small firms are much greater than with large, established companies. A high proportion of small companies fail, especially in the first three years of life. For the shareholder who does not have sufficient shares to exercise a controlling or major influence the risks are greater because it is difficult to affect decisions.

Shares can be difficult to sell. There is no difficulty in selling shares in, say, ICI because thousands of these shares are traded every day. Small company shares cannot be sold until a buyer is found. Because trading in shares is more difficult and uncertain it is not always easy to know what the share value actually is. In the case of private companies it is even difficult to obtain information. The balance sheet and profit and loss account should be filed at the Companies Registry each year but many are late and the Registry does not have the resources to pursue every company that is overdue with its accounts. In some cases the delay is as much due to the company's auditors as to the company management.

Today the limited liability of directors is not absolute. They may lose this privilege if they continue to trade after becoming insolvent.

It is usually suggested that it is safer to make a loan to a small company than buy equity. However, if the company fails it may be unable to repay loans in spite of its legal obligations to do so. On the other hand the lender to a successful company does not share in that success because loan terms are not usually changed - in contrast to ordinary shares where the value rises with success, resulting in increased profits and higher dividends or the strong prospect of higher dividends.

Any investment is a risk but the risks of investing in small firms are greater than buying ordinary shares in a major company.

Question 19

Successive British Governments have shown concern to assist small firms through financial aid or by changes in the law. There are a number of possible reasons for this.

- Small firms are more helpful in regional development because they are likely to spend a higher proportion of their revenue in their home district - in contrast to large national firms with head offices and purchasing departments in London or some other major commercial centre.
- The 'per job created' cost of promoting employment through small firms is generally thought to be lower than with large firms which are more likely to replace labour by increasingly advanced technology and expand their labour forces much more slowly than their capital assets.
- Small firms are traditionally regarded as the seed bed of new technology and ideas and large firms look to the them for future developments which they can then put into large scale production. An economy without a significant small firm sector is likely to be less vigorous and enterprising than one in which small firms thrive.
- There is some evidence that labour relations tend to be better in small firms than in large.
- Small firms play an important part in the production of services and as the economy becomes increasingly services orientated so small firms also become more important.
- Although a Labour government, under Mr Wilson, set up the Bolton Committee which made a valuable report on the whole issue of small firms and which later set up an advisory service under the Department of Industry, small firms are politically attractive to a Conservative government because of the political support usually given by small business owners.

Question 20

Moving from a large to a small firm (and vice versa) can be a traumatic experience for many people, especially those with managerial training and responsibility. There are several reasons for this.

- The extent and importance placed on specialisation in large firms are often foreign to the small firm experience. For example the manager in a small firm wishing to send out an urgent letter would usually type, write or word process this him/herself. Doing this in a large firm, assuming it to be possible, tends to upset typists or word processor operators who feel threatened and downgraded when an 'amateur' does work which they regard as their special preserve. People in large firms have learned to keep to their specialism and to respect the boundaries of other specialists. In small firms people at all levels have to join in whatever work needs doing. Moreover the attitude that some work is 'inferior' to other work and, therefore, not touchable by people above certain grades does not exist in small firms. All work is equally important to the success of the enterprise and the important thing is that it gets done as speedily and as inexpensively as possible.
- People trained in formal, bureaucratic structures as described in this course, find it extremely difficult to adapt to the personal structures of the small organisation. Similarly anyone used to the small firm personal system finds the bureaucratic structure frustrating.

- In small organisations workers recognise more easily the objectives of the enterprise and the link between costs and profits. Provided there is no personal resentment towards the employer and no sense of being exploited, all workers realise that their earnings have to come out of profits. This association is harder to recognise in the large organisation where departments operate to budgets a large budget may be justified by heavy spending. There is no obvious link between cost saving and personal earnings.

Question 21

Small firms can be flexible in many ways. Decisions can be made quickly without having to be formally justified and presented to a decision making committee. Employees are not generally defensive over their specialist areas of operation when they can quite clearly see that change is necessary for survival or for improved pay and work opportunities. The flexible working practices noted in Question 5 extends to readiness to learn new ways, and consequently a small firm can sometimes make some major changes - in product, design, materials and production method - quickly and with little opposition from those most closely involved.

However, there is one matter where the small firm is often much less flexible than the large organisation. This is geographical location. The small family firm is often tied very closely to one particular location or district. The owner and key workers often have very strong personal reasons why they should not move to another area. Consequently they are frequently at the mercy of shifts in the economic climate of that area. Large firms, on the other hand can relocate subsidiary operations fairly easily.

Flexibility in the small firm depends, of course, on the attitudes and abilities of the owners; for example if a dominant shareholder cannot cope with change then nothing in the firm will change.

Question 22

The possibility that labour relations in small firms may be better than in large firms has already been noted. To be more accurate, most of the available research indicates that it is in small production plants that labour relations are better and this would apply to small units which are part of large concerns. However, the small firm can only operate from small establishments so for the purposes of this discussion we can simply compare small and large firms. There are a number of possible explanations.

In the first place, where research uses the standard measures of days lost in industrial action, the difference is not surprising as there is plenty of evidence that workers in small firms are less unionised than in large. A small firm employee is much more vulnerable to employer retaliation in response to industrial action. It has always been accepted that unions find it easier to organise and gain power in large working establishments, especially where much of the work is routine, and where individual workers have little chance of promotion or of improving their pay without union action or formal bargaining procedures.

Lack of industrial action does not, in itself, indicate good labour relations. It may simply indicate worker weakness and employer dominance. Nevertheless this evidence is supported by other measures such as low labour mobility and the findings of attitude surveys.

The general condition of better labour relations in small firms can be accounted for by the closer proximity of workers and their managers and often the owner-managers. Communications are shorter and more informal and depend on personal relationship instead of formal procedures. If owner managers are seen to work hard and are prepared to do any necessary work this attitude encourages more co-operative attitudes among employees. Workers do not lose their identity in the small establishment to the extent that they can in large plants. Often the atmosphere is more friendly and human even though physical working conditions can be below minimum standards tolerated in large firms.

2
The growth of organisations

What is meant by growth?

Firms grow in two ways:

- Internally, i.e. by expansion of their activities through increased sales production capacity, investment in buildings, equipment and so on.
- By merger or take-over. Strictly merger takes place when two or more companies come together to form a new organisation while take-over refers to the purchase of one or more companies by another. In practice the terms now appear to be used almost indiscriminately and in any event there is usually one dominant company in any merger and this eventually imposes its own objectives and policies on the new organisation.

Either form of growth usually means that the organisation controls more capital, workers and land and, of course increases its total production capacity and sales revenue. It is, however, sometimes possible for growth to mean an increase in total capital employed in production without an increase, or with a less than proportional increase, in the number of people employed. More capital may have enabled the company to acquire more technologically advanced equipment allowing production to be raised without any increase and sometimes with a decrease in the number of workers.

Why do firms grow in size?

Growing to survive

When the author started work in a commercial company one of the first comments made to him by his first departmental manager was, 'You can't stand still in business. You either expand or decline.' Many similar remarks, from all kinds of people in all kinds of organisations have been made before and since. This belief that survival in the market place requires continual expansion is very strong among all levels of business managers and this, in itself, is a powerful source of pressure for growth.

Managerial preference for growth

In addition to this general attitude it is widely recognised that professional managers have as much, and often more, to gain from growth as they do from increased profits. The manager of a department of 50 workers handling an annual budget of, say, £500 000, normally expects to receive a higher salary and more business expenses and enjoy more status and privileges than a manager with similar professional skills who controls a department of 15 workers and has an annual budget of £100 000. The business owner manager has less to gain from pure growth unless it is accompanied by increased profits. Growth to the small business manager usually involves increased work and a greater diversity of work and work problems. The pressure to grow is thus less intense among small business owners although few observers would deny that it is still there, especially in the early years of the firm where size is often seen as evidence of increased security, and a visible symbol of having become established in the chosen market.

In the public sector there is almost always a direct relationship between size of department or unit controlled and salary/expense entitlement. All kinds of managers from head teachers to local authority accountants are rewarded according to the size of the unit they control. It is often difficult to see any economic logic in this system which is a positive encouragement to excess spending, resource waste and naked 'empire building' and it seems likely that it stems from the origins of organisations, when they were modelled on the armed forces where command over a larger group of men led to higher rank, privileges and financial reward.

Economies of scale

The traditional economic explanation for business growth is been based on the idea that larger organisations can make more efficient use of resources and so gain the benefits of **economies of scale**. Such economies are possible whenever a given increase in resources employed by the firm leads to a proportionally greater increase in production. Thus, if a firm manufacturing chairs employs 10 per cent more capital, labour and other production factors and, as a result, increases chair production by 15 per cent then economies of scale are being realised. These are **real** scale economies involving an increase in the **productivity** of the producer, as opposed to the purely **financial** economies gained when a large firm is able to use its market power to purchase materials at a lower price than that charged to its smaller rivals. Real scale economies usually arise from the increased skills resulting from specialisation and from the ability to make fuller use of specialised labour, capital and land. This is looked at in more detail in unit 3.

If a business firm enjoys economies of scale denied to smaller rivals and is then able to charge lower product prices, it should be able to increase sales and achieve growth with a significant reduction in its average production costs in the long run. This reduction is shown in the long-run average cost curve of Figure 2.1.

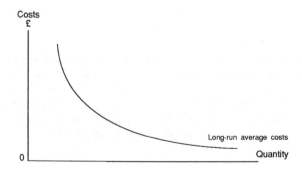

Figure 2.1   *The firm operating with economies of scale. Unit (average) cost falls as output increases*

Firms can also experience **diseconomies of scale**. If, for example production resources (inputs) are increased by 15 per cent and, as a result, production output is increased by

10 per cent, i.e. by a smaller proportion than inputs, then increased size is leading to reduced factor productivity and the firm is suffering scale diseconomies. These usually arise through managerial and organisational problems such as breakdowns of communication, poor co-ordination of activities or loss of control over subordinates. If these diseconomies start to outweigh economies then average or unit costs will start to rise. This is illustrated in Figure 2.2

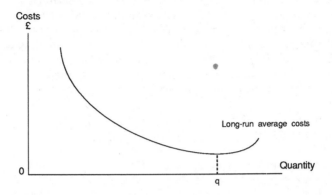

Figure 2.2 *Economies and diseconomies of scale. If the firm operates beyond quantity level q it experiences diseconomies of scale*

An increase in long-run average costs is a reflection on managerial skill and sets a limit to managerial ambitions of further growth. Managers will seek to overcome the problems producing the diseconomies and, if they succeed, they will be able to flatten the curve. Growth can then be continued. It may not be possible to achieve further significant economies of scale but diseconomies will be avoided. The output level beyond which significant scale economies are no longer achieved is an important one and is called the **minimum efficient scale** of output (MES). Growth above this output level cannot be justified on the grounds of cost savings but there is ample evidence that it does frequently take place. Consequently further reasons must be sought. The L shaped long-run cost curve produced by such growth is illustrated in Figure 2.3 where quantity level x represents the **MES**.

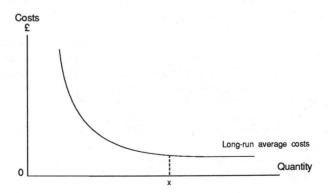

Figure 2.3 *The Minimum Efficient Scale of operations. At quantity levels above x there are no further significant economies of scale*

Pressure from government

So far, all the pressures for growth have developed from within the organisation but there are also exterior forces reinforcing these. In trying to explain past periods of rapid growth of organisations, such as the period from around 1966 to about 1973 when the business world was accused of suffering from 'merger mania', a powerful force to be taken into account is that of the Government which believed at the time that larger companies were needed to compete with overseas competitors. An organisation, the Industrial Re-organisation Corporation, was set up and provided with substantial public funds to encourage growth and a number of important, though not entirely successful, mergers resulted, including British Leyland, later the Rover Group. However, a later period, roughly 1984 to 1988, saw a similar wave of company mergers. No one accused the British government of encouraging this trend which contained a strong element of foreign take-over of some large and famous companies.

Financial advantages

Another explanation for earlier periods of business organisational growth was the ability of large companies to borrow money at fixed rates of interest. This proved to be a cheap source of finance during a period of rapid inflation when the real value of the fixed interest payment declined rapidly. Much of the money was provided by insurance offices which were operating pension schemes for smaller companies. Bigger groups had their own pension funds. It is possible that many small companies were unwittingly providing the funds for their own extinction but this situation has also proved to be temporary as financial institutions have learned how to cope with almost permanent inflation. Few are now willing to arrange loans at fixed rates of interest. Most large scale suppliers of finance now reserve the right to increase interest charges or to ensure that they obtain the right to share in future profits instead of or in addition to charging interest.

Pressure from the financial markets

Nevertheless there seems to be little doubt that the suppliers of finance have encouraged growth in the size of business organisations. Companies that accumulate profits are expected to use these to acquire other firms and are criticised if they do not. Take-over battles and rumours of future take-overs provide the main source of interest for financial journalists. Companies that grow rapidly become favoured by institutions that make their profits from supplying take-over finance.

Any change in the structure of a business firm provides work and profit for a financial adviser and supplier of finance. Banks, therefore, live off business change and encourage it whenever possible. In the 1960s and 1970s the banks were encouraging mergers and take-overs. These were not always successful and the more difficult economic conditions of the early 1980s led to much re-organisation, involving the sale of companies to other companies and often to their own managers through what has become known as **management buy-outs**. By the late 1980s some of the newly independent companies were beginning to pursue growth by take-over. All this activity provides profits for the financial institutions.

TEST YOUR UNDERSTANDING

1   Some owner-managed firms refuse to grow beyond their present size. Suggest reasons for this and also suggest possible dangers.

2   Discuss the economic arguments for relating managerial salaries to the size of the operation managed.
3   Under what conditions are firms operating
    * with economies of scale
    * with diseconomies of scale
    * beyond their minimum efficient scale of output?

Some consequences of organisational growth

Market dominance by large firms

When there is a significant amount of growth by take-over and merger with an increase in the average size of business organisations then it is inevitable that the number of firms operating in many industries will decline and there will also be a concentration of power in the hands of the dominating firms in each industry.

As a result of the merger activity in Britain since the early 1960s the level of business concentration in most industries has increased. In 1977, for example, the largest five suppliers to over half of the product groups in manufacturing and mining supplied 80 per cent or more of the production for their group. In over a third of these groups the largest five firms supplied 90 per cent or more of the production for their group. Many firms are very large suppliers to more than one product group so that a high proportion of total British manufacturing output is accounted for by relatively few large companies. In 1970, for instance, over half of British net output was produced by the 100 largest firms.

Although figures seem to be more readily available for manufacturing than for other sectors of the economy, similar trends towards market concentration in the hands of a few large firms are clearly visible. For example, 45 per cent of the total retail sales of soaps and detergents in 1987 were made through four of the largest supermarket groups (Sainsbury, Tesco, Asda and Kwiksave) with another 40 per cent of sales made through the Co-operative societies and 30 other large multiple stores, leaving only 15 per cent of sales through the smaller independent shops. The manufacture of washing powders, was dominated by two giant firms, Lever Bros (part of the Anglo-Dutch Unilever group) and the American Proctor and Gamble, which between them supplied 87 per cent of the market.

Survival of the small firm

In the face of such dominance by large firms you might be forgiven for wondering whether there was any place at all for small firms. Indeed one feature of the 1980s in Britain has been the marked increase in the number of people working for themselves - the self-employed. This number increased from under 2 million in 1977 to nearly 2.9 million in 1987.

Small firms in general, though not always, individual firms, survive because they have important functions in a modern economy. These include:

* **Innovation**
  Some firms owe their origins to the desire of their owners to develop new ideas which larger firms have rejected or not considered at all. If a person believes in an idea strongly enough and can show that it is potentially profitable that person is likely to wish to test it through an independent business venture. Some important new developments have come from new ventures rather than from established large firms.

Microcomputers, for example, were developed by individual entrepreneurs in the face of some hostility from the large monopolists in the supply of mainframe computers.

- **Supplying small markets**
  Where a market is too small for a large firm to operate at a sufficiently low cost the small firm can continue and may even gain a local monopoly. Rising incomes and the desire to have a wider choice of product than is provided by large firms is tending to increase the number and range of small markets. For example, the 1980s has seen a revival in demand for hand-made local cheeses which are often preferred to the mass-produced versions sold through the large supermarkets.

- **Supply where the minimum efficient scale of production is small in relation to market size**
  In these markets, which include many service and highly specialised activities, the large firm has few production advantages over the small organisation, which is thus able to compete and survive. Often the specialist services are provided to the large firms themselves, e.g. for repair of machines, computer programming and industrial photography and design. A substantial proportion of small firms work under contract to large firms either providing specialised services or enabling them to supply small orders which would otherwise not be worthwhile.

- **Survival through co-operation**
  One way to obtain some of the economies of large scale operation while retaining the managerial benefits of a small firm is for the small organisation to sacrifice a degree of independence through membership of groups of small and larger organisations, e.g. retail voluntary groups such as VG and Spar, or through co-operation with larger organisations through franchise arrangements. The large organisations usually provide expertise and marketing and sometimes assist with finance and equipment. Actual production or service provision locally remains in the hands of the small independent firm. Co-operation and specialisation of function is also a feature of some activities, notably computer software production where the **organisation of what is to be produced and the marketing of products** is carried out by one controlling organisation but the **actual work of production** is carried out by numbers of small producers, often self-employed people working at home or in their own workshops. There are some interesting similarities with this form of modern organisation and the old pre-industrial revolution style of manufacturing of the eighteenth century. Possible implications of this development are examined later.

TEST YOUR UNDERSTANDING

4   Comment on the extent of domination by large firms you would expect to find in the following sectors of business:
    Computer manufacturing; computer software production; clothing manufacturing; accountancy; motor components manufacturing.
5   Is there a future for any small retail shop?
6   Have small firms gained or lost from recent developments in computer technology?

Managerial specialisation and growth

Specialised areas of management

It is often instructive to talk to people who have successfully started a small business. The experiences of one lady who, with a partner, started an electronic office equipment and supply firm in England Midlands is typical of many. She had a background of successful selling and her partner was a highly skilled service engineer. They quickly found that these skills were not enough to run even a small business enterprise. Their first need was to acquire a degree of financial competence because they ran into cash flow problems at a very early stage. They would advise anyone contemplating starting a business to go through a course of basic bookkeeping. Many would advise a rather broader financial accounting course. All would agree that anyone attempting to run a business must be financially educated. The management of finance is thus one of the most important of the specialised managerial sectors whatever the size of the enterprise.

During the first two years' trading, as the business began to grow, they discovered that there was more to purchasing than they had realised. The partners found that they could negotiate purchase prices and that some suppliers were better in some sectors of the trade than in others. Many other business managers have also found that skilled purchasing is an essential element in successful and profitable marketing. If the customer is to be supplied with the right goods at the right time and at a price that satisfies the buyer while providing a satisfactory return to the seller, then that seller must be a very careful buyer. Perhaps the most familiar example of the importance of purchasing to successful selling is that of the local greengrocer. This is an extremely competitive trade, with fresh fruit and vegetables sold in a wide range of shops and stores. People want the freshest possible produce at the lowest possible price, consistent with quality. Only by extremely skilled buying can the independent greengrocer hope to survive and prosper in this very tough sector of retailing.

The partners found they had to learn another specialised area of management when, after a year or so, they employed an assistant. They found it to be something of a burden. The partner who had become used to handling all the administration found it difficult to delegate work without going over it herself, in the process, no doubt, increasing her own total work load. At the same time she had worried about the personal safety of the assistant when left alone for long periods. It is commonly said that all managers are personnel managers and to some extent this is true. However, not all managers are as effective in the management of people as they are in their use of equipment or their own working skills. Personnel management is highly skilled and specialised and as people are the most important resource for all but very small firms, it is a specialism that deserves considerable attention.

Growth and its implications for managerial functions

In view of the importance of growth as a business objective it may come as something of a surprise to find business owners who appear to have limited growth ambitions. At an early stage the partners of the office equipment firm had decided that, however successful they were, they would not expand beyond what could be handled by four people. Whether they would be able to keep strictly to this decision in practice is open to question. Nevertheless this conscious desire to limit growth on the part of small enterprise owners is by no means uncommon. There are probably two main reasons for this. The owners recognise that growth beyond a certain point will bring managerial problems that they are not certain they can handle. They recognise their own managerial skill limitations, not least of which is an unwillingness to delegate specialist responsibility to subordinates. They also recognise that continued growth requires injections of capital from outside the organisation and this brings risks that they are unwilling to accept. The major problems of growth, for any scale of enterprise, are managerial and financial, and firms wishing to grow must overcome these if they are to succeed.

The main, broad managerial functions are:

- **Production**

  This relates to the production of the good or the performance of the service which is the principal economic activity of the organisation. In the office equipment example production was the sale and servicing of office equipment. These are really two separate, though related, production activities and in practice one of the partners managed the selling side of the business while the other, the engineer, managed the servicing.

- **Finance**

  In the same firm the sales partner also managed all the financial work of the firm. This ranged from determining re-sale prices of stock and service charges, negotiating with the bank, invoicing, checking and chasing overdue accounts, determining the propor- tion of profit that could be drawn by the partners and the proportion allocated to reinvestment in stock, vehicles and equipment and, of course, communicating with the Inland Revenue with the help of the firm's accountants. Since the partner's main skill and strength lay in selling, the time spent on financial matters was lost to the job she did best and enjoyed the most.

- **Personnel**

  The partner in the office equipment firm admitted that having an employee took up a proportion of her time, thoughts and energy. The management of people, though part of every manager's job, is also a specialised activity.

- **Purchasing**

  The office equipment partner found that increasing her purchasing skills helped her increase sales and profits.

- **Marketing**

  The partner was highly skilled and very competent at selling. Indeed, her selling skills had been crucial to the firm's survival in its first months. However, it also became clear that she was in danger of falling behind in a competitive market because she was so involved in day-to-day work that she did not have time to look to the future. The knowledge limitations of the two partners were already forcing them to specialise in one sector of the office equipment market and to ignore other areas. As long as their specialised sectors continued to expand the firm would prosper, but if further tech- nological change took place or if they were overtaken by areas of development which they had been ignoring, e.g. laser printing, the firm was doomed. Concentration on sales was in danger of leading to the neglect of marketing.

Further growth for large numbers of firms, perhaps even their survival must depend on paying attention to all the managerial functions and finding ways to include those being neglected. Clearly there is a limit to the working capacity, skills and knowledge of just two people. Somehow additional managerial labour and expertise needs to be gained.

Expanding management

When a very small business starts to grow it is tempting simply to recruit routine workers. Often, of course, this is necessary, but, as we have already seen, this adds to the workload and stress of the owner-manager. The owners really need to be able to share their managerial duties and to free their time and energies to pursue their own specialist strengths. In practice owner-managers find this a very difficult thing to do. There are frequently practical financial difficulties. The turnover of the firm may not justify the kind of full time salary that a specialist manager would require and the work involved may not completely fill that manager's time.

If, however, this financial hurdle can be cleared there are often much more serious difficulties in matching the personalities of the owner-manager and the new assistant. If the assistant has worked for a large organisation the transition to a very small firm can prove to be a traumatic culture shock. Accustomed perhaps to the company of other specialists and being able to pass problems to them, and to the back-up of secretaries, ample stocks and equipment, to suddenly be thrown on one's own resources, to do one's own typing, to make speedy decisions in an unfamiliar environment, to make do and improvise with what may appear to be inadequate equipment and stocks, can prove too much for some people. At the same time the owner-manager may find it almost impossible to make the mental adjustments necessary to train, delegate and trust the new assistant. Too often the unfortunate newcomer is blamed for not acquiring in a few days information, customs, practices and customer idiosyncrasies that the owner has learned over many years. The new manager has usually been recruited to bring new skills and knowledge into the firm but when he or she tries to introduce these the innovations are met with hostility and declarations that they are unsuitable for the special conditions of this particular firm. Sometimes it appears that the owner is looking for a clone of him or herself, with enterprise but without independence, able to generate income and profit but without any ambition to share in that profit beyond the agreed salary. Because the requirements are often inhuman they are rarely found in any normal human being.

These difficulties, however, are not insuperable if the owner-managers are able to analyse their own real needs and resources and then seek to find someone capable of meeting the most urgent needs within the financial resources available. It may be that a full time managerial appointment is not justified. One or more part-time assistants may be more satisfactory. Part-timers are likely to be less costly but able and willing to offer a greater personal commitment and be less likely to feel that they have been misled about working requirements. The changing structure of the modern workforce with its increased supply of people wishing to work part-time is likely to make this option more attractive for many firms. The increased supply is coming from those returning to the workforce after a period of full time responsibility for the family and from the 'early retireds'. Another possibility may be to hire specialised help as and when this is needed. This option, however, can be expensive and people working under contract do not have the personal commitment of the part-time worker.

The aim of any arrangement must be to allow the firm to grow and in the process, allow the owner-managers to pursue their own strengths. Suppose, for example, the sales manager partner of the office equipment firm were to hire a sales manager. This might seem a strange choice given her own selling skills. However, if she were freed from the routine selling, and willing to trust her most loyal customers to deal with the new manager she would have the time and opportunity to explore new, expanding markets in, say, laser printing. This kind of market development could ensure a more stable future for the firm.

TEST YOUR UNDERSTANDING

7   Identify the specialised areas of management in your own firm or one well-known to you. Are these all in the hands of specialised departments?

8   Discuss the implications of the statement that 'concentration on sales was in danger of leading to the neglect of marketing'.

9   What are the attractions and disadvantages of part-time working for
    • the employer
    • the employee?

Managerial growth and co-ordination

The need for co-ordination

At an early stage of managerial growth the need to develop an entirely new kind of managerial skill will arise. This is the ability to get other managers to work together and pool their different skills and personalities in the pursuit of common objectives. The managerial co-ordinator must be able to formulate clear and practical objectives and communicate these to subordinates, breaking down overall objectives into targets that have meaning and which are attainable by the subordinates. In addition the co-ordinator must be able to inspire in subordinates the desire to achieve these objectives and the willingness to operate as part of a team.

The owner-manager who starts to develop a managerial structure must, therefore, acquire new skills and assume a new role - that of co-ordinator. This also involves a change of attitude. The owner must be prepared to delegate work and responsibility. If this is not done, the additional role becomes an extra burden which could prove too much for both owner and firm. However, delegation is not easy. The delegator must be prepared to see work done in a different way, possibly, especially in the early stages, in an inferior way. However this must be accepted if the owner is to assume the new role and perform managerial tasks which, ultimately, will be much more important for the future of the firm. How often are heard comments such as, 'The only way I can be sure that the job is done properly is to do it myself', and 'It's nearly always quicker and easier to do the job myself'. These are always danger signals indicating that the manager is failing to delegate, failing to train and failing to allow adequate time for effective learning to take place.

Some features of co-ordination in small firms

By no means all small firms make the errors described here. If they did, no small enterprise would ever grow. Many do and are successful. Some of the problems of continued growth are outlined in the next stage. It must be noted that, provided the true nature of co-ordination is understood and if personal attitudes are favourable, then the process of growth is not too difficult and in some ways is much simpler than with large organisations.

When a small business is operating successfully, and when the managers are working effectively together then, whatever their particular specialist skills, they all share some common features. For example, precisely because there cannot be full time specialist managers for every managerial functions each must be prepared to take on unfamiliar work and have a flexible approach to day to day tasks and problems. They must all know something of each other's work. In the office equipment firm, for example, the sales manager would not claim to be able to repair an electronic printer but she would know enough to ask relevant questions when a customer reported a problem and would be able to inform her technical partner what the trouble was likely to be. At the same time she would be aware of the kinds of technical problems that were being encountered with different kinds of machines, making her a more skilled salesperson and helping her customers to avoid making costly errors in purchasing. In small organisations the managers meet constantly, getting to know each other's problems and learning from comments about customers. All would know the customers who pay bills on time and those who take the longest possible period of credit. They all adapt their own service to fit this type of knowledge.

If communication is easier, so too is the understanding that is the basis of good communication. The co-ordinating manager understands the problems of subordinates because he or she has actually done much of the work they do or has been very close to it. A parallel can be drawn with the functions of the professional football manager. This person's task is to create a team from a group of individuals, each with different skills, but all sharing some common skills and qualities. Most successful managers have themselves been successful players but by no means all successful players become competent managers. To the ability to play football the manager must add the abilities, outlined earlier, of formulating objectives, communication, motivation and the ability to inspire others to work together as a team.

Another example of management at this kind of level is that of the head teacher in a small primary school. This head must have all the qualities of a good classroom teacher and indeed, is likely to spend a fair proportion of time teaching in the classroom. A head who is not an effective classroom teacher is unlikely to command much respect from the other teachers. In addition the head must be able to perform the co-ordinating managerial functions we have identified and, because the school is part of a larger educational structure, must be able to communicate with and influence others else-where in that structure, e.g. to work with and perhaps manipulate local authority inspectors, councillors and school governors.

These examples, from some very different activities should help you to recognise that there are important managerial functions which are common to all activities and, perhaps, it may make you suspicious of the claim that 'This may be very true for other organisations but it doesn't apply to ours because we are different'. Every organisation, like every person, is unique but all share many common features. You should be able to identify these and be able to make practical use of that knowledge.

TEST YOUR UNDERSTANDING

10 What advice would you give to the owner of an expanding small firm who is about to recruit an assistant for the first time?
11 What different skills and qualities, if any, should be possessed by the head of a large comprehensive school in contrast to the head of a small primary school?
12 In the early days of the large retail superstores at least one of the new firms deliberately sought to recruit personnel managers from outside retailing.
Suggest reasons for this policy.

Personal structure of management

Meaning of personal and bureaucratic structures

In a well-known book, *The Reality of Management*, Rosemary Stewart outlines what is implied by the term bureaucracy. The popular idea of bureaucracy is of a set of unimaginative officials determined to sink every action under a weight of paper and to pass anything approaching a decision to the next level of authority. The term is related to the French word bureau, meaning office. A bureaucratic structure of organisation is one that is built round a system of offices or, more accurately, office holders. The office, or its holder, has clearly defined functions, duties and responsibilities. In order to fulfil these the office holder must possess just as clearly defined skills and qualities. Filling the office, therefore, implies seeking a person with the qualities needed for the office or training a person in the necessary skills.

In contrast to this stress on the office the personal structure implies a stress is on the person where the functions, duties and responsibilities of the office are adapted to the skills, interests and personal qualities of the person holding it.

Clearly all organisational structures, to some degree, are a mixture of both bureaucratic and personal. A structure would not be a structure if all office holders did as they wished and interpreted their responsibilities with complete freedom. No firm would last very long on that basis. At the same time everyone in a bureaucratic structure brings an element of individual interpretation to the role established by the organisation. Shakespeare wrote the role of Hamlet but there are as many ways of acting Hamlet as there are actors playing the part. Nevertheless it is important to distinguish the two broad systems of management as this helps us to understand some of the problems experienced by firms as they grow and some of the problems that individuals have in fitting into the managerial structure of particular firms.

Strengths of the personal structure

The personal structure is the natural way for a managerial system to evolve as a very small firm starts to expand. Many small firms start as partnerships on a very informal basis. Two people find that their skills and interests interlock so that by working together they can produce and market a product or provide a service more effectively than could either working alone. The division of work and responsibility then comes naturally, with each respecting the other's skills and qualities. In the office equipment firm described earlier, one partner looked after purchasing, marketing, administration and finance - the commercial side of the enterprise. The other partner was the technical expert and his skills in the servicing and repair of electronic equipment provided the foundation for much of the commercial success of the firm. Suppose they were to hire an assistant. Although they would have a reasonably clear idea of the work they wanted that assistant to perform they would most probably choose a person with little initial commercial or technical training on the basis of that person's personal qualities, on reliability and trustworthiness, the ability to communicate with customers and willingness and ability to learn. Above all the new person would have to be someone they liked having around the office - whose personality fitted into that small social group. Such a person could then most probably start to create a role, depending on his or her interests and skills. He or she might develop skills on the commercial or the technical side, perhaps even developing an interest in new forms of equipment, enabling the firm to extend the range of services and activities it offered.

It is common to find this kind of extension and development in the small family business when it is joined by a son or daughter, particularly when the son or daughter has spent some years in a different firm or has undergone business training outside the organisation. Provided the introduction of new ideas and interests does not come into conflict with the existing, established authority it can often bring new life to an enterprise and stimulate new enthusiasm among other employees. A typical example of this is the case of a small family engineering company in the West Midlands which faced possible extinction in the early 1980s when economic recession and the shrinking of the local motor industry took away many of the company's traditional customers. The son of the firm's founder then took control and introduced new production techniques that could be applied to working with plastic materials. He also made a vigorous effort to seek out new markets with the result that, by the end of the decade, the firm was enjoying a renewed prosperity and security.

It is the ability to see a business problem as a whole and to be capable of applying and even learning the skills needed to solve it, regardless of the usual management demarcation lines, that marks the successful small business manager. This is one of the reasons why it is sometimes difficult for a people trained in a large firm to adapt to the requirements of a small one. They are used to organisations made up of specialists and to respecting the barriers that people erect to protect their specialism and can find it difficult to think in more general terms. They may also find it difficult to free themselves of the 'social caste' attitudes that frequently abound in the large organisation. The manager in the large firm would not usually dream of sitting at a secretary's word processor to produce an urgent letter or printed set of figures. In the small firm everyone must be ready to turn a hand to almost anything. This gives the whole organisation a flexibility and ability to respond to unexpected emergencies - and opportunities - denied to the large organisation.

This flexibility and willingness to judge people by their attitudes, readiness to respond to the needs of the firm and by their achievements, also provides people with much wider opportunities. Personal progress depends on what people can and are willing to do and not on what paper qualifications they possess or how they can manipulate committees. In small firms it is not unusual to find people in control who have achieved their positions by their ability to cope with problems as they arose, although they may have entered the firm in apparently routine jobs with no obvious prospect of upward progression. The author's experience brought him into contact with a successful, expanding frozen food distributor, where the person in day-to-day control was a lady who had joined the firm as a secretary/driver to the managing director. Control involved scheduling the movements of a fleet of insulated and refrigerated vehicles and their drivers and ensuring that sales, purchases and distribution were handled promptly and efficiently. It involved quick thinking, resourcefulness, ability to recruit, manage and occasionally fire drivers and maintain good relationships with large numbers of busy shopkeepers. The firm was growing rapidly with the expansion of frozen foods and the requirements of the job were constantly developing. It needed a person who was capable of developing the skills and knowledge required as they became necessary. Personality and character were clearly much more important than training in any specific managerial specialism. A person trained in a large organisation would have had considerable difficulty coping at that stage of the firm's development.

Weaknesses of the personal structure

Personal management structures are successful as long as the people in managerial roles are able to meet the challenges and changing requirements of these roles. If they do not do so then the firm is likely to fail to adapt to a changing economic and social environment and may simply collapse.

For example, a firm that starts life in a period of economic growth, operating in an expanding industry or service sector, is likely to face problems in organising production and distribution. Marketing may not be a major managerial concern. Managers whose attitudes are formed under these conditions may have considerable difficulty adapting to an environment where growth is harder to achieve and dependent upon developing new products and markets. Future success, if not survival, can then depend on existing management recognising the marketing challenge and either rising to it themselves or recruiting someone able to do so. This may also mean recruiting someone with a different personality and attitudes who then has difficulty in becoming assimilated into the existing team.

Identifying the type of person required for a developing or changing organisation is often a major barrier for the small owner-managed firm. The owner tends to assume that what is needed is someone in the same mould as the people who brought the firm to its present stage of development, with an interest and willingness to work for the firm, but also ready to accept without question views and decisions of the owners, and work for a fraction of their remuneration. Clearly this is an impossible job description but attempting to fill it can lead to a great deal of friction, bad feeling and waste of time and money.

Most small firms are family controlled and financed. The need to accept into the firm a member of the family can be a serious problem. The newcomer can bring into the firm some valuable advantages such as knowledge of the firm's history, activities, customers and other workers, all built up over a number of years. If these are added to new attitudes, ideas and skills the firm can gain much. However, bringing in a new family member can also be a disaster. If the newcomer has little interest in or knowledge of the firm, no skills to offer and sees the job as just a way to extract money from the business without having to do any serious work it is not difficult to judge the effect on other workers and on other members of the family. Even between these two extremes there can be problems. A dominant owner who has managed a successful firm for many years may find it difficult to accept that a newcomer has anything worthwhile to contribute. Slight disagreements can blow up into full scale business and family rows and many long standing and bitter family feuds have their origins in the failure of two members of the same family to work together successfully. The breakdown of the more structured family relationships in native English society and the virtual disappearance of the extended family make family recruitment less of a problem. However, the retention of the extended family among other ethnic groups in Britain, many of which are clearly doing much to restore the tradition of small (and some large) family firms in Britain, is likely to ensure that the issue remains a live one in the current period of economic and social change. It should be noted that among some of the oldest and most successful family firms, including those in merchant banking, there is a rule that members of the family are welcome, but only when they have proved that they have the qualities required by the firm and if they can contribute skills and abilities that are of value to the firm. The firm is not to be weakened by tolerating family members who do not meet its high standards.

TEST YOUR UNDERSTANDING

13 It is sometimes found that a successful small company performs badly after being taken over by a large group. If the groups then allows the company to be bought back by its own management it again becomes successful. Discuss possible reasons for this.
14 Many small companies encourage recruitment of relatives of existing and former employees, favouring these applicants even though better qualified applicants may be available. Is this a short-sighted policy?
15 Is it possible to train a person to become a manager of a small family business?

The bureaucratic structure

The strengths of the bureaucratic structure

The bureaucratic structure, based on offices with clearly defined duties and responsibilities, has the major strength of contributing to clear lines of responsibility. In an ideal structure each person should understand his or her duties and responsibilities and be aware of their own positions in the wider managerial network however that is structured. The bureaucratic structure assumes a high degree of specialisation and a system of rules to define areas of responsibility and the conduct of individuals when faced with problems. Success in such a structure is assumed to depend on the degree of competence with which responsibilities are discharged and on the ability to meet consistently any performance or financial targets that may be set. Rules have to be followed because there is inevitably a high degree of co-ordination with other specialised areas of operation within the organisation. Since each office contributes to the total work of the enterprise all activities must fit together, much as all components of a complex manufactured product have to fit if the final product is to work effectively.

Such a structure is designed to enable the large, complex organisation to function without splintering into its individual parts. If lines of communication and responsibility are clearly established then people know how to obtain information and instruction, and what they are expected to do irrespective of who is in a particular office at any given time. Because people are likely to come and go in any large organisation this continuity of the functions of the office, regardless of the personality of the office holder, becomes important. In the personal structure the office holder frequently determines the boundaries of the office and its functions to suit personal preferences in the light of the strengths, weaknesses and attitudes of other office holders. In the bureaucratic structure the office holder must adapt to the requirements of the office or find another, more congenial office.

Problems of the bureaucratic structure

You may be thinking that a somewhat inhuman structure in which human individuality is subordinated to the needs of a particular working community is being described. It is true that there is only limited scope for individual initiative in the actual performance of one's daily work. Individual ability and initiative lies more, perhaps, in gaining additional skills in order to move to another 'office' and gain wider responsibilities and more challenging work. In practice the scope for this is often limited and people may seek instead to widen the boundaries of their particular 'office' so that it encroaches on the territories of others, or to increase its standing within the organisation by extending the volume of its work. You may recognise the symptoms of the typical organisational disease of 'empire building'- a disease encouraged and made more contagious by the common practice of relating the scale of monetary and non-monetary remuneration to the size of the 'office', e.g. by the financial budget for which it is responsible or by the number of people for whose work the office holder is directly accountable.

It is often possible for one office to expand because the holder of another is unable or unwilling to fulfil the requirements of that office. Both office holders, therefore, acquiesce in a situation which appears to satisfy each. The true position is either concealed from superiors or they too acquiesce in the belief that as long as the work gets done any distortion to the managerial structure does not matter too much. If such a situation is repeated throughout the organisation it becomes, in effect, a personal structure and, as such, extremely vulnerable to pressures and strains from a changing economic environment. It also becomes frustrating for many trained specialists, especially those coming into the organisation from other firms, and the rate of managerial turnover can rise to dangerous levels.

The term 'bureaucratic structure' is a general one which can be employed for any system of managerial organisation based on a set of organisational duties and responsibilities rather than on the personalities of individual people. It is a basic requirement for any large organisation which needs to employ specialists and to co-ordinate their work. It embraces many styles and types of managerial organisation and some of these are examined in the next section.

TEST YOUR UNDERSTANDING

16 Why are formal communication structures usually necessary in large organisations?
17 Is a bureaucratic structure less efficient than a personal structure

18 Are bureaucratic structures inevitable in the public sector regardless of the size of working establishments?

The structure of management

What is management structure?

The term management structure refers to an organisational system whereby a coherent set of rules can be established governing the duties and responsibilities of managers, their lines of communication, control and accountability and the means whereby their work can be co-ordinated in the pursuit of organisational goals and objectives.

Clearly the more managers there are, and the more specialised their work and skills, the greater the need for a structure which they all know and understand. This implies that it is essentially for the large firm that structure becomes very important. It might be said that it is the organisational structure that binds managers together. It is a kind of cement that provides strength but which can also be very rigid. If the organisation has to face harsh economic winds it is the rigid structure that is most likely to fragment. The structure, therefore, must be strong but it must also be flexible and adaptable, especially in a time of rapid technological, economic and social change.

Types of structures

The structure of the organisation must help managers meet its goals and objectives. The precise form it takes must, of course, depend partly on size but also on the firm's activities, the way these are spread through the market in which it operates and the kinds of other organisations, including political organisations, with which it has to deal. At one time, and even as late as the 1950s, there were constant attempts to devise an ideal business structure towards which all firms could direct themselves. Few would attempt this search today. There is a greater readiness to accept that any organisational structure must meet the needs and particular circumstances of the individual organisation. What is effective for firm A may not be effective for firm B nor may it continue to be appropriate for firm A if its circumstances and the environment within which it operates change.

Hierarchies

The most common way an organisation responds to the challenge of growth, and possibly the organisational style with which most people are familiar, is based on a **hierarchical pyramid** with a clear line of command running from the top to the lower levels and with accountability running from the bottom to the top.

Offices within the hierarchy are usually based on **functions**, the most common being those of finance, personnel, production, purchasing or marketing. The hierarchical business structure accepts that authority and direction flow down from the Board of Directors, within which the Managing Director usually has considerable power to act personally in the name of the Board, to various levels of managers.

Figure 2.4 shows a simple functional structure with management based on the functions of production, marketing, purchasing and finance. Attempts to distinguish between the levels of management in order to indicate status and authority within the firm have led to the adoption of titles other than 'manager' in some firms. The most common practice is to designate managers at the more senior levels as 'directors'. The term 'director' has thus become a little confusing. In a large company it could indicate membership of the main company board, the board of a subsidiary company or management at a senior level.

The diagram of a hierarchical organisation may suggest a very clear structure of authority and direction but, in practice managers cannot operate in the kind of watertight vertical funnels that it might appear to indicate. Each specialist area is dependent on the others and in some degree influences the others. The purchasing manager, for example, buys the materials etc. which, say, production managers need but their requirements and even production processes can be modified by information supplied by purchasers, and both must operate within constraints imposed by finance. Similarly, personnel departments recruit and hire workers for other departments but they also have to ensure that the requirements of legislation are met, and they will also influence company training and education.

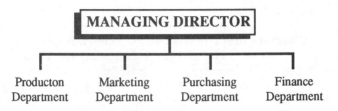

Figure 2.4 *Simple functional organisation*

It is clear that there are two kinds of relationship within a managerial structure. On the one hand a senior manager can give directions to a subordinate, e.g. the production manager can instruct a works manager to produce a given quantity of a product to certain specifications by a certain date. On the other hand one specialist manager can advise another that certain rules or senior management instructions have to be observed in relation to certain activities. Consequently the line between 'direction' and 'advice' can sometimes be very thin. Nevertheless the distinction between the two is the basis for the well known managerial division into **line and staff** relationships. Line management refers to direction and control, e.g. production and works management in the diagram. Staff management refers to specialist advice which can certainly modify or set constraints on the authority of line managers within their spheres of influence, e.g. finance and personnel management in relation to production. These divisions are not watertight. A personnel manager has line responsibilities for the people in his or her department and often for training. A marketing manager is likely to have a staff relationship with production. A simple example is shown in Figure 2.5.

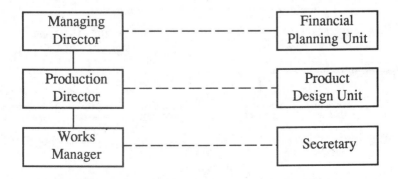

Figure 2.5 *Line and staff relationship. Solid lines show line, broken lines staff relationships*

The kind of blurring of functions noted above becomes increasingly important as production becomes more varied and complex. It makes the hierarchical structure somewhat difficult to maintain when the firm is engaged in anything other than routine mass production of fairly simple products. It can lead to indecision and disagreement, so that decisions frequently get passed up the hierarchy to levels senior to both the line and staff managers involved. In some circumstances top managers can find themselves snowed under with calls to make operational decisions, to the neglect of their strategic decision-making roles. On the other hand any attempt to erect a level of top management above all operational responsibilities may make the managers remote from reality and lead to unrealistic decisions.

Attempts to overcome the problems faced by hierarchical structures has led to the development of other organisational structures.

Divisionalised structures

In this kind of structure the firm is divided into sections with each responsible for an individual product or territory. The division is frequently established as a separate private limited company with its shares owned by the parent company. For convenience we can refer simply to divisions and ignore the legal way in which these may be constituted. Functional specialisation takes place within each division which thus has its own managers for production, sales and distribution, marketing, purchasing, personnel or any other pattern of specialised function which is considered appropriate to the firm's activities and size.

As long as a division successfully achieves the objectives set by the senior management of the parent company it is likely to operate with a considerable degree of independence, though under its firm financial control. Any major investment project will have to meet the conditions established by the parent and be in accordance with its general business strategy.

There may be some loss of the benefits of specialisation but there may also be gains from the feeling among divisional managers that they have considerable control over their own operations and are responsible for their own successes - and failures. In practice the specialist managers in the divisions co-operate with each other and also compete with other to some extent.

A very simple form of divisionalised structure is represented in Figure 2.6.

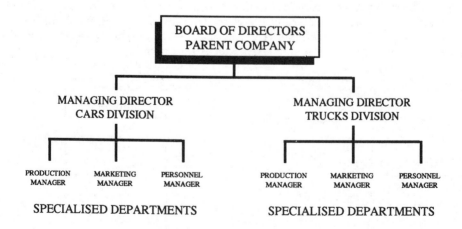

Figure 2.6   *A divisionalised management structure*

Matrix structure

This seeks to achieve the benefits of both hierarchical and divisionalised structures. People are assigned to particular functional departments but each product or project is made the responsibility of a project leader who draws people as required from the functional departments. The main advantage of this is that people are given specific duties in relation to particular products and are brought into direct contact with others whose specialist skills are required to complete the project. There is, however, the danger that individuals find themselves having to meet conflicting requirements from more than one 'boss'.

A simple matrix structure is illustrated in Figure 2.7.

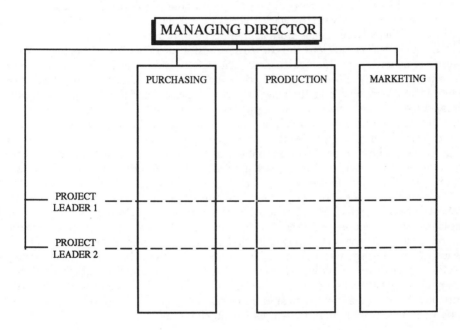

Figure 2.7 *Matrix organisation for two major projects*

Other structures

There are other structures, most of which emphasise team operation and the need to give individuals a feeling of responsibility for particular activities or projects. They also aim to shorten and clarify lines of communication between those whose work has to be co-ordinated to achieve a finished product. Detailed examination of these can await more advanced studies of business organisations.

TEST YOUR UNDERSTANDING

19 Is there a best kind of management structure?
20 What kind of management structure best fits your own company - or another company well known to you?
21 The terms 'line' and 'staff' really describe functions of management rather than positions in the company. How far is this true?

Some management problems

Motivation

When an organisation grows and when strategic decision making moves to a management level which appears to be remote from the people who must eventually put the decisions into effect, there is always the possibility that individuals become alienated from the environment in which they are employed. Working in a small firm brings individual employees into personal contact with their employer. In a period of reasonably full employment it can be assumed that workers will only remain with a small employer if they have some respect and liking for that employer. If there is personal friction or disagreement with the work objectives and methods of the employer then the employee will leave and seek a more congenial place of work.

In a large firm the situation tends to be rather different. There may be aspects of work that are liked and those that are disliked. The dislike, particularly if shared by groups of workers, can lead to a kind of passive resistance in which workers maximise their own benefits from work but do as little actual work as possible. If this attitude spreads to managers it can be especially damaging because it means that managers are not contributing any initiative or much beyond the minimum skill and energy.

A major problem, therefore, for the senior management of large organisations is that of motivation - how to persuade managers and workers to identify with the firm's objectives and to work positively and energetically and with initiative. This is an organisational rather than a personal problem because even the most charismatic business leader cannot transmit personal magnetism to more than a small proportion of the total workforce. The reconciliation of possible conflicts between worker and employer expectations of work is examined later. At this stage it is sufficient to recognise that high pay is not always the answer and, in some circumstances, may even aggravate the difficulty. The organisation has to be structured in a way that enables the manager to retain a high degree of individuality in spite of having to meet the requirements of his or her 'office', to obtain personal satisfaction through the achievement of objectives that contribute to the success of the firm and to recognise that subordinates also have to be motivated to work with and not against the objectives of the firm.

Co-operation, co-ordination and communication

These are often known as the three 'C's. In the modern large business organisation very little can be achieved by individual effort alone. Not only is it normally impossible for an individual to manufacture a complete product, it is also difficult and often impossible for an individual to carry out a complete commercial service function. More and more business activity depends on team work. A typical example might be the promotion of a new product and its introduction to the market. Although the marketing manager may be in overall charge of such an operation, numerous specialists will also be involved, including many who will be employed by other firms. The preparation of leaflets and display advertisements, for example, will involve photographers, advertising agents and the support of people in production departments to make products available and explain them to people outside the firm. The larger the promotion the greater the number of people involved and the greater the need for careful co-ordination of all the various activities. The marketing manager is likely to spend much time in securing the co-operation of others, co-ordinating their work and communicating the necessary information.

Leadership

It is not only the major projects that require the three 'Cs' which have just been noted. A fairly simple task such as preparing a report is likely to involve the co-operation of several people. If we regard the ability to persuade other people to work, co-operate and co-ordinate the work of others as essential elements in a quality that can be described as leadership, then we must recognise the need to develop leadership qualities in people at many layers of the organisation.

Leadership is much discussed by those concerned with modern business education and training. There is no universal agreement on precisely what constitutes a leader, no certainty that it is even a separate quality in itself. Some would argue that if a group of people is subjected to one set of circumstances one person is likely to emerge as the leader but if the same group is put under an entirely different set of circumstances then another leader would emerge. If this is correct then a person appointed to a demanding management role in one period might be very successful for a time but could prove inadequate if conditions changed.

There is even less agreement on the best ways to identify and recruit leaders and on how to foster and develop leadership qualities in those believed to be capable of leading and managing. Most would agree that leadership skills can be improved with training though there are different views as to the form that training should take. However realistic training simulations are made, no one really knows how a person will react in an emergency until he or she is faced with that emergency. Anyone who has lived through active service in war knows how surprising can be the character revelations under conditions of extreme danger. Many people with distinguished records in war have survived to become successful leaders in business or politics but by no means all were able to make the difficult transition from war to peace.

It is possible that there are different styles of leadership and not all of these are suitable for people in bureaucratic organisations. Some imaginative, creative and charismatic leaders find it difficult to temper their enthusiasm to the need to be part of a team and to communicate with others in the team. Such people can be very destructive and frustrated in a large business organisations and may be better running their own firm, however small. On the other hand the large organisation does need people with imagination, initiative and charisma. How to harness people with these qualities and help them to develop the other skills required of organisational leaders is an important organisational problem in a country such as the UK, which is trying to adapt its economic and social structure to the rapidly changing conditions of the modern world.

This discussion has stressed the issue in terms of the large organisation and a major difference between leadership in large and small organisations should be recognised. In the small unit the leader will generally have the same skills, training and background as the subordinate members of the group. Respect for the leader will depend on the possession of competence in skills which all possess and recognise. The head teacher of the primary school, for example, must be a competent classroom teacher to be accepted by the other teachers in the school. Given this common background the leader understands and often shares the problems and anxieties of the subordinates. Leadership is likely to involve the ability to assist subordinates to overcome these problems. Leading by example is likely to be a successful and even essential technique.

However, in the large organisation this common background of skill and knowledge is less likely to be present. No one would expect the Head of a large comprehensive school to teach to A level standard every subject offered in the school. The leader in the large unit must be much more of a co-ordinator, a person capable of understanding the needs of people whose skills he or she does not possess and respecting their special skills and abilities. Indeed, subordinates may be superior to the leader in some of the specialised skills and abilities valued in their institution. Nevertheless the leader has the task which they do not have of combining their work to achieve organisational goals. To do so the leader must be able to gain the respect of subordinates without being able to lead by example in the ways normal in the small unit. This difference poses further problems of leadership selection and training which by no means all organisations have been able to overcome. It is only too evident that subordinates in many large organisations do not respect and do not accept the authority of some of their most senior managers.

TEST YOUR UNDERSTANDING

22   All large organisations have to face the problem that they require leadership of ability and that somehow they must produce leaders. There remains the question of how these are to be produced. Are leaders born or made?
23   Many young army officer cadets have been given the advice, 'Never ask any of your men to do something you could not or would not do yourself.' Is this sound advice for the aspiring business manager?
24   What additional skills must the manager in a large company display when he or she reaches a managerial level above that of a functional specialist such as finance or marketing?

Ownership, control and business enterprise

Profit maximisation and its problems

The traditional assumption of economics has long been that the objective of the firm is to maximise its profits. This results from the classical economic belief that 'economic man' always tries to maximise self interest. The self interest of the business owner is assumed to be profit. Consequently classical economics operates on the belief that business firms attempt to maximise their profits. This does not just mean that firms seek profits. Few would wish to challenge the importance of profit for the survival of all business organisations which are not protected from financial collapse by the State. **Maximise**, however, means the largest possible so to say that firms try to achieve profit maximisation suggests that their overriding goal is to make the largest possible profit.

To achieve this firms need to be able to choose the output level and, if they have freedom to choose their own price, the price level, which will ensure that the additional revenue they receive from the last unit of output sold is just equal to the additional cost of producing that unit. Given that production decisions have to be made well in advance of actual market sales, this may seem an impossible task. If we also think in terms of firms producing a range of products in many different product and geographical markets and making long run decisions about product development, location, prices, marketing strategies and so on, the goal of profit maximisation begins to look even more unattainable.

Accepting these practical difficulties the modern supporters of the profit maximisation theory suggest that firms profit maximise within the limits of their knowledge and that, given two possible courses of action, they will tend to choose the one offering the greatest profit.

Nevertheless those who think that profit maximisation is not the objective pursued by large firms point out that a number of important aspects of their behaviour do not accord with what we would expect if they were profit maximising. Among these are advertising expenditure, which rarely appears to accord with a desire to make the largest possible profit, and responses to some types of cost change.

The ownership and control controversy

Much of the debate over business objectives revolves around the question of who really controls the large public company. The legal position is that the company is financed by a joint stock of capital. This stock is divided into shares which are then bought by people who thereby become shareholders. These shareholders have most of the legal rights of ownership but they cannot exercise direct control. Instead they elect a board of directors to act on their behalf and in their interests. In turn, the directors appoint managers who actually manage the day to day operation of the company, usually under the leadership of the Managing Director who is a member of the Board (and sometimes also the company Chairman) and has authority to act in its name on most practical management issues.

The interest of the shareholders in the company is primarily financial so that it is frequently assumed that shareholders favour profit maximisation because this would ensure the largest possible financial return from their holding of shares.

However, it has been suggested that neither the shareholders nor their representatives, the directors, have either the knowledge or the real power to challenge the people who control the day to day operation of the company - the managers. Because the large public company can be expected to have significant power in the market place as a result of its importance to market supply, it can achieve substantial profits with many output and price combinations without seeking to *maximise* profits. This opens up the possibility of a trade off between profit and some other objective or objectives that offer satisfaction to managers. If we accept the possibility that the company is really controlled by its managers then it is feasible to think that managers are able to pursue their own interests with little or no interference from directors or shareholders as long as profits are in line with shareholder and financial market expectations.

Before examining possible managerial objectives it is fair to point out that not all observers believe that the modern large company is managerially controlled. Some accept that it may have been in the past but that from around the early 1970s finance markets have become dominated by financial institutions (described more fully in Unit 4), mostly pension funds, insurance offices and banks. It is these institutions that are now the major shareholders and they have restored shareholder power. They have the knowledge and resources to analyse company performance more thoroughly than any individual shareholder and they can topple boards of directors if they lose confidence in their ability to make the profits they consider possible. Other observers dispute whether there ever was a significant 'divorce' between company ownership and control. They argue that the really wealthy have always been able to exercise power in company board rooms although their identities and influence have frequently been concealed by devices such as trusts and bank nominees. Perhaps more significantly they suggest that the senior managers of large companies tend to come from the same social groups as the major shareholders and have always had their interests at heart. Senior managers are likely to be shareholders themselves, though not usually major holders of shares in the companies they manage.

Clearly the issue is arguable and involves matters of social and political debate beyond the scope of this course. Of relevance, of course, is the question of control over the financial institutions. Are these controlled by a relatively small group of wealthy international bankers as some sociologists maintain - or are these also managerially controlled companies in the same mould as the business companies in which they invest their clients' funds?

TEST YOUR UNDERSTANDING

25 Why is it believed that the managers of large companies have more to gain from growth than from maximising profit?

26 Can shareholders exercise any control over large public companies?
27 In what ways can a policy of growth be pursued at the expense of profit?

Managerial objectives

There is, at least, a case for examining possible managerial objectives which may have replaced or modified profit maximisation as the overriding business goal. Notice that it is profit maximisation that is in dispute. No one doubts the importance of making profits to the survival and success of the shareholder-owned public company. The question is whether managers pursue additional objectives at the expense of some profit. A number of possibilities have been suggested.

Revenue maximisation subject to making a minimum profit

The minimum profit is necessary to satisfy shareholders and the financial markets but once this is achieved managers seek to maximise sales revenue. You should not, of course, confuse revenue and profit. Revenues are the receipts from sales **before deduction of costs**. Revenue is seen as the symbol of success in the market place. Managers who can boost revenue tend to gain credit in the organisation and the rewards that accompany success. To achieve revenue they are likely to incur advertising costs beyond the point where these are adding to profits and they will also push up production levels so that additional costs become greater than additional revenue, i.e. they will sacrifice some profit to achieve increased revenue.

The maximisation of managerial utility

This is an interesting view because it manages to incorporate multiple managerial objectives while keeping the idea of maximising one goal. It achieves this by taking managerial utility as the goal and then identifying three elements in that utility. The elements are:

- **Discretionary profit**
  This is profit above the minimum needed to satisfy shareholders and financial markets. It is recognised that managers do not ignore profit once this minimum is obtained but still see it as a desirable objective. One reason for this is that profits increase the amount of investment finance available and managers achieve satisfaction from being able to control large investment budgets. Critics might see this a form of enjoyment gained from spending money that properly belongs to the shareholders - a similar satisfaction to that gained by politicians who appear to enjoy money which properly belongs to the taxpayers!

- **Staff expansion**
  Managers also gain satisfaction from controlling large departments. Salary, status and other rewards frequently depend on the number of people for whose work a manager is responsible. Expanding the size of the organisation can sometimes appear to be an end in itself. There can be few workers who have not seen 'empire building' in progress in their organisations.

- **Managerial emoluments**
  A more common name for this is **perks** and it includes all the non-salary rewards that

come from climbing the managerial ladder. They include such items as the company car, the expense account and the right to use company credit and charge cards, the right to first-class travel by rail and air or even rights to use the company aircraft and helicopter. The corporate gravy trough grows ever deeper and the right to dip one's snout into it is valued not only for the pleasures of the perks gained but also for the status and prestige attaching to it.

O. E. Williamson, who developed the theory of managerial utility maximisation (outlined in his book, *Corporate Control and Business Behaviour*), saw it as a consequence of the loss of shareholder control over managers, associated mainly with the hierarchical style of company organisation. He suggested a remedy in the form of the divisionalised structure but with an 'elite group' situated between divisional management and the main board of directors. This group's function was to monitor divisional performance and ensure that profit, properly recorded and accounted to the shareholders, was retained as the prime objective of the firm.

Maximisation of the rate of company growth

The idea of growth as a desirable managerial objective is never far from any theory advanced as an alternative to profit maximisation. It underlies the theories of sales revenue and managerial utility maximisation. Growth as an end in itself appears in a number of theories and one of the most developed of these, that proposed by Professor Robin Marris (especially in his book, *The Economic Theory of Managerial Capitalism*), suggests that there is no limit to the size that the successful firm can grow and that managers will push for the fastest possible rate of growth subject to the fear of takeover. Growth, whether by internal expansion or by merger/takeover, requires finance and if it is pursued at too fast a rate the finance used for growth will reduce the share of profit that can be allocated to the individual shareholder. Shareholders who fail to receive the returns they feel they should have are likely to sell their shares. Share prices will fall and the company becomes vulnerable to takeover. The first casualties in a takeover are the senior managers of the company taken over so management will seek to avoid this fate and this will set a limit to the speed of growth of the company.

Behavioural theory

The theories based on management power so far outlined have all suggested objectives other than or in addition to profit that managers may seek to maximise. Behavioural theory follows the line of argument outlined by H.A. Simon whose major book, *Administrative Behaviour*, eventually earned him a Nobel prize. Simon argued that firms do not try to maximise anything but seek to satisfy a number of conflicting objectives as they react to the problems presented by an uncertain and changing environment. Two American writers, Cyert and March, whose book *A Behavioural Theory of the Firm*, remains one of the clearest descriptions of this concept, developed the behavioural approach to form a fairly coherent behavioural theory of the firm based on four fundamental behavioural concepts:

- **Quasi resolution of conflict**
  Managers were forced by the nature of the firm and the forces influencing it, (shareholders, customers, professional managers etc.), to pursue conflicting objectives. This conflict could never be fully resolved but the different forces could be partially satisfied, i.e. the conflict was partially resolved.

- **Uncertainty avoidance**
  Day to day management would be impossible if every issue had to be resolved as an

individual matter. In practice managers develop decision making rules and they seek to control both the internal environment of the firm and the external environment within which it operates. In this way the degree of uncertainty against which managerial decision making has to take place is reduced.

- **Problemistic search**
  A theory based on maximisation assumes constant search so that the managers can adapt to change. If maximisation is abandoned then search need only take place when existing decision making rules fail to provide a satisfactory solution to a problem that threatens the stability or survival of the firm. Such problems would include declining profits and share price, loss of customer orders, high turnover of specialist managers and so on. Faced with this kind of problem, and failing to solve it with procedures based on past experience, forces managers to undertake search activity designed to achieve a satisfactory (not the best possible) solution to that problem as perceived by the decision makers. Search ends as soon as a satisfactory solution has been achieved.

- **Organisational learning**
  Achievement of a new and satisfactory solution becomes part of the learning mechanism of the firm which adapts its decision-making rules accordingly. Goals are also modified in the light of perceived experience and perceptions of the achievements of comparable organisations.

Behavioural theory is essentially descriptive. It gives a good account of the way many large firms really do behave. It is also adaptable to a range of different organisations. Although Cyert and March suggested a number of goals which they believed were relevant to the business firms of their day, the same framework could be applied to different organisations with different goals. The theory provides interesting insights into the behaviour of non-profit seeking public sector organisations which are not easily analysed with the conventional tools of economic analysis.

On the other hand it is not a complete theory of the firm in that it says nothing about what firms *ought* to do. There is no comment on welfare or about the efficient use of resources. Indeed the concept of efficiency does not seem to come into this theory.

Other theories

There are other theories, among them game theory which is really an explanation of the options available in situations involving conflict between rivals with very similar objectives. These also add interesting insights into behaviour within organisations but none provide a complete alternative to the traditional concept of profit maximisation, still an essential starting point for understanding most of the major decisions that organisational managers have to make.

TEST YOUR UNDERSTANDING

28 Is managerial control of large business companies desirable from the point of view of the community?

29 Is a high level of company take-over activity desirable from the point of view of the community?

Implications for enterprise

As soon as you start looking closely at the behaviour of managers in large organisations you are faced with the need to reconcile with modern reality one of the traditional concepts of classical economics, that of **enterprise**.

Enterprise is still often explained as the quality of risk taking on the part of the **entrepreneur**, who risks personal capital in the search for profit through organising and controlling a business organisation. While this may be a plausible explanation of business motivation in an economy made up of large numbers of small, owner-managed firms it has an air of unreality when you come to look at the large multinational group whose profits are shared among thousands of shareholders, most of whom have only the slimmest idea of the group's activities. Who are the entrepreneurs in **Unilever, ICI, British Gas or Shell**? Whoever they are they are certainly not the shareholders.

More modern economists, adopting ideas introduced by what has become known as the 'Austrian school', have taken a fresh look at the idea of enterprise and explain in terms of the ability to foresee opportunities for profit in the conditions likely to be found tomorrow. This involves not only looking forward to future market demand but also to future production possibilities and seeing how the two open up new ways of meeting needs to the satisfaction of both buyer and seller. Seen in this light enterprise is a dynamic concept and the driving force is the desire to profit by being first in a new field. The entrepreneur is a pioneer rather than a risk taker though, of course, risks are involved because the entrepreneur's vision of the future may be wrong or simply mistimed. The entrepreneur will, of course, wish to use modern techniques of advertising and product promotion to support and encourage the vision to become reality.

This kind of enterprise is not just the privilege of the business owner or the managing director of the public company. It can be shown by employees with decision-making powers at any level of the organisation. It can also be a team quality. Many business leaders and analysts believe that future success for a large corporation depends on the ability to foster this kind of enterprise throughout the organisation. Without it the company is likely to sink under the weight of organisational bureaucracy.

How to promote and reward enterprise within a corporate structure which often tends to be intolerant and intensely suspicious of original thinking, except at the very top, is one of the challenges facing the modern organisation. Recognition of the need to make managers at all levels more profit conscious and more aware of the ways they, as individuals, can improve profits, underlies the modern tendency to introduce a strong profit sharing element into managerial remuneration. Whether this is one path towards encouraging greater enterprise and leadership remains to be seen. It could simply be viewed as a further device to channel revenues due to shareholders into the pockets of managers.

There are no easy solutions to these problems but you should be aware that they exist and be ready to discuss them.

TEST YOUR UNDERSTANDING

30 Who are the entrepreneurs in modern business?
31 How should business enterprise be rewarded?

NOTES TO QUESTIONS

Question 1
Among the common motives for starting a business are the desire for independence and the desire to be in control of an enterprise. If a firm grows beyond a certain size these

qualities are lost because additional finance has to be gained at the cost of giving up total control over the firm. We have already seen that the style and structure of management change as firms grow. Owners who have built up their own personal management structure are reluctant to move towards the bureaucratic structure. In summary we might say that the owners recognise that growth will change the whole nature of the firm and running the new operation is likely to require qualities and skills they do not posses while their own style and attitudes are unlikely to fit into the changed firm.

However, refusal to grow in a market where demand is rising can be very dangerous and this refusal will leave unsatisfied customers and create opportunities for new suppliers. The firm that refuses to grow may soon find itself in decline. The most common solution to this dilemma is to sell the firm to a larger organisation or to a business owner who does wish to pursue growth. This solution can be a very difficult one to accept for someone who has devoted a working life to a particular firm. It can also have serious consequences for employees who are likely to find it difficult to fit into the changed firm.

Question 2

It may seem to be beyond argument that the larger the area of responsibility the higher should be the salary. The economic justification would seem to be that the larger organisation is likely to be making the greater contribution to the activities and profits of the firm. The personal justification would be based on the view that the larger responsibility requires a person of more ability, skill and experience.

However, there is no guarantee that size and profitability are closely correlated nor any certainty that controlling a long established, well staffed department requires any more skill than building up a small, new one. When pay and size are linked there is no incentive for any manager to keep administrative costs low. On the contrary the incentive is to build empires. This is particularly prevalent in public sector institutions.

Question 3

- Firms are enjoying economies of scale when the proportional increase in output resulting from a given increase in factor inputs is greater than the proportional increase in input, e.g. when 5 per cent more factors produce 10 per cent more production.
- Firms suffer from diseconomies of scale when the proportional increase in output resulting from a given increase in factor inputs is less than the proportional increase in input, e.g. when 10 per cent more factors produce 5 per cent more production. The factor inputs can be labour, capital or most probably both.
- The minimum efficient scale of operations is the output level beyond which no significant economies are achieved from further increases in size. A firm operating above the MES is not achieving savings in unit costs as it grows larger. Consequently if it does continue to grow there must be some other explanation for that growth.

Question 4

In general, dominance by large firms is more widespread in manufacturing than in services but there are exceptions. Computer manufacturing is becoming increasingly dominated by large firms after a period when small firms appeared in the new microcomputer market. However, after some years of intense competition the market is now settling towards a position where the giant international firms are gaining control.

Computer software production offers more scope for small organisations because much of the best work can be achieved by several individuals working in isolation. Nevertheless software marketing requires large international networks so that software firms tend to combine the advantages of the two extremes of size. Actual production is carried out in very small units but marketing is handled by much larger institutions. Nevertheless the position is changing all the time. The development of author languages may make the production of much routine software fairly simple and suitable for larger scale production.

Clothing manufacture is not dominated by large firms. Manufacturers have to be flexible and able to switch production quickly to new styles. Again distribution is in the hands of large firms but manufacture is often in very small units. Motor components manufacturing tends to be dominated by large firms able to deal with large motor manufacturers in world markets.

We might expect accountancy to be mainly the preserve of small firms. It is a service activity and one with a long tradition of resisting limited liability or incorporated structures. There are indeed very many small firms and by industrial standards the level of concentration is not high. On the other hand most of the large scale business of services local authorities, other public sector organisations and public companies is handled by a small number of very large firms which now operate on an international scale. A multinational company requires a multinational firm of accountants to handle its auditing and associated financial business.

Motor components manufacturing is less heavily concentrated than motor manufacturing itself but again there is a growth in the power and influence of large multinational companies. It is difficult to resist the modern trend towards reliance on large organisations.

Question 5

People have been asking whether small shops can survive for the past quarter of a century at least. They still do survive though not in such large numbers and often very precariously. Retailing is now dominated by the giant superstore and national chain groups but there are still sectors within retailing where skill and personal service are important and there are areas where the potential demand is too small to interest large firms. Franchising is one method of associating with a big group but remaining small and independent to a large group. Co-operation through voluntary groups and chains is another. Nevertheless small shopkeepers have to be prepared to struggle to survive and the further they are from the major superstores the better their chances of achieving a satisfactory living.

Question 6

In recent years advances in computer technology have been in the direction of producing small computers at steadily reducing costs. Financially, therefore, equipment that would have seemed extremely advanced a decade before has moved within the reach of most small firms. The main limitation has been the ability to make use of the available technology. Lack of managerial and technical skill has been the major problem of many small firms. Time is likely to overcome this problem and it is possible that modern computer technology will enable an increasing number of small firms to survive and compete with large organisations in some specialised fields of activity.

Question 7

Your answer, of course, must depend on the type of firm you have chosen. However, look for the way such activities as financial control and marketing are carried out. If the firm is too small to have specialised departments for each managerial function consider how the functions are combined and the extent to which some might be neglected.

Question 8

The difference between selling and marketing is an important one. The person whose background has been in sales is in danger of concentrating on the task of selling a particular range of goods without looking at changes in the market place and whether the range of goods should be changed to meet new conditions. This difference is stressed when marketing is considered in more detail.

Question 9

- For the employer the benefits of part-time working are those of greater flexibility, especially the ability to vary the quantity of labour employed to fit changing market conditions. It is often said that 'You can't employ half a worker.' In fact this is possible through part-time work. Part-time work can also be used to provide a kind of probation for new workers to find out if they are suitable for full-time employment. The cost is usually lower as certain statutory benefits need not be provided for workers employed for less than a stated number of hours.
- The dangers for the employer lie largely in the fact that part-time workers often lack the commitment of full-time workers. They may not be able or willing to increase their working hours to meet special needs. When the workers decide they prefer full-time work they may decide to seek different employment and their experience and knowledge is lost to the firm.
- For the employee part-time working has a number of attractions including: the chance to combine work with personal interests or responsibilities; the opportunity to continue work when full-time work would not be possible or available. The flexibility offered by part-time work is attractive to many people at certain stages of their working lives when they do not want to become committed to a particular employer or, sometimes, an occupation.
- The dangers to the employee include: the loss of statutory employment protection rights; often lower rates of pay; lack of pension provision and lack of opportunity to progress in a chosen career.

Question 10

Advice to the small firm owner might include the following:

- Think very carefully about the work to be delegated and identify the kind of person most capable of doing this work.
- Take trouble and care in selecting a person most likely to meet the needs that have been identified. The person prepared to work for the lowest wage may not be the least expensive person in the long run.
- Be prepared to take time and trouble to train the person and do not expect work to be done exactly as before. Differences may well be improvements!
- Evaluate the benefits and costs after a reasonable period and be prepared to accept an honest evaluation and act accordingly.

Question 11

This question concerns the kind of managerial leadership required in different circumstances. The leader of a small scale institution such as a small primary school will be 'one of the staff', with roughly the same training, experience and skills as other members of staff. To gain respect this head must also be at least as good a teacher as any other on the staff. This head must set an example of good teaching as well as efficient management of the school.

The informality that is likely to characterise the small school will be absent in the large comprehensive. Here the head cannot hope to share the specialisms of more than one or two of the staff. Ability to display the skills of a teacher are likely to be much less important and subordinate to the ability to manage and co-ordinate the efforts of many different kinds of specialists. Stimulating others and co-ordinating their work are qualities most to be desired in the manager of the larger school.

Similar comments could be applied to other kinds of operation in both the public and private sectors.

Question 12

The superstores were different from other retailing establishments at that time. They represented something new in retailing and it was felt that new kinds of managers were needed. These should have specialist managerial skills and not just the skills and experience of working in a shop. It was hoped that a personnel manager trained and coming from industry would be able to identify the managerial needs of the store and be able to select and train people with the necessary skills. These managers would soon gain retailing experience and bring their other skills to solve the new problems being faced by the new trading establishments.

Question 13
The management buy-out has become a feature of modern industrial life and many have been successful in that prosperity has been restored to a small company which had become a problem for a large group. Often the company with regained independence had been successful before take-over. In many cases this z-turn has been achieved under broadly the same group of managers so that it cannot be explained in terms of managerial competence. The more likely reason lies in the difference of approach between small and large organisations. A company which had flourished under a personal style of management lost its way when forced into a bureaucratic structure. Customers who had become used to a personal style of decision making were likely to become impatient with the delays and uncertainties of dealing with a large organisation, especially when the local managers were themselves uncertain how to obtain decisions. Frustrated managers were likely to become demoralised, seeing no personal advantage in pursuing the objectives of the parent organisation. Restoration of independence and removal of the bureaucratic structure enabled the managers to regain their confidence.

Question 14
Nepotism, the favouring of relatives at the expense of others apparently better qualified for available work, has come to be regarded as something of a business crime in a modern Western industrial society. It was seen as the natural way of doing things in nineteenth century Britain and in many Eastern societies today. Clearly to ignore job competence and to employ people solely on the grounds of their relationship to owners or employees is a recipe for disaster. It could even be criminal if the lives and safety of others were put at risk by an incompetent or dangerous worker. However, assuming that a person has attained or has the ability and desire to attain a satisfactory level of job competence then employment of people having personal connections with the firm can have definite advantages. These can include:

- An awareness of the objectives and structure of the company and the actual working relationships of employees
- The worker quickly becomes part of the informal communications structure of the organisation
- Loyalty to the family becomes integrated with loyalty to the firm
- The family exercises an informal code of discipline and standards of behaviour which reduce the need for formal discipline control procedures within the firm
- The worker quickly gains acceptance and fits into the working group

In spite of the apparent unfairness of favouring families it is not difficult to see why many employers do adopt the practice. Moreover the rate of labour turnover is likely to be lower than if relationships are ignored as workers are less likely to move to obtain a temporary wage advantage. If other members of the family approve of the employer sufficiently to want the worker to join them they are likely to point to the long term advantages of staying with the firm.

Question 15
In the case of the potential manager who is a member of the controlling family it may seem unnecessary to suggest formal training as the person concerned is likely to have an intimate knowledge of the firm, its personnel and objectives already. However, in modern business all managers need a range of managerial skills which are increasingly being taught through practical, business related courses. Since other managers in the

firm may not have been exposed to outside influences for some time it is more than ever necessary to ensure that a new generation brings in the highest possible level of skill and training.

Among the more obvious areas where up-to-date training is desirable are financial management, information technology, company law, marketing techniques and personnel management, including labour law. In addition, of course, it is desirable for the manager to be up-to-date in the specialised technology of the business itself.

Question 16

Any business decision or action has both vertical and horizontal consequences, in that it affects people at levels below and above the decision maker and other specialists at the same level. To take the simplest possible example. The sale of an article affects finance, especially if it is a credit sale, stock levels (hence future purchasing) and marketing (which is affected by sales trends). However, it would be ridiculous to pass a message to everyone in the company every time a sale took place. Those who need to know require the information in a form which they can understand, at times when it is required. In fact modern technology can ensure that every sale is recorded, that stock levels are automatically adjusted, that stock managers are warned when stocks reach a predetermined re-order level, that cumulative sales figures and trends are available to marketing departments and that customer accounts are adjusted and prepared. The larger the organisation the more important is it to ensure that information is passed to those who need it, when it is needed and in a form likely to be most helpful to those who have to take action on it.

Question 17

It is, perhaps, unfortunate that the term bureaucracy has become associated with inefficiency. Clearly it is inefficient if it imposes unnecessary work, delays and costs on those who have to take action to further the interests of the organisation. Writing a formal report to a person you meet each day at coffee break is likely to be an example of this kind of inefficiency, unless a written record is required to meet some other legal or business obligation. Administrative procedures must meet the needs of the organisation, be sufficient to meet those needs, but should involve no more work than is absolutely necessary for this purpose. It is desirable for people to know **why** certain tasks have to be performed, **who** uses the information they are recording and **what** happens if the information is not recorded or recorded inaccurately. If people do not know why they are doing things and do not feel that their activities are of any importance they are unlikely to do the tasks well or accurately.

Question 18

Bureaucracy is most closely associated with public sector organisations and there are special reasons for its prevalence in the public sector. All public sector institutions have to operate according to powers granted under the authority of Parliament. If they act outside those powers the individual responsible could be held legally and financially accountable for the action. Many public sector organisations can have their actions questioned by Members of Parliament and/or Parliamentary Committees or by local councillors in the local government sectors. All public servants, therefore, have to be able to justify and explain their actions and be able to show that they were taken within the bounds of the legal powers granted by Parliament. It is thus inevitable that public servants have to make many more records and act within much more formal procedures than workers in the private sector.

Question 19

Most students of management now agree that there is no ideal form of management structure but there is likely to be a form that is more suitable than any other for any given firm. The structure must take into account the firm's size, its activities, the geographical range of its activities, its product range, its history and traditions and the personalities of its most senior managers. It must also be remembered that the structure that is right for 1989 might not be right for 1999. Change itself can sometimes revive a tired organisation but too frequent changes can be destructive.

Question 20
Things to look for in your company are the presence - or absence - of organisation charts and the lines of authority. At this stage you may also care to note the extent to which the formal organisational structure is actually modified in practice by informal structures, e.g. when people know that they need to get support or approval from A before approaching the formal decision maker, B.

You may find that none of the patterns identified in this text actually fits your firm perfectly. In this case try to decide how the differences have arisen. Have they just developed over time in response to changing circumstances and people or have they been deliberately planned to meet particular conditions?

Question 21
Most staff managers are also line managers in their own specialist departments so in this sense the terms describe functions rather than positions. However, the question also draws attention to the role of the adviser and of advice itself. Under what conditions does 'advice' actually convey line authority. If the computer manager tells a works manager that the company's information system requires the completion of certain records in a certain way by a given date, is this advice or instruction? If the personnel manager tells a production manager that workers can only be dismissed after a stated number of written warnings and after notification of the worker's union representative, is this advice or instruction? Very often the formal limitations of staff advice are preserved by the temporary delegation of authority from a line manager of sufficient status. In many cases, however, staff advice is generally recognised to be a powerful influence on the actions of subordinate managers.

Question 22
When questioned about this issue, Sir Peter Holmes, Chairman and Managing Director of Shell, gave an example of leadership qualities emerging in response to a particular situation. He was clearly of the view that these could be developed if the basic ability was there in the first place. If it was not there was little that could be done.

Some people believe that leadership can be shown by different people in different situations. In any given group A might emerge as the leader in one set of circumstances but B would emerge in others. If you have experience of an industrial dispute or of any other kind of emergency or crisis you may be able to offer views as to what enables some people to respond more effectively than others.

Question 23
The advice really refers chiefly to leadership under conditions of danger where people have to be inspired by example and not driven. It does, however, have a more general message. No one respects a manager whose abilities are questioned. A manager is not expected to be master of every skill he or she is called upon to direct but competence in some skill is expected and the person recognised to be competent in one skill can usually be trusted to respect the skills of others. The good manager must have the respect of others and respect has to be earned by example.

Question 24
When a manager rises above his or her specialist activity the essential qualities required involved the ability to co-ordinate and to persuade others to co-operate with each other. The manager must understand the contribution that the various specialists can make and how they fit together. The manager must, therefore, be the leader of a team.

Brilliance and skill at one particular specialist activity is no longer enough at this level.

Question 25

Until comparatively recently managers of large public companies were rarely rewarded in direct proportion to the profits of the company. Even today it is usually only the most senior managers who have a significant profit element in their pay in spite of some trends towards making pay more profit related. It is much more common to find that managerial salaries and their scale of perks depends on the size of the unit for which they are responsible. Size is measured either by the number of workers under their control or the amount of finance they are responsible for spending. This gives encouragement to build empires of staff and spend money. Managerial status also depends on size of empire. It is much more satisfying to announce yourself as the finance director of a major household name company than to admit to being an accounts manager for an unknown company - even though the latter job may require a great deal more skill. In spite of alluring advertisements and the activities of head hunters it becomes more difficult to move to a larger firm the older and more senior one becomes. Consequently the easiest path to increased status and salary is to encourage your existing employer to grow bigger.

Question 26

The majority of individual shareholders who hold relatively few shares in the large public companies have no power to exercise control at all although a few organised groups can attract media publicity at annual general meetings. Nevertheless there are some shareholders who can and do exercise considerable power. These are:

- **The financial institutions**
  These are insurance offices, pension funds, trust fund managers and so on whose investment managers have the staff and the expertise - and contacts - to find out how firms are performing and to put pressure on senior management to improve perform-ance if this is felt to be necessary.

- **Very wealthy individuals**
  Some are former owners, many are overseas people with considerable wealth. Their identities are often concealed by trusts and other devices but their power to influence fund managers and to put pressure on companies is often very real.

Firms now have to go to considerable efforts to achieve and retain the support of the fund managers and their wealthy clients, not only because their support is needed to obtain the finance needed for continued expansion but also to keep their loyalty in the face of any hostile take-over bid. In the modern stock market even very large companies can fall victim to determined take-over raiders. No company is safe unless it can count on the loyalty of the big fund managers.

Question 27

It is sometimes thought that the larger the firm the bigger the profit. Consequently there does not seem to be any serious conflict between the two. However a shareholder is interested in profit **per share** as it is this that determines the amount of dividend that can be paid. Doubling profit is not much gain for a shareholder if the process has been achieved by trebling the number of shares entitled to dividends. The previous notes will have already indicated how growth can be at the expense of profit when this involves managerial empire building and the expansion of expenditure plans. Thick carpets, china tea sets and luxury cars do not add to profits. They are paid for out of revenues that would otherwise have been available to pay dividends to shareholders. Sharehold-ers are not opposed to company growth provided that profits grow at least as fast and preferably faster. Too often, however, growth is achieved at the expense of some of the profit.

Question 28

Economists are divided over the desirability of managerial control - if indeed this exists. Peter Drucker in *The Practice of Management*, probably the best known of all books on business management, argues that it was to the benefit of the community because professionally trained managers were bound to be more efficient that owner-managers who owed their position to the accident of birth. He described professional management as the 'officer class' of modern business. O. E. Williamson, on the other hand saw managers as hiving off profits that properly belonged to the shareholders and regarded their power as arising from loss of shareholder control which should be restored.

The community interest is that business firms should be efficient in both the absolute (use of resources) sense and the allocative sense in that business should provide the goods and services that are most desired by the community. Traditional economics suggests that the market and the profit motive are the most effective means of achieving total efficiency. If this view is accepted, anything that interferes with the profit incentive is likely to produce inefficiencies so that managerial control should be looked at with suspicion.

There is no certain answer to this question but it is an important one as it concerns the use of scarce resources in economies which are, to a great degree, dominated by giant business companies.

Question 29

Another related question, and one that is being asked increasingly as the pace of take-overs increases on both sides of the Atlantic, is the desirability of take-overs. On the one hand the economic justification for take-overs is that they ensure that companies use resources efficiently because if they do not they will be taken over and managements will be replaced by more efficient teams.

The opposing view is that too high a level of take-over activity destabilises business, threatens jobs and undermines the finances of otherwise sound and profitable companies. The resources used in the 'take-over' industry are considerable and can be regarded as unproductively used - if the first argument is not accepted.

The question then is, do take-overs prevent managements from becoming lazy and encourage them to improve performance or do they prevent managers from getting on with their more desirable work of producing goods and services, creating real wealth and providing employment and incomes to the work force? Again there is no certain answer and you should try to form your own judgement.

Question 30

Traditionally the entrepreneur is seen as the organiser of production factors and the person who risks his or her own finance to engage in business for the pursuit of profit. The growth of large companies and of public sector activities has made this explanation unsatisfactory, but the general value of the entrepreneurial outlook and spirit remains important.

There are some entrepreneurs in the traditional style. A few outstanding individuals have created their own business empires and their success has been rewarded by the achievement of great wealth but these cannot run their empires single-handedly and they must employ other people of skill and enterprise to work for them. At the same time the giant companies continue to prosper and to show enterprise though few know the identities of their senior managers.

A more recent interpretation of enterprise is given by the Austrian school of economists who believe it can be shown by people at all levels and can be encouraged in all companies. In this view the function of the leaders of the large corporations is not to show immense individual enterprise but to develop entrepreneurial attitudes throughout the organisation.

Question 31

How then should enterprise be rewarded? The traditional return to enterprise has always been regarded as profit, but the profits of large companies belong to the shareholders who take no part in the activities and decision making of the firm. Extending the traditional view there are some who argue that enterprise among employees should be rewarded by a share in the profits they create. In practice this tends to become simply a device to raise the incomes of the most senior managers - some of whom make most unlikely looking entrepreneurs. It might be argued that the successful and enterprising individual is likely to rise and prosper in the company. Anyone with experience of large company bureaucracies is likely to be a little suspicious of that claim. Once more we have to admit there is no easy answer to this problem. Business requires the entrepreneurial spirit. How to foster and reward it remains one of the problems still facing the large business company.

3
Production and the organisation

The production of goods and services

Production defined

When applied to business organisations the term production has a rather narrower meaning than when used in economic theory. The economist applies the word to any activity which assists in the satisfaction of a human want although when it comes to measuring national production some of these activities, by convention, are not counted. Within the business organisation, however, there is usually a clear distinction between production and what are usually referred to as the commercial services. Production is then applied to the direct provision of whatever activity is the main source of the organisation's revenue if it is in the private sector of the economy or the main reason for its support by the State if it is in the public sector.

The production of goods

The term is most familiar when applied to the manufacture or assembly of physical goods. Production to the manufacturer means the actual work of making or assembling the product that is to be sold. Production management relates to the organisation of this activity, i.e. organising and controlling the machines and workers who make the actual goods.

In contrast to these the commercial departments are those that provide services to production, i.e. the purchasers of materials, the providers of finance and those who organise marketing, sales and distribution. In addition there are departments or functions which are neither production nor commercial but which support both these activities. The main support service is the personnel function including, in many cases, training.

The production of services

In recent years it has become common to use the term production to apply to services if they form the main revenue earning activity of the organisation. Accordingly an insurance office might refer to its underwriting and claims handling departments as 'production', and it will also have supporting services such as marketing, finance and personnel.

It is often helpful to identify the various activities within a service organisation in this way as it emphasises that there are similar organisational needs and problems whatever the nature of the revenue earning activity. Resources have to be provided, workers recruited and trained, finance provided and managed and marketing has to take place whether the activity is a service or a physical product.

Notice that what may be a commercial or support service in one organisation may be the main production activity in another. The example of insurance has already been given. Others would include accountancy, market research, advertising agencies and banking. The growing tendency to contract work to specialists is producing an increasingly diverse sector of firms providing all kinds of commercial and support services. Among fairly recent developments of this kind are direct mail companies, book distribution companies (for book publishers) and companies which organise conferences and sales promotions. Often it is the larger companies which support these specialists on the grounds that they can handle the work more efficiently and at less cost than their own staff.

Production in the public sector

Efforts to improve efficiency in the public sector have tended to encourage organisations to learn from the private sector, where firms must be profitable to survive. Increasingly public sector organisations are called upon to earn revenue from their activities, in order to reduce the burden on the public purse and to force them to be more responsive to demand in the markets in which they operate.

Introducing the terminology of private sector business organisation does more than just change a few names. For example, if the function of marketing is introduced to an institution of higher education it tends to change the whole approach to the educational services provided by that institution. Instead of seeking to 'recruit students to fill our courses' the institution starts to engage in market research to locate gaps in the current educational provision and to set up courses to fill these gaps. This then has major consequences for the buildings, equipment and personnel employed by the institution, for the way courses are taught and even for where they are taught. The college that thinks in terms of 'producing', marketing and financing a service behaves in a totally different way from one that thinks only in terms of supplying educational courses in a given area.

TEST YOUR UNDERSTANDING

1   How might the functions of production and marketing be applied to a firm of accountants?
2   To what extent could the concept of production be applied to a public sector hospital?

What is involved in production?

The work of planning and managing the work of production is often referred to as production engineering. This involves a number of processes which are both related to each other and to the work of other departments within the larger organisations.

Design and production method

There is more to production than simply making goods or providing services. Decisions have to be made about design, the way goods are made, and the machines to be used in manufacture. Design and production method are not, of course, independent issues. Ease and cost of production will be taken into account in the choice of design and some compromise may be necessary between the desire of the production manager to have a simple design and the requirements of the market. As Henry Ford said, customers could have any colour car they wished as long as it was black! At the time it was difficult and costly to introduce different colours into a mass production system and technically difficult to ensure that different batches of the same colour were all exactly the same shade. Consequently, if customers wanted a cheap, reasonably reliable car, it had to be black.

Design also includes choice of materials. This too involves compromises between what is desirable for the market and costs and methods of production. The choices open to producers depend on the level of technology available while the desire of producers to move in a particular direction will influence the areas of research. As steel became increasingly expensive in the 1950s car manufacturers sought substitute materials. They experimented with plastics but their favoured choice was glass. Increasing the proportion of glass to metal not only reduced production costs but also provided desirable market features in that it improved the vision of drivers and the appearance of the vehicle. To exploit this change fully, however, required new types of safer, tougher glass, that could be shaped more easily and cheaply. Here we see changes in design interacting with changes in technology to produce changes in production method. Changes of this kind also influence production systems, to be examined later.

Control over production

The management of the actual production process involves a number of related functions. These include:

- Ensuring that the materials and components needed are acquired and are available at the place and time required. Delays caused by shortages of essential materials can be very expensive as workers and machines are kept idle. In addition, workers become frustrated if they are on any form of payment by results system and may suspect managerial motives for the delay and loss of earnings. At best management will be shown to be inefficient and will lose employee confidence and respect. On the other hand keeping materials in store is expensive in terms of idle capital and the costs of providing security, storage space and the capital and labour needed to administer stores. A balance has to be struck between the conflicting objectives of avoiding delays and avoiding unnecessary expense. The introduction of computers has helped in the task of inventory control but some firms may have erred on the side of risking breakdowns. These issues will be examined more fully in the sections on purchasing and stock control.
- Production has to be planned and the whole process kept under supervision to ensure that plans are being followed through. This can mean keeping track of work during production and ensuring that completion times are met, that measures are taken to meet any disruption caused by worker absence or machine failure, and sometimes interrupting normal production to fit in urgent orders.
- The chances of machine breakdown will be reduced if machines are carefully maintained. Allocating time for maintenance and repair and ensuring that engineers are available when required involves careful planning. This is an essential part of the management of production.
- The aim is not, of course, just to produce goods but to produce saleable goods that will not cause after-sales problems. Quality control is an essential part of the production process.

The various elements involved in production are illustrated in Figure 3.1

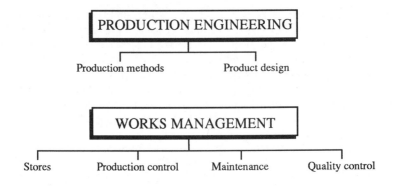

Figure 3.1   *The elements in production*

TEST YOUR UNDERSTANDING

3   Why is design an important element in production?
4   Typically most production departments operate at less than full capacity. Suggest
reasons for this.

Production costs

Whatever the objectives of the firm it will seek to produce at minimum costs at the level
of production it desires and at the quality level it believes to be appropriate. It is
necessary to understand some aspects of costs because of their implications for
production decisions.

Sunk costs

These are costs which have been incurred and which cannot be recovered other than
from revenues. If production is stopped the money has been spent and cannot be
retrieved. Examples would be research and development costs or the cost of specialised
equipment which may have no resale value. A computer software house might have
devoted many hours of work to developing an individual set of computer programs for
a specific purpose. If, for some reason, that purpose cannot be achieved the work is lost.
Before stopping production, therefore, a firm needs to examine whether it might not be
better to continue and seek to obtain some contribution from revenue towards these
costs.

Variable costs

These are costs which change as production levels change. They include costs of
materials used in production, some distribution costs and any part of wages that
depends on the quantity produced by workers. It is difficult to imagine any circumstances under which a firm would wish to continue production when its variable costs
were greater than its revenues and there was no prospect of reversing this or where
there was not some special reason for subsidising one activity from the profits of another.

The change in variable costs may not be in direct proportion to the change in production. As production levels rise the increase in variable costs should be less than proportionate, e.g. a 10 per cent increase in production may be achieved with a 5 per cent increase in costs, perhaps because the firm was able to obtain larger purchase discounts, or use its materials and labour more efficiently. At a higher level of production the changes would become proportional, but at higher levels less could be achieved from further increments of materials etc, indicating that the firm was experiencing diminishing returns.

Fixed costs

Some costs remain constant over a given production range. These are said to be fixed. They would include land or building rents, depreciation of machines, insurance of buildings and equipment, staff salaries where staff are paid an annual salary. Do not misunderstand the meaning of 'fixed'. It does not mean that the costs do not change. They can and do, of course. They are merely fixed in relation to production levels. Even if all production is halted machines will go on depreciating and rents will have to be paid. Many fixed costs will be sunk costs as already described. Some need not be. Buildings, for example will have a sale value as will most vehicles and non-specialised machines. Firms using highly specialised machines and equipment are thus more vulnerable to changes in the economic climate than those using multi-purpose buildings and equipment.

Indivisibilities

In some cases a minimum amount of cost has to be incurred if production is to take place at all. For example, a particular machine, essential to a production process, may require one operator and be capable of producing, say, 500 units of product per hour. Thus a firm wishing to produce 200 units will face the same costs as one able to handle 500 units. On the other hand a firm wishing to produce 600 units per hour and already using one machine to full capacity must acquire another with its operator. Buying another machine will only be worthwhile if production can be raised from 500 units to something above, say, 800 units. Smaller production units can find these indivisibilities a major problem. Larger units can often combine different production methods to make it easier to move from one production level to another. The problem, however, is rarely completely eliminated, and firms typically operate with spare production capacity. Efforts to reduce unit costs by making fuller use of that capacity is often a powerful motive to extend markets and to move into further production activities.

Marginal costs

No mention of costs would be adequate without mention of marginal costs. These are the additional costs incurred as a result of increasing production levels. It is normal (for good mathematical reasons) to relate the marginal cost to a very small (or unit) change in production even though changes may actually take place in larger 'steps'. Thus if production is raised from 2000 units to 2500 units per week, at an increase in total costs of £500 per week, then the marginal cost at this production level is £1. Many production decisions have to be taken with this marginal cost in mind. The decision makers have to ask 'What is the extra cost of raising production?' and 'What extra revenue can be expected as a result of such an increase?' Only if the extra revenue is greater than the extra cost will profits be increased. Other factors may be taken into account when making a final decision whether or not to increase production but the marginal cost-marginal revenue relationship should not be overlooked.

This brief review of costs has assumed the production of physical goods but the same principles apply to the production of services. The cost and organisation implications are also the same in the public sector although there may be no direct revenues to relate to costs. However, costs still have to be met from taxation or other government revenues and taxpayers are increasingly questioning the value received for the cost.

TEST YOUR UNDERSTANDING

5   Modern production costs tend to contain a much higher proportion of fixed costs than, say, 50 years' ago. Why?
6   What has to be considered in relation to costs before deciding whether or not to cease production?
7   A leading economist once stated that the economist's attitude to costs was to 'let bygones be bygones'. What do you think he meant by this? Is this attitude always sound?

Types of production systems

Unit production

Unit production refers to a system in which each item of production is individually produced, usually for a particular customer. Although often associated with small scale production, producing hand-made musical instruments for example, it can also apply to producing on a large scale, e.g. building an ocean going cruise ship to the specification of a cruise company.

Although the finished items are individual the production processes are likely to follow a routine pattern and may include standardised parts or components. A Rolls Royce car especially produced and adapted for a head of state is likely to have light bulbs manufactured on a production line.

Many services are similar in their characteristics to unit production. The interior decorator faces a different task or set of tasks for every customer although many of the details are the same for each. The company auditor sees each set of company accounts as an individual issue and each is likely to have its own special features and problems. At the same time there is a great deal of routine and repetitive work in the actual auditing process - though the auditor cannot 'buy in' ready-made materials.

Unit production may appear to be a simple process but there are important planning issues. Each unit has to be individually sold and selling has to take place in advance of production if gaps between units are to be avoided. Each order is likely to have special features and producer and buyer must be in agreement on these. Details must be clearly recorded if expensive mistakes and damaging misunderstandings are to be avoided. In many small firms communications between buyer and seller are often verbal and recording systems rudimentary. An example of the possible consequences concerns a regular customer of a bespoke tailor, who went for his first fitting of a new jacket to find that it was made of a cloth that he had earlier considered and rejected in favour of another. The tailor and his customer were able to overcome the problem with goodwill and some sacrifice on each side. The customer had two jackets at significantly reduced prices but the former relaxed and informal relationship could never quite be restored.

In some rather larger issues it is not unknown for disagreements between buyer and producer to lead to expensive lawsuits. It is common for buyers to negotiate changes in production while this is in progress and many disputes arise from this. Interior decorators know that most householders ask for some extra work to be carried out while the original order is being carried out. Consequently few jobs can be precisely timed. Changes also alter previously agreed prices and this can be a fruitful cause of dispute. Some contractors may even encourage customers to change orders so that resulting price adjustments are scrutinised somewhat less carefully than an original, detailed estimate.

Even when there are no changes to the order, planning remains essential before and during the production process. The producer must establish the most efficient order of production so that work does not have to be repeated and all materials and components are available at the time and place required. When the carefully chosen paint is already drying on the woodwork it is not desirable to tell the householder that the equally carefully selected wallpaper is not actually available, or that it cannot be delivered for several more weeks!

Mass production

In this system, production units are produced in very large numbers. It is only entered into when marketing has established that a large enough market exists to produce a sales quantity that can justify the heavy financial costs of acquiring the equipment and labour needed for mass production.

To be profitable a mass production system has to be kept in continuous production for as much as possible of the effective lifetime of the equipment used. This can mean continuous marketing to ensure that orders are obtained to absorb the goods produced and, in most cases, labour will need to be employed on a shift system so that the idle time of capital equipment is kept as short as possible. At the same time equipment has to be maintained and repaired and this will need planning. Production managers will wish to keep production levels as steady as possible throughout the year whereas demand may have seasonal peaks and troughs. Arrangements will then be necessary to store goods during periods when supply is greater than demand, for release when demand is greater than supply. To reduce storage costs it may be worthwhile to offer special prices to distributors able and willing to share the burden of storage. Marketing efforts are also likely to be made to try and reduce the range of the seasonal differences in demand. In the motor trade sellers are more likely to offer high discounts and 'trade in' values and low interest credit facilities during periods of low customer demand.

A major objective of mass production is to try and achieve economies of scale. These occur when large scale production allows the firm to obtain reduced unit production costs through the efficient use of equipment and workers. Production planning is thus extremely important and will involve ensuring that the least possible time is lost from handling and moving materials and components and that machines and workers are kept fully occupied in the actual work of production. In the 1970s people wondered why it was possible for Japanese car manufacturers to transport cars from Japan to Britain and still sell them at prices lower than similar cars made in the UK. One of several reasons was that Japanese factories were very carefully planned to ensure that components were made close to the final assembly line so that little time was lost between manufacture of the component and its assembly within the finished vehicle. In some factories, for example, tyres were still warm from the tyre making process when fitted to the vehicle. In contrast, many of the components fitted to British cars had already travelled long distances, often from overseas before arriving at the vehicle assembly line. When this is taken into account the car assembled in Britain may well have travelled more miles than its Japanese competitor before arriving at the dealers' showroom.

Batch production

This process involves the production of goods in substantial quantities, partly for store in anticipation of future orders and partly for specific orders. The system is used when the firm is producing a number of different goods from similar machines and with the same labour force. Machines are 'tooled' for one product and are run for a specific time. They are re-tooled for another product and so on. The length of each product run depends on expected sales and is adjusted in the light of experience and the sales predictions of the marketing specialists. The production manager will try to ensure that customers are not kept waiting for delivery while maintaining stocks of finished goods at the lowest possible levels. This requires skill in scheduling the various production runs and in deciding the quantity to produce from each run. Errors are likely to prove expensive, but making additional product changes or moving input materials may be necessary to avoid costly storage problems or disgruntled customers.

Continuous process production

This is similar to mass production except that, instead of making large numbers of individual items, the product is produced in bulk. This system is suitable for the processing of many kinds of basic materials, e.g. for refining oil or making plastics from chemicals and it is common for it to be highly dependent on automated machines, involving relatively few workers, who are employed mainly to check, monitor, control and service the equipment, rather than work directly with the materials.

Process work is often rather dull and monotonous, involving long spells of dial or screen watching but carelessness can lead to heavy losses from damaged equipment or lost production. In chemical factories the potential for damage is often enormous and the risk of injuries from leaks or other failures can be high. Process workers may have to be carefully selected on the basis of their personal qualities rather than on their possession of special skills.

TEST YOUR UNDERSTANDING

8   Which of the production processes described in these notes is most likely to ensure constant quality standards?
9   Which production process is most likely to make the greatest use of automation?

Some implications of production for management

Specialisation

The basic economic principle of specialisation establishes that any group of people will achieve more if each person concentrates on a limited range of tasks, contributing to the total work. Production is increased because wasteful duplication is avoided and each person becomes skilled in his or her particular task or tasks. The more complex the product the more important this principle becomes. Adam Smith, in *The Wealth of Nations*, used the simple example of a pin factory to illustrate the universal application of specialisation or, as it is also known, the division of labour.

The same principle can be applied to machines. A machine adapted to one purpose is often more productive than one able to perform many functions. It is the ability to keep highly specialised people and machines fully employed that contributes towards the economies of large scale production previously mentioned.

Notice, however, that it is wasteful to employ expensive, specialised people and machines if they cannot be kept fully employed. Although specialisation in some degree is a feature of all but the tiniest of businesses, the extent to which it can be taken depends on the quantity of production that the firm can sell. For example, the small firm is usually better served with a single computer with software packages for word processing, stock control, accounts preparation and so on. The large firm is quite likely to have a number of computers each set up to carry out a limited range of tasks and employed solely for those tasks.

Specialisation, therefore, provides the means of increasing production provided it is in relation to the volume of sales - hence the different production processes which we have been describing. Specialisation pursued for its own sake can be very wasteful. It is a means to an end rather than an end in itself.

Specialisation can create problems. Sometimes it is argued that it reduces quality. The term 'mass produced' often carries an implication of low quality - A Mini, for example, being compared with a Rolls Royce car or a piece of chain store furniture with a Chippendale - but the differences in quality are not due to specialisation but to differences in materials used and methods of assembly. The Rolls Royce is built for a small number of buyers able to pay large sums of money, and is produced with extreme care on a relatively small scale. The Mini is a remarkably reliable and functional product built for a mass market.

In the production of services, as often in the manufacture of goods, specialisation is the key to improvements in quality. Few solicitors are able to gain an adequate working knowledge of all the legal issues that can be brought to the smallest practice. Most modern solicitors have to specialise, and to bear the costs of specialisation legal firms now usually have to grow larger. In the 1980s and 90s service organisations have been facing the kind of pressures for merger and growth that manufacturing companies experienced in the previous two decades.

Another problem is that highly specialised, mass production systems can make work extremely boring for the assembly line worker. Workers fail to associate their work with the finished product, lose interest and develop feelings of hostility to work and their employer. It should, however, be recognised that once work becomes purely mechanical then it is better performed by machines than people. Indeed much of the most soul-destroying assembly line work is now carried out by robots. Some degree of repetition and monotony is inevitable for all kinds of work.

Overcoming worker hostility and reluctance to work is one of the tasks of management and is examined in more detail later.

Opportunity to plan ahead

The scale of operations has been identified as one of the issues affecting production. Another is the opportunity to plan ahead. No one can be certain of the future, but forecasting future demand is one of the major functions of marketing. However, it is one thing to be able to predict the volume of future sales; it is another to be able to know precisely what is to be produced and to plan accordingly. If a firm is producing, say, electric cable, it is likely to receive orders or be meeting a demand for a given quantity of cable to be supplied over a period of some months. The production manager is thus able to plan ahead for a reasonable period. On the other hand the motor engineer, concentrating on repairs and servicing to vehicles, may know with some certainty how much work is likely to be offered for the coming months but does not know precise details of the jobs until each individual order is received. Production planning must, therefore, be extremely flexible and subject to changes at short notice. The managers in each of these cases must possess rather different training and skills. They would have difficulty taking on each other's work without considerable preparation and re-training.

Clearly all production managers seek to reduce the extent of future uncertainty to enable them to plan and avoid waste of resources. It is often possible to do this through marketing. Customers can be encouraged with discounts, for example, to arrange regular servicing of vehicles. Market uncertainties can never be removed but they can be reduced. Nevertheless the desire to have too much certainty can be dangerous. The production manager may feel comfortable if it is known that there are orders sufficient to keep the department fully occupied for the next six months. This means, however, that some customers may be kept waiting for the goods they want and there are always other producers waiting to receive dissatisfied customers. When waiting lists for Land Rovers and Range Rovers grew their suppliers assumed that they held a commanding position in the market only to find that their failure to meet market demand had provided Japanese manufacturers with exactly the kind of market opportunity they needed to launch a rival product.

Notice that in these examples we are beginning to show how closely the various specialised areas of management are related. Some of the solutions to production problems lie in marketing, purchasing, stock control and personnel management. At the same time the work of these functions all have implications for production. It is no use having a big promotional drive for a product if some of the orders generated are lost because not enough of the product has been produced. Producing too much, too little or the wrong products can all lead to business failure. Production must serve the market place. If it forgets this the market can be unforgiving. If, however, it serves it well then the market can often be surprisingly tolerant of temporary misjudgments, provided they do not occur too often.

TEST YOUR UNDERSTANDING

10 In eighteenth century England, Walsall, in the West Midlands, was a major centre for making spurs. At that time the spur consisted of a number of metal and leather parts. Each part was made in a different workshop and each of these was individually owned. Product orders were placed by a merchant who delivered materials to the workshops, collected the finished parts from each and delivered them to the next in the production chain, collecting finished spurs from the last.
    What similarities with modern production practices do you see in this system?
11 A self-employed painter and decorator remarks that he is fully booked for the next eight months. Should the decorator be pleased or worried?

NOTES TO QUESTIONS

Question 1
The accountant is in business to provide a range of financial services to clients. The actual provision of these services - auditing, financial advice, etc - can be seen as 'production'. As accountancy firms grow in size they become involved in other activities associated with maintaining operations and providing the accountants with the material they need to do their work.

Question 2
A hospital's production is the provision of care for patients, e.g. the diagnosis of disease etc, the carrying out of operations and the treatment of patients requiring hospital care.

A modern hospital is likely to be involved in other work such as the training of medical staff, the arranging of appointments and administration of transport for sick people.

It is, of course, possible to define the objectives of a hospital in various ways and these would affect what would be regarded as its core production activities. If the function of a hospital was seen in terms of raising the level of health of the community, i.e. reducing accidents and disease, then its productive work would involve more preventative medicine and services aimed at reducing accidents.

Question 3
Design is an important part of production because it affects both the marketing of the product and its actual manufacture. One function of design is to please the buyer at the lowest possible production cost. At the same time the makers of physical goods recognise that goods need to have aesthetic appeal as well as utility. When early warriors started to carve the handles of swords they did not do this to make the swords more effective for fighting. Design, is the function where production and marketing come closest together.

Question 4
Demand is rarely completely constant and predictable so that firms need to have some reserve production capacity in order to meet fluctuations in demand, without causing too many delays or forcing buyers to go to competitors. Spare capacity is also necessary to provide reserve production facilities in the event of machine breakdown, worker illness and other disruptions to the normal flow of production. Provision also has to be made for machine maintenance. If there are reserves available outside the firm, and if availability of these can be guaranteed, then firms are able to operate closer to full capacity. For example widespread use is made of 'temps' for office work and other business activities and there is a constant demand for plant and vehicle hire facilities.

Larger firms are often better able to absorb spare capacity than smaller organisations for which keeping a reserve machine or vehicle could be a major additional cost.

There are always indivisibilities in business costs. If the firm finds that it cannot meet demand with its existing resources it may have to purchase an extra machine and hire another worker. However, these may produce more than is needed to meet existing demand, providing an incentive to obtain more orders. Success will create the need for another machine - and more spare capacity. Some observers suggest that it is this kind of process that helps to account for the pressure in most business organisations to grow ever larger.

Question 5
The increased reliance on equipment is often the most common reason for fixed costs to become a rising proportion of total production costs. Once equipment is acquired, whether by purchase or hiring, it represents a definite cost whether or not production is taking place. In most sectors of business the ratio of capital to labour has been moving in favour of capital, for much of this century, so that the ratio of fixed costs has also been rising.

However, the falling cost of computers and other electronic equipment in the 1980s has meant that powerful computers and software packages are now available at a fraction of the cost of a decade or so ago.

Question 6
The decision to cease production is a major one, usually taken when the product fails to reach its target contribution to profits within a specific time, as it implies that the resources employed in that product could be more profitably employed in some other sector of the business. In practice this is not always the case. There may be specialised equipment which is not suitable for any other purpose, so that any contribution to its actual cost may be more profitable than simply stopping it from generating any more revenue. There may also be sunk costs which can only be recovered if production continues. However when the marginal cost of continuing production is greater than the marginal revenue likely to be received, then there is clearly no point in continuing. If it there are transferable resources that can generate higher profits in other activities then such transfer should be made unless wider considerations make some sacrifice of profit desirable. This is an application of opportunity cost. This concept of cost is based

on the gain likely to be made from transfer. If this is greater than the loss of sunk, non-transferable and irrecoverable costs then the profit maximising firm will make the transfer.

Question 7
'Let bygones be bygones' is another way of reinforcing the idea that it is the opportunity cost that has to be considered, not the historic cost. Accountants sometimes calculate the average total cost, including the purchase price of specialised machinery. If average revenue is less than this average total cost they may recommend stopping that form of production on the grounds that it is losing money. If, however, the machinery cannot be used for any other purpose then its historic cost does not really come into the calculation. The important issue is its opportunity cost which is now very low or even nil. As in question 6 the decision then rests on whether transferable resources can be more profitably used in some other activity.

The value of the economist's view of costs is to stress the present options and the importance of considering all current potential revenues and costs. This does not mean that past costs, now sunk, should be ignored entirely. If any contribution can be made to reduce the amount of loss then this should be sought. Also, of course, the lessons of any loss should be carefully and honestly learned. The reasons for the loss should be investigated and care taken that past errors are not repeated.

Question 8
Continuous process production and mass production systems offer the best chances of maintaining consistent quality standards. For example, when a giant company took over Golden Wonder crisps and started to produced them by continuous, mass production methods, consistent quality enabled Golden Wonder to expand at the expense of the former dominant producer, Smiths, which was still operating batch production methods. To survive and seek to regain their position Smiths had to change the production system.

Question 9
The continuous process production system offers the most opportunities for extending automated methods as it enables the cost to be spread over a large quantity of product and the system lends itself to the replacement of routine human operations by automated methods. Some of the crucial decisions on when to make changes in the process can also be made more accurately by electronic measuring devices than by humans. However, you must also recognise that advances in robotics have introduced extensive opportunities for developing automation in mass production assembly line methods.

Question 10
The production system for spurs in eighteenth century Walsall was based on a high degree of specialisation and the travelling merchant was, in effect, a moving assembly line. The pace of production was, of course, much slower than it is today but it was well adapted to the size of the contemporary market and it was efficient.

Question 11
The decorator will be happy to have work assured for some months but should not be complacent. Many people will not wait once they have made up their minds to have work done. There is clearly an opening for a rival firm. The decorator may consider taking on an employee but then risks a reduction in the quality of work and will have to spend time supervising the employee's work. The decorator must decide how to proceed, whether to expand the firm or insist on maintaining very high standards at a reasonable price so that a sufficient number of customers will be prepared to wait. This is a familiar problem in small service organisations.

4
Finance and the organisation

Short-term finance

What is short-term finance?

Short-term finance refers to finance obtained from sources outside the organisation on terms that require repayment within a short period. The short period has been defined in various ways, often depending upon whether or not a distinction is made for the medium term. If no such distinction is made then the short term can be anything up to around four years. If the medium term is recognised separately then short relates to periods of not more than two years and often less. Very short-term lending can take place on call, i.e. subject to immediate recall without notice, overnight, or for 24 hours. These very short periods usually relate only to very large sums of money and chiefly concern the banks and the large multinational companies.

Need for short-term finance

It may seem strange that a profitable and well-managed business should need to obtain finance of any kind from outside sources and particularly short-term finance. There is a need, however, and it arises because of the gap that frequently arises between incurring costs and receiving revenue. This is not a new problem, nor is it confined to industrial economies. If you have lived in a traditional rural community you will be familiar with the old farming practice of taking credit from as many traders as possible until money has been received at harvest time. Farmers have to buy their seed and bear all the costs of running the farm until their crops had been harvested and sold.

Business firms frequently face similar situations. They have to buy materials, pay labour and generally bear the costs of running plant over a period of some months until their product is sold. Even then buyers in competitive markets frequently expect a period of credit so that the receipt of revenue can be further delayed. The longer the time gap between incurring costs and receiving sales revenue the greater is likely to be the need for raising money to cover the gap. Long gaps are often suffered by manufacturers of capital goods, and by exporters, where several months' credit is normal and where highly organised services are available to meet the problem.

A need to raise short-term finance, therefore, is by no means a sign of financial difficulty. On the contrary it may arise from expansion and growing demand when the receipts for earlier production may not be sufficient to cover the rising costs of an expanding production system.

Nature of short-term finance

Any lender of finance needs to have some security that the money will be repaid. The problem with short-term lending is that it is usually for a diversity of purposes, few of which provide physical assets which could be sold, if necessary, to repay a debt. If money is needed to pay wages the employer cannot offer the lives of the workers as securities or hostages to guarantee that the money will be repaid. The real security is the future revenue that the lending will make it possible to generate, so that most lenders will seek to have some claim on this revenue to reduce their risks. One of the best assurances that money is due to be paid in the future is the invoice for goods actually sold or services provided but not yet paid for. A number of methods of financing have been developed based on the invoice. These include:

- **Factoring**
  In the financial world a factor is an institution, usually a subsidiary of a bank, which takes over agreed financial responsibilities and obligations on behalf of a client. The factor, in effect, purchases invoices representing debts owed to the business by its customers. The factor usually pays 75 per cent or 80 per cent of the value of the invoices immediately with the balance being paid, less charges, when the invoice is paid by the debtor. The factor administers the sales ledger and accounts collections. In some cases the factor provides credit protection so that, if any debt remains unpaid, the factor will pay, thus protecting the business from the risk of bad debts. Where credit protection is not provided the factor has to make good any payments not collected after a period of three to four months.
  Because finance is available against each invoice a factor is often able to provide considerably more funds than conventional borrowing from a bank, as security for the funds lies primarily on repayment from a wide spread of debtors rather than from a single business. Before taking on a firm's debts a factor will make credit assessments of all the debtors and will normally expect all invoices to be factored.

- **Invoice discounting**
  This is similar to factoring in that the finance company purchases invoices from the client. However, the sales ledger administration and collection of accounts is carried out by the client. Technically the client administers these as agent for the finance company which must, of course, be fully satisfied that these financial duties are carried out to a high standard and that the client can be fully trusted to handle the debts.
  In some cases the debtors are aware of the discounting agreement. In others, however, the invoice discounting agreement is entirely confidential. Invoice discounting is less costly than factoring because the finance company does not handle the physical work of accounts collection.
  A brief outline of factoring and invoice discounting appears in the copy of Barclays Commercial Services advertisement, Figure 4.1.

Borrowing supported by physical security

Most established firms keep some stocks of finished or semi-finished goods and these can sometimes be used as security for loans. The readiness of lenders to accept stocks as security depends to a great extent on the ease with which such stock can be sold. Importers of basic materials have little trouble obtaining loans to finance their trading as these materials have a ready market. Grocery chains can also rely on the co-operation of lenders as their stocks have a high rate of turnover and can usually be sold easily with

Figure 4.1

little loss of value. Most groceries can be stored for several weeks without too much loss. Manufacturers and distributors of more specialised goods, or goods facing uncertain or fluctuating demand conditions are likely to face more reluctance from lenders.

Unsecured borrowing

Short-term borrowing, either through a loan over an agreed time period or through an overdraft facility, is sometimes possible without any definite physical security. The reputation of the borrower may be sufficiently high for a lender such as a bank to be able to trust in the borrower's ability to honour any agreement.

Medium-term finance

This is a natural progression from the short term and is often handled by the same institutions. Medium-term finance up to around, say, five years is usually required to acquire machines, vehicles or other business equipment. In many ways this is quite straightforward as the equipment that is being acquired can be used as security. However, some equipment is likely to be more marketable than others and so is more likely to keep a reasonable re-sale value for a longer period. Specialised equipment, with little re-sale value offers much less security.

Where the security can be re-sold at a reasonable price, borrowing can be based on a hire purchase or leasing arrangement whereby the physical goods remain the legal property of the lender for an agreed term, during which the borrower pays regular instalments towards the full purchase price and interest on the money made available. During this term the borrower has effective use and control over the equipment and gains legal ownership as soon as the final instalment has been paid. If the hirer fails to honour the terms of the hire purchase or leasing agreement the lender has the legal right to take possession of the property to reduce the debt. Non-corporate borrowers have some statutory protection in these cases but limited companies need to look very carefully at any contracts they make.

Where property does not have a re-sale value lenders are likely to insist on some kind of credit sale arrangement under which they can sue for the debt should problems arise; borrowers would not then have the right to hand back the goods. In practice, of course, the best protection for lenders is to ensure that agreements are made only with reliable firms and people and to make use of credit reference agencies and the credit and financial records of banks.

Improving cash flow

Although not strictly borrowing or raising finance careful management of finance can sometimes serve to reduce borrowing requirements and so reduce expense. Careful timing of purchases and payments, linked with times of receiving revenue, and ensuring that debtors keep to their agreed obligations can avoid unnecessary short-term borrowing. Financial control is of very great importance. This involves rather more than just keep watch on outstanding debts. Businesses may delay payment because of uncertainties, insufficient information or errors in invoices and accounts, or even because of delays in sending out accounts so that they become difficult and time-consuming to check. The most important part of credit control is accurate and up-to-date accounts administration.

TEST YOUR UNDERSTANDING

1   What is meant by 'security' for a loan?
2   Suggest reasons why small, non-corporate firms enjoy more statutory protection as
    borrowers than do limited companies.
3   What benefits can be gained from using a financial factor?

Long-term and permanent finance

Marketable securities

In the early days of industrial development in Britain most finance was raised on short
term arrangements and often on the personal security of the business owners. This could
- and did - cause the failure of many sound and reputable business ventures as the
owners had to live under the constant pressure of having to repay debts even when little
cash was available, in spite of owning assets of high worth. You cannot pull down half
a factory to repay a debt or sell a machine essential for continued production! Clearly
if finance is to be used in a business in a form which makes it difficult to repay then it
must be raised on terms where it is clear that repayment cannot be made for a period
of some years and in some cases not as long as the firm continues in operation.

At the same time it has to be recognised that few people can afford to make money
available to others for terms of, say, 20 or more years, or permanently, without having
some means of recovering cash. This conflict of interest - the firm needing money without
fear of having to repay it at an inconvenient time and the provider of finance wanting
to have means of recovering cash if this is needed unexpectedly - can be resolved if the
money is made available in return for a clear written agreement which then itself has
a value and which can be sold. In practice the agreements take two forms:

Bonds

These are promises made to a lender to repay money borrowed on or within certain dates,
and in the meantime to pay interest at an agreed rate. This promise, or undertaking, is
independent of the profitability of the organisation making it. The bond is a legal
contract and enforceable by law. Nevertheless the bond is of little value if, in the event,
the organisation has no funds to meet it. The lender, therefore, may require additional
security in the form of a claim on specific property held by the organisation. If the
borrower fails to meet the terms of repayment or payments of interest the bondholders
can then exercise their rights to take possession of the property and dispose of it in the
best way possible to recover their money.

The general term 'bond' covers a range of different financial agreements, including
those issued by the government and certain other public sector organisations, such as
debentures (this simply means 'loan'), loan stock, secured loan stock and mortgage
debentures. Debentures and loan stock are roughly interchangeable terms, as are
secured and mortgage stocks. All these stocks can usually be traded in agreed units.

The holder of a bond can sell it to another person and the promise of interest and
repayment is transferred to the new buyer. Consequently a 20 year bond can become a
fairly liquid asset (one readily transformed into cash) without upsetting the security of
the borrower who is not called upon to repay until the end of the 20 year period.

Shares

A share is a portion of the **joint stock** of funds contributed by members of a company to form the share capital which the company can employ in its agreed operations as long as it remains in being. Share capital is thus the permanent capital of the company. Shares, however, cease to be permanent under some conditions. These include:

- **Ordinary shares redeemed by the company under the provisions of the companies acts**
  Within certain limits and subject to certain conditions companies may redeem a proportion of their shares. They may do this to make take-over more difficult, a defence only open to small companies, or to support their share price.

- **Redeemable preference shares**
  Preference shares are those which have a measure of preference over other shareholders in a division of profits. They usually provide for payment of a fixed percentage of their nominal value in dividend (division or distribution of profits). Thus a 10 per cent preference share 1995-98 would pay a shareholder with shares having a nominal value of £1000, an amount of £100 per year, ignoring tax, until the company decided to repurchase them at a time of its choosing between 1995 and 1998.

Whereas a bond undertakes to make a regular payment to the bondholder, regardless of profit earned, a company only undertakes to pay shareholders (ordinary or preference) a division of the profit. If there is no profit there can be no dividend payable. Unless stated otherwise preference share dividends are cumulative, i.e. any dividends missed have to be paid in subsequent years before ordinary shareholders can receive any payment out of profits.

Companies do not usually pay out all the profit earned each year to their shareholders. Some, often around half, is retained for replacing or extending the physical assets held by the company. The proportion of profit distributed as dividend to ordinary shareholders is decided by the company's directors, subject to approval by Shareholders at the Annual General Meeting. Shareholders can either accept or reject the directors' recommendation. They have no power to change the recommendation.

Shares can also be traded in the same way as bonds and in Britain the International Stock Exchange provides an active market for such trading. Shares and debentures in private companies can also be traded but must not be advertised for sale. Consequently they cannot be traded on any of the stock exchanges.

Other methods of raising long-term finance

If the company owns property it may **mortgage** this. Under the terms of a mortgage the lender takes over the legal rights of ownership of the mortgaged property but the borrower still retains physical possession and can use it - as long as the terms of the mortgage agreement are honoured. If the borrower fails to make repayments or pay interest as agreed then the lender, the mortgagor, can take over possession and sell the property in order to eliminate or reduce its outstanding debt. Once the debt and all interest has been completely paid full legal ownership reverts to the former borrower (mortgagee).

Another way to raise long-term finance from property is actually to sell it as part of an agreement under which the seller has the right to lease (occupy as tenant on payment of rent) the property for an agreed period, say 50 or more years, usually with a stipulation that the annual rent is reviewed at regular intervals. This is known as **sale and lease-back**. The device unlocks cash from the value of property and provides the buyer with a long-term investment which is likely to increase in both capital value and income over the years. Provided the seller can generate more wealth from the business activity than the value of the rent and **capital appreciation** (increased value of the property) this arrangement is beneficial to both sides. A summary of the main types of finance is shown in Figure 4.2.

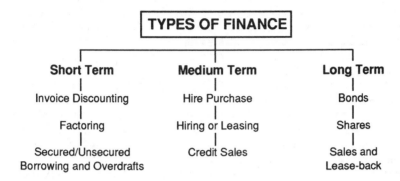

Figure 4.2 *Many types of finance available to firms*

TEST YOUR UNDERSTANDING

4   Shares are permanent capital but they are also a liquid asset. Explain and comment on this statement.
5   'Bonds are safer investments than shares.' Are they?
6   Obtain the published annual accounts of any public company. Identify and suggest reasons for the various kinds of finance that it appears to be employing.

Structure of the banking system

What is a bank?

To qualify as a full bank an institution should fulfil all three of the basic functions of banking. These are:

1   The safe keeping of money
2   The lending of money
3   Exchange and transfer of money on behalf of customers

Most modern banks now carry out a fourth function which can be described as the assisting customers with the management of money. This is becoming increasingly important and now involves providing a wide range of what the banks usually term their 'fee earning services', including stockbroking, insurance broking, acting as trustees, administering share registers for companies, providing financial management advice for businesses and generally selling their financial skills and resources.

In practice in the United Kingdom an institution can call itself a bank if it is recognised as such by the Bank of England in its capacity as regulator and supervisor of the British banking system under the provisions of the Banking Act 1987. The Bank of England must satisfy itself not only that the services provided are such that it can legitimately be regarded as a bank, but also that it fulfils the solvency requirements established by Parliament.

The high street banks

When the word 'bank' is mentioned most of us think immediately of one of the 'Big Four' banks - Barclays, National Westminster, Lloyds and Midland. These, together with a number of others, including the Co-operative Bank, the Trustee Savings Bank, the Scottish and the Northern Irish banks are often known as the high street banks or, because most are members of the London Bankers' Clearing House, as the clearing banks. These institutions are also sometimes known as branch banks to distinguish them from the merchant banks and accepting houses (described later in this unit) which usually have few or no branches.

The high street banks provide services for all kinds of firms as well as individuals. Customer accounts range from the very small to those of very large, international companies. The range of services provided by the high street banks is very wide. The bank has specialised divisions and also acts as the parent for a family of specialised subsidiary and associated companies, each operating in particular financial sectors or areas of the world. For example, Figure 4.3 shows the group structure of the U K financial services available through subsidiaries and associates of the National Westminster Bank while Figure 4.4 shows the National Westminster's group structure for corporate and institutional banking and the support services. These illustrations show something of the diverse financial services offered. Note that they include investment services, home mortgage finance, factoring and invoice discounting, insurance, hire purchase and many others. These copies are taken from the bank's published report and accounts for the 1988 financial year. The accounts show two further pages of, mainly, overseas organisations. You should obtain or look up in a reference library similar published accounts for one of the other major banks and you will see a similar spread of activities.

Although the high street banks are frequently described as **retail** banks indicating their readiness to deal directly with almost any kind of business or individual customer, they are also active in the **wholesale** and **merchant** banking sectors, and in the financial services sectors such as insurance, stockbroking, investment management and advice. The wholesale sector of banking is concerned with amounts of $1m or more but, as with retail banking, wholesale banking is more a function than a distinct group of separate institutions. The major high street banks can now be fairly described as **financial composite companies** to indicate the diversity of their financial interests.

Merchant banks and accepting houses

In view of the tendency for large banking institutions to broaden their activities merchant banking should now be seen more as a type of banking function than an institution. At the same time many institutions see themselves as merchant banks and/or as accepting houses. Merchant banks deal primarily with business organisations. They fulfil the basic functions of banking already identified but they also take a direct interest in the financial management of their business customers. They seek to provide the finance and the financial support skills to increase the profitability of their clients and, by taking equity in the companies they support, they also seek to share in the profits they help to generate.

The **accepting houses** include some of the leading merchant banks and take their name from their business of **accepting** commercial bills of exchange. To understand this term you need to understand what a bill of exchange is and how it operates.

A bill is a kind of highly formalised 'IOU', usually for a substantial sum of money and most frequently related to foreign trade. The bill is actually drafted by the seller of goods (or the seller's bank), at which stage it is often referred to as a draft, and is then sent to the buyer who signifies **acceptance** of the draft's terms under which the money is to be paid by signing across its face. The draft then becomes an accepted bill and the acceptor has a clear, legal obligation to make the payment to the amount, in the currency, on the date and at the place stipulated in the bill. Bills are either **sight**, i.e. payable immediately on presentation, or **term**, i.e. payable after a stipulated period (often 30, 60 or 90 days) after presentation. A term bill thus allows the buyer a period of credit but gives the seller a considerable amount of legal protection because an acceptor cannot refuse to honour a bill on the grounds that goods or services provided were not as agreed or were defective. Failure to honour a bill is a major 'crime' in the commercial world and effectively destroys the credit worthiness of the defaulter. Of more practical significance in most cases is the fact that the holder of an accepted term bill can either use it to settle another debt by **endorsing** (signing the reverse side) and passing it on, or sell it for cash at an agreed **discount** off the face value. The amount of discount depends on current market rates of interest, the time left to the bill's maturity and the financial standing of the acceptor.

Clearly a bill of exchange is only of value if trust can be placed on the acceptor to honour the obligation to pay. So important is this trust that it has become normal for bills to be accepted on behalf of business firms by internationally respected banks known as accepting houses. The most prestigious of these are members of the Accepting Houses Committee. Bills accepted by institutions whose 'paper' is recognised by the Bank of England as eligible for use as security for loans from the Bank are virtually as secure as a Bank of England note. These can be discounted through the banking system at the keenest rates.

Accepting bills on behalf of business clients, effectively guaranteeing that the client will honour debts, is potentially very hazardous. Banks could only transact such business if they had a very thorough knowledge of clients' affairs, of their industries, of economic conditions and of political conditions in relevant countries. With this kind of knowledge and experience the houses can provide a much wider range of financial services to business. These services, often referred to as merchant banking, include: advice on investments; lending and arranging loans for short and medium terms; arranging the issue of securities through the capital market as **issuing houses**; advice on carrying out or resisting mergers and take overs; advising on the sale of subsidiary companies, including setting up **management buy-outs** (sale to existing company managers) and general financial advice and business consultancy. Many of these activities are highly specialised, and require specialised companies or divisions within the bank.

Foreign and consortium banks

Finance markets are now highly competitive and international or multinational groups often prefer to deal with their own national banks as far as possible. Consequently London is one of many financial centres which attracts a wide range of foreign banks. The main banks operating in Britain are those from the USA, Japan, the Middle East (representing the oil exporting nations), European Community and Commonwealth countries.

A consortium bank is one which is jointly owned by a United Kingdom bank and a foreign bank. There are often practical advantages in this kind of arrangement.

The discount (very short term money) market

This is a major part of the wholesale market. For a long period it was dominated by a small group of **discount houses** whose special position arose from their right to borrow from the Bank of England on the security of certain approved securities (mainly the government's own paper and bills accepted by banks approved by the Bank. For their part the houses undertook to underwrite the British Government's weekly issue of its

GROUP STRUCTURE, UK FINANCIAL SERVICES

SUBSIDIARY COMPANIES

Coutts & Co
Banking and Investment Services
Chairman D B Money-Coutts
Managing Director A J Robarts
Head Office 440 Strand, London
WC2R 0QS

Coutts Finance Company
House Mortgages
Chairman D B Money-Coutts
Managing Director G T Spencer
Head Office New London Bridge House,
London Bridge Street, London SE1 9SG

Isle of Man Bank Limited
Banking Services
Chairman W L B Stott
General Manager J C Allen
Head Office PO Box 13,
2 Athol Street, Douglas, Isle of Man

Lombard North Central PLC
Banking Services, Credit Finance,
Leasing and Contract Hire
Chairman Sir Hugh Cubitt CBE JP DL
Chief Executive B A Carte
Head Office & Registered Office
Lombard House, 3 Princess Way,
Redhill, Surrey RH1 1NP

**Lombard NatWest Commercial Services
Limited**
Factoring Services, Invoice Discounting
Chairman B A Carte
Managing Director M A Maberly
Head Office & Registered Office
Smith House, PO Box 50
Elmwood Avenue, Feltham, Middlesex
TW13 7QD

Lombard Tricity Finance Limited
Instalment Credit and Credit Card Facilities
Chairman B A Carte
Managing Director J M Morgan
Head Office & Registered Office
Lombard House, Baird Road, Enfield, Middlesex
EN1 1TP

National Westminster Growth Options Limited
Venture Capital for Small Businesses
Chairman G A Robinson
Director R C King
Head Office 41 Lothbury, London
EC2P 2BP

National Westminster Home Loans Limited
Home Mortgage Finance
Chairman M A Lydon
Managing Director H A Gillis
Head Office PO Box 156
38 Colmore Circus, Queensway
Birmingham B4 6AL

**National Westminster Insurance Services
Limited**
Insurance Brokers
Chairman M A Lydon
Managing Director F S Frost
Head Office PO Box No 106,
37 Broad Street, Bristol BS99 7NQ
Registered Office 41 Lothbury
London EC2P 2BP

NatWest Export Finance Limited
Financial Services
Chairman J J Botevyle
Director J E McIntosh
Head Office National Westminster Tower
25 Old Broad Street, London EC2N 1HQ

NatWest Stockbrokers Limited
Retail Brokers and Investment Managers
Chairman M A Lydon
Managing Director N F Stapley
Head Office & Registered Office
Garrard House, 31 Gresham Street,
London EC2V 7DX

Ulster Bank Limited
Banking Services
Chairman Dr W G H Quigley
Chief Executive D Went
Head Office 47 Donegall Place,
Belfast BT1 5AU

Ulster Investment Bank Limited
Merchant Banking
Chairman M Rafferty
Chief Executive B W McConnell
Head Office 2 Hume Street,
Dublin 2

Lombard & Ulster Limited
Medium Term Finance, Hire Purchase, Leasing
and Deposits
Chairman H S E Catherwood
Chief Executive J H Torney
Head Office Canada House,
22 North Street, Belfast BT1 1JX

Lombard & Ulster Banking Limited
Medium Term Finance, Hire Purchase, Leasing
and Deposits
Chairman M Rafferty
Chief Executive R A Robinson
Head Office Lombard & Ulster House,
54-57 Lower Mount Street, Dublin 2

Ulster Bank (Isle of Man) Limited
Deposits
Chairman J C Allen
Managing Director D J McCawley
Head Office 46 Athol Street,
Douglas, Isle of Man

Ulster Bank Dublin Trust Company
Trustee and Income Tax Services, Investment
Management
Chairman F J O'Reilly
Managing Director P Caulfield
Head Office PO Box 145,
33 College Green, Dublin 2

Ulster Bank Trust Company
Trustee Services, Home Loans
Chairman R D Kells
Managing Director J T Hart
Head Office PO Box 233
35-39 Waring Street
Belfast BT1 2ER

Ulster Bank Insurance Services Limited
Insurance Brokers
Independent Life Assurance and
Pension Advisors
Chairman D Went
Manager G P Davidson
Head Office Ulster Bank House,
Shaftesbury Square, Belfast BT2 7DL

Ulster Bank Commercial Services (NI) Limited
Factoring Services, Invoice Discounting
Chairman R D Kells
General Manager D F Moynihan
Head Office 11 Donegall Square South,
Belfast BT1 5PH

Ulster Bank Commercial Services Limited
Factoring Services, Invoice Discounting
Chairman K R Wall
Chief Executive W Glynn
Head Office Felix House,
7-9 South Leinster Street, Dublin 2

PRINCIPAL ASSOCIATED COMPANIES

**The Agricultural Mortgage Corporation PLC
(26%)**
Agricultural Mortgage Finance

**International Commodities
Clearing House Holdings (22·2%)**
Clearing Services for Futures Markets

3i Group plc (23·4%)
Permanent and Long Term Investment Finance

Signet Limited (30%)
Credit Card Operations

Switch Card Services Limited (33·3%)
Ownership of Switch Scheme

Figure 4.3

GROUP STRUCTURE, CORPORATE AND INSTITUTIONAL BANKING

NatWest Gilts Limited
Gilt Edged Securities Market Maker
Chairman Dr J M Owen
Managing Director G R Southern
ad Office 41 Lothbury, London EC2P 2BP

National Westminster Financial Futures Limited
Worldwide Financial Futures and
Options Broker
Chairman Dr J M Owen
Managing Director & Controller J Jarvis
Head Office 41 Threadneedle Street
London EC2R 8AP

NatWest Capital Markets Limited
Capital Markets Activities
Chairman Dr J M Owen
Managing Director G R Southern
Head Office 41 Lothbury, London EC2P 2BP

ational Westminster Bank of Canada
Banking Services
Chairman of the Board
The Hon A W Gillespie PC
President A S Yankovich
Chief Financial Officer D T Aylward
Head Office Suite 2060 South Tower
PO Box 10, Royal Bank Plaza, Toronto
Ontario, Canada M5J 2J1

International Westminster Bank PLC
International Westminster Bank PLC and National
Westminster Bank PLC merged by Act of
Parliament on 1st December, 1989 and with the
exception of certain deferred facilities, all assets,
liabilities and functions of International
Westminster Bank PLC have become assets,
liabilities and functions of National Westminster
Bank PLC.

National Westminster (Hong Kong) Limited
Medium Term Finance
Chairman J W Melbourn
Director and General Manager
R J Lacey
23rd Floor, 1 Exchange Square
8 Connaught Place, Hong Kong

SUPPORT SERVICES

Centre-file Limited
Computer Services
Chairman A Morris
Managing Director J M Graycon
Head Office
75 Leman Street, London E1 8EX

PRINCIPAL ASSOCIATED
COMPANIES
BACS Limited (22%)
Provision of Automated Clearing Services

BCH Property Limited (34.5%)
Property Investment Company

Figure 4.4

own IOUs, the treasury bills, through which it borrowed money for short periods.

More recently, however, the Bank of England has sought to widen the market by increasing the number of banks with which it is prepared to deal directly, provided these banks are prepared to join the discount houses in underwriting the treasury bill issue.

The very short term money market handles large amounts of money, often on call or very short notice, most of which are sums lent between banks or between the major multinational companies (some of which operate their own banking divisions) and banks. This specialised market ensures that even the most liquid of funds are kept at work oiling the wheels of international business and that the banks are always able to balance their books whatever unexpected calls they may have on their funds. It is an essential guarantee of the stability and integrity of the financial system.

TEST YOUR UNDERSTANDING

7   Does the National Savings Bank offer all the banking functions? Give reasons to explain your answer.
8   If banks have a duty to keep clients' funds safely why then do they lend much of their customer deposits to borrowers?
9   Suggest possible reasons for the efforts made by banks to extend and develop their 'fee earning services' in recent years.
10 Identify the main points (a) of similarity and (b) of difference between branch and merchant banking.
11 What is meant by the statement that the major high street banks have become financial composites? How do you explain this development?
12 Suggest reasons why bills of exchange still play an important role in international trade.

Finance available to business through the banking system

We can now summarise the main forms of finance provided to business through the banking sector.

Short-term finance

You will be familiar with bank lending and overdrafts - the most familiar forms of bank finance. Loans may be for a fixed term with the loan repayable in full at the end of the term, though there is often provision for renewal, or with the loan repayable by instalments during the term.

Loans may also be provided in the form of invoice discounting or factoring as outlined earlier in this unit.

Notice that the distinction between short-, medium- and long-term borrowing becomes clouded when loans or overdrafts are renewed over a long period of time though, of course, the bank always has the right to refuse renewal.

Medium-term Finance

Where finance over several years is required ,e.g. for the purchase of equipment or vehicles, a bank will usually seek to persuade customers that their interests are best served by one of its specialised subsidiaries or divisions. Some kind of instalment credit or leasing arrangement is usually appropriate, depending on the purpose of the finance and the current tax position. The customer is then using the additional equipment to generate the funds to finance its own acquisition. The borrower is obliged to calculate whether in fact the additional net revenues likely to be generated by the acquisition do, in fact, justify its cost.

Long-term capital

Traditionally banks have not been providers of long-term capital, though, in effect renewable loans and overdrafts have been used by firms for this purpose. However, during the 1980s there was an increasing interest in the promotion of the small firm and personal business sector, partly in response to pressure from Government which initiated a limited and not altogether successful loan guarantee scheme. All the major high street banks now have small firms advisory services, staffed by specialists and if a proposal is regarded favourably the provision of long-term finance may be recommended by whatever method is considered most appropriate, taking into account the nature of the business and experience of the owners. Finance may thus range from simple loans repayable by instalments during the loan term, to the taking of equity or debentures under the care of the bank's merchant banking subsidiary or division.

Finance for foreign trade

This is a specialised sector of the financial market and one in which the branch banks have long been pre-eminent. It is virtually impossible to conduct foreign trade, either exporting or importing, without the active and close support of one of the major branch banks. Both importers and exporters may require loans and overdrafts to finance purchases or the provision of credit and so the bank's creditworthiness checks and advice will be needed. Where a substantial and regular trade is conducted payment is likely to involve various forms of schemes based on bills of exchange. These are normally operated by banks and documentary credit arrangements, involving the release of accepted bills against the production of agreed export documents, and are handled almost entirely within the banking system. Payment systems based on commercial bills of exchange enable the banks to satisfy the conflicting needs of importers and exporters. The importer gets time to pay while the exporter can obtain payment as soon as goods are shipped and the necessary documents are lodged with the bank.

The growth of European trade on open account, where payment is made directly through bank accounts - much as in home trade - is replacing the older bill based structures. However, the banks remain essential intermediaries, mainly to finance the credit that exporters have to extend to buyers, to report on creditworthiness and to arrange currency exchange or to provide deposit facilities in a range of European currencies. In view of the costs of currency exchange there is likely to be growing pressure for more widespread use of a single European Community currency unit or for making all Community currencies legal tender throughout member states.

TEST YOUR UNDERSTANDING

13 How is it possible for a firm to use short-term finance for long-term purposes? What are the dangers of this practice?
14 How is the growth of European Community trade likely to affect the financial needs of business?

The Capital Market

This has developed separately from the markets for short- and medium-term finance. It is customary to separate two sections of the capital market although it should be recognised that the two are closely linked and the same institutions are involved in each.

The new issue market

This is the market where firms raise new or additional equity or new or additional debenture/loan stocks. The money paid by investors goes to the firms issuing the stocks.

Firms recognise that few people or institutions would invest money on a long term or permanent basis unless they had some means of recovering cash should this be needed in the future. Consequently a new issue is not launched until the firm is sure that the new stocks are going to be accepted for trading in a recognised part of the capital market. This means that the firm has to satisfy not only the Government, represented by the Department of Trade and Companies Registry, that the law has been observed but also the ruling and regulatory authorities in the relevant sector of the capital market. Firms, therefore, need specialist help in securing the necessary approvals and in establishing when and on what terms the issue should be made. Although there is no longer any formal queuing system in the new issue market no firm would wish to launch its issue on the same day as a major new issue from, say, ICI or BP. The specialist advisers on new issues are called issuing houses and many are now subsidiaries or divisions of large stockbroking institutions.

In all but very large issues the issuing institution is usually able to ensure that the issue is fully sold to its institutional contacts (pension funds, life assurance offices, unit and investment trusts, etc.) in the capital market. The cost of making the issue is reduced if the issuing house is able to launch it as a placing or introduction direct to institutional investors as, of course, advertising costs are saved. If a full public issue has to be made costs can be high and this is really only practicable if the amount of the issue is substantial. If you keep an eye on the *Financial Times* you will see details of public issues from time to time.

Since the start of the British Government's privatisation programme it has been almost wholly public liability companies that have raised finance through the new issue market. If there is a change of policy from a future government we could expect to see a resumption of new issues from public sector organisations. Bonds issued directly by the British Government (gilts) are launched by a different route administered by the Bank of England.

Companies will go to the new issue market when they are raising additional finance through new equity or loan stocks, on formation or, more likely today, on converting to a public company after a period of successful trading as a private company.

The stock exchanges

The London exchange is now the home of three distinct markets.

- **The Main Market**
  This is the market for securities which are listed in the exchange's official list. This is the most familiar market and the one from which the share price lists quoted in the daily business press are taken. The cost of an issue through this market is substantial so that it is practicable only for large companies. Very large multinational companies can raise capital not only through London but also through the capital markets of

other countries. As there are no exchange controls in Britain money raised in a foreign country can be used for development in Britain if desired. Similarly, money raised in Britain can be used for development in other countries.

- **The Unlisted Securities Market (USM)**
  This was introduced for the benefit of smaller companies which were believed to be having difficulties raising capital because of the expense of entry to the main market. It has proved successful and USM prices are now quoted daily in the main business press. For its first few years costs of entry were kept low but they have since risen and the old problem of costs for small issues arose once more. At the same time a thriving market in securities outside the official exchange started to develop as an Over-the-Counter market. This caused worries as it lacked the regulatory protection of the official exchange so further developments seemed desirable.

- **The Third Market**
  This is the name by which this latest addition to the exchange continues to be known and you will also find quoted prices in the major business press. The third market has become firmly established and is the door through which most smaller companies are likely to enter the exchange. A number of larger private companies will continue to enter the USM and a small number will be large enough to justify direct entry to the main exchange. It is possible, of course, for a successful and growing company to proceed through the Third Market and USM to take its place on the official list.

  Strictly it is an issue of securities which is quoted on one or other of the markets. Different securities of the same company can be traded on different markets. For example a company's ordinary shares may be traded actively and justify inclusion in the main market but its debentures may be traded only infrequently and so remain in, say, the USM.

Other sources of capital

Entry to an official sector of the national capital market has always been expensive and impossible to justify where amounts required are relatively modest. Moreover a market where stock is on offer to the public is not an option available to a private company. It has always been possible to raise long term and even some permanent capital by other means.

Before the severe inflation of the 1970s it was not too difficult for small companies to borrow from insurance offices and some other financial institutions, particularly if the borrower could offer freehold land or property as security for a mortgage type loan or for sale and leaseback. Inflation, however, has meant that loans are only available at very high rates of interest, while many institutions are no longer prepared to lend any money at fixed interest rates.

There has also been a long history of local markets where successful business people have been prepared to invest in other small, local firms, becoming holders of equity with the right to take an interest in management, if necessary, to protect funds. These have usually lacked any formal organisation and have depended upon informal, personal contacts.

In the late 1980s, however, these local **venture capital** markets have become more formal and better organised. By late 1989 at least two of the 'big four' banks had venture capital subsidiaries, and the major banks also have interests in Finance for Industry Limited, which is prepared to take an equity interest in approved small companies. In some areas venture capital brokers put firms seeking finance in touch with groups of potential private investors. Other sources of finance include the Local Investment Network Company, which operates a series of local enterprise agencies acting as further channels of communication between potential borrowers and investors.

Following years of consistent inflation most venture capital investors are looking for a substantial equity stake, on the same terms as the company founders, to provide a substantial share of future profits. Despite tax concessions available under the Government's Business Expansion Scheme the provision of venture capital is risky and by no means all investments will generate profits; many will produce losses. Consequently very high returns will be looked for from companies that are successful. For the small business owner this means that capital acquired on this basis will mean loss of much of the profit earned from success. Moreover, if the entrepreneur is not careful, outside investors will gain a controlling interest in the shares and the original founders and managers will lose control. Business people must recognise that the providers of venture capital are not philanthropists. Expansion of the sector suggests that profits are available and individual entrepreneurs may well feel that they are being deprived of some of the fruits of their labour.

There is still no completely fair solution to the problems of financing small business enterprise. Investors feel that fixed or even variable interest loans do not provide adequate compensation for risks nor opportunities to make good losses on failures. On the other hand surrendering a large share of profit and perhaps control of the enterprise is not hugely attractive to the entrepreneur attracted by the idea of independence and the chance to build up some personal wealth. As always, those who seek to make use of the capital of others must balance the risks, problems and opportunities that this course of action must involve.

TEST YOUR UNDERSTANDING

15 What must a small business owner take into account before seeking to raise finance through a local market for venture capital?
16 Why are there three distinct markets operating in the London stock exchange?

Introduction to financial appraisal

The purpose of financial appraisal

We are all familiar with the idea of financial appraisal in that it describes the process of deciding whether or not the expenditure of a sum of money is going to be worthwhile. If you are in a shop wondering whether or not to buy a pair of shoes and you are thinking 'Do I look good in these shoes? Do they feel comfortable?' you are carrying out a financial appraisal. What you are really thinking is, 'Is the benefit I am going to get from wearing these shoes, the feeling they give me of looking good and feeling comfortable, greater than the pain of parting with £x?' If the answer is 'Yes', you will spend the money on the shoes. If not, you will keep the money or spend it on something else.

The business firm goes through much the same process when it undertakes a financial appraisal exercise. It seeks to determine whether the value of the benefit it is likely to receive by spending money on a project is greater or less than the cost it would incur from going ahead with the project. Although this kind of decision is a daily one in every business organisation the term financial appraisal, or the alternative term, capital budgeting, is only used where the firm is considering significant expenditure capable of affecting future production.

The assumptions of financial appraisal

Before examining the way in which appraisal is carried out we should recognise that certain assumptions are normally made. These can be summarised as:

- Before examining spending projects the firm will have made strategic decisions regarding the direction in which it intends to expand in the future. Marketing appraisals will have been made concerning the markets and product range to be entered or expanded and, perhaps, other markets and products where activity is to be reduced or abandoned. The firm will not wish to examine detailed proposals for updating production techniques for a product which it proposes to cease producing in a few years' time.
- The benefit sought by the firm from any significant financial spending is an increase in its net profits. This is not necessarily the same as assuming that the firm is seeking to maximise profits in all its activities but it is reasonable to assume that, other things being equal, the firm will choose the most profitable course of action when considering any change or development of production methods or product range. If, for example, the firm had made the strategic decision to seek to be a market leader in the sale of pet foods, it would only decide to produce a brand of flavoured rabbit food if its market research indicated that this would increase its profits.
- All financial expenditure has a cost. If the firm has to borrow money from a bank in order expand its production plant then the cost will be closely linked to borrowing the money. However, if the firm has money already available spending that money will still involve a cost in that the money is spent it may no longer be earning interest in a bank deposit or it is no longer available to spend on some other project. This cost, measured in terms of the benefit sacrificed by not choosing the best alternative use for the money, is the **opportunity cost**. The actual calculation of the opportunity cost is not always a simple one, but at the very least it may be the interest lost from sacrificing the chance of investing the money in the finance market. Consequently the cost of investing in a business project will always be related to, though not necessarily the same as, the market rate of interest, so that as interest rates change so too will the costs of business investment.
- As already indicated business investment will have production and marketing implications, and it will not be possible to carry out worthwhile investment appraisal unless there has already been a full investigation of these implications. Production changes will influence both present and future costs and market conditions will affect the returns that can be expected from the investment. For example, an office manager who decides to replace, say, two electronic typewriters with a computer and laser printer has to consider not only the capital (purchase) cost of the new equipment but also the future cost of maintaining and servicing the printer and the re-training or replacing of office staff. In this case the market is internal within the firm so the manager must also consider whether the volume of output actually demanded by the firm's activities justifies the increased production capability of the new equipment. You may think this is simple common sense but there are many instances where managers take pride in ensuring that their offices contain 'state of the art' equipment, regardless of the true implications for the financial condition of their organisations.

The decisions involved in financial appraisal

Two questions that financial appraisal is required to answer may be identified. The first assumes that there is no practical limit to the supply of finance available to the firm so that all that has to be asked is, 'Will the proposed investment project increase profits?' If the anticipated return is greater than the estimated cost then we can expect the answer to be, 'Yes' and the profit seeking firm should undertake the project.

The second question arises when the total supply of finance available to the firm is not limitless so that choosing project A may mean that project B cannot be undertaken because of the limitation on the amount of finance that the firm can acquire. In this case the firm needs to be able to rank possible projects in order of profitability so that it can use the finance available for the projects that offer the greatest contribution to profit.

TEST YOUR UNDERSTANDING

17 All finance has an opportunity cost, whether it comes from the firm's own accumulated funds or from the external finance market. Does this mean that financial managers should be indifferent as to the sources of investment finance?
18 What considerations, other than the level of anticipated profit, do you think might influence business managers in the choice of investment projects?

The techniques of investment appraisal

Some simple techniques

In looking at appraisal techniques we assume that the costs and anticipated returns have been carefully estimated, using all available information. Also, because we wish to concentrate on the techniques, we can use very simple figures. As a further simplification the examples used normally assume that the total cost of the project is paid in one lump sum at the beginning of its life.

Undiscounted payback

This simply involves calculating the length of time before the cost of the project just equals the total amount of additional net return it provides. For example, a project costing an initial £10 000 produces a net return of £2000 at the end of the first year, £4000 at the end of the second year, a further £4000 at the end of the third year and £2500 per year for two further years. Thus, at the end of the third year the project has produced a net return of £2000 + £4000 + £4000 = £10 000, the same figure as the initial cost. The payback period is, therefore, three years.

Firms usually have target payback periods depending on the cost of finance, the current state of the economy and the degree of economic and political uncertainty prevailing at the time. If the project achieves a payback period within the target it is acceptable if there is no limit on the availability of finance. If finance is 'rationed', so that only a proportion of potential projects can be accepted, then the usual rule of thumb is that those with the shortest payback periods gain priority.

This method is really a typical 'back of an envelope' kind of approach but it is easily understood and widely used, and often employed as a preliminary hurdle which projects have to clear before more resources are devoted to a detailed appraisal. It is open to the criticism that it ignores profitability after the payback period. For example, project A has a shorter payback period than project B but project B has a longer life and total anticipated profits are greater than for project A. Nevertheless if the normal payback rules are observed project A will be the one adopted under conditions where the firm has to choose between the two.

Return on capital

In its simplest form this method, also known as the **book rate of return**, involves adding all the anticipated returns, before tax, over the estimated life of the project, taking the annual average and expressing this as a percentage of the total cost. It is usual for estimates to take into account depreciation, which is the reduction in value of an asset caused by the passage of time, e.g. a three year old car has a lower market value than the equivalent two year old car, even if both have the same mileage, simply because it is a year older.

In the example quoted under **payback**, the total return from the project over the full five years of its life was £15 000. The annual average is thus: £15 000/5 = £3000 so that, on a total cost of £10 000 the annual return of £3000 represents a rate of 30 per cent.

Discounting appraisal techniques

Neither the undiscounted payback nor the return on capital method distinguishes between £1000 received at the end of the first year of a project's life and £1000 received at the end of the second or third years, i.e. they ignore the time value of money. It is desirable that time should be taken into account. Methods of appraisal in which anticipated future flows of cash are discounted are commonly known as **discounted cash flow (DCF)** techniques.

Present values

£1000 payable today is not the equivalent of £1000 payable at some date in the future. If I were to offer you the choice of a payment of £1000 now or £1000 in a month's time you would be foolish not to ask for the money now even if you had total trust that I would make the future payment. If I were to ask you why you wanted the money now you would probably say that, with inflation a constant factor in modern economies, £1000 would be likely to purchase fewer goods and services than it could today. This is certainly a good reason for preferring money in the hand rather than having it promised in the future. Nevertheless this is by no means the only reason why payment now is preferable to payment of the same sum in the future. If you have the money now and you have no immediate spending use for it you can lend it on deposit with a bank, building society or other financial institution and earn interest. If, say, you receive interest at an annual rate of 10 per cent then £1000 becomes £1100 in a year's time. We can say, therefore, that £1000 is the **present value** of £1100 payable in a year's time, **discounted** at a rate of 10 per cent. The discount rate represents the rate of interest that the present value payment would earn in the period up to the future payment.

When considering an investment project, however, the firm is more likely to look for a stream of future payments. The simple example below assumes that payments are received at the end of each year in the life of the project. In practice, of course, revenues come into the firm more frequently.Payment of an initial lump sum is assumed to be paid at the beginning of the project's life which is expected to last six years. The firm's management believes that 12 per cent is an appropriate rate of discount to use. In this case,

$$\text{The Present Value (PV)} = \frac{R_1}{(1+d)} + \frac{R_2}{(1+d)^2} + \frac{R_3}{(1+d)^3} + \frac{...R_n}{(1+d)^n}$$

where

R = The anticipated net return from the project at the end of year 1 (R_1), year 2 (R_2) etc
n = The lifetime of the project, in this case 6 years
d = The rate of discount adopted to calculate the present value

Notice that discounting is simply the reverse process to accumulation at compound interest. £1000 put on deposit now and increased by 10 per cent will accumulate as shown:

$$1000(1+i) = £1100$$

where i = the rate of interest, here, 10%, expressed as a decimal fraction.

The present value of £1100 payable in a year's time, discounted at 10 per cent per year is:

$$1100/(1.1) = £1000$$

The discounting methods

One modification of the simple payback method is to base the calculation on the present value of anticipated future payments.

The following table is based on the payback example used earlier. The start of the project's first year, and the time of payment is year 0.

Year	Undiscounted Return	Return discounted at 10% p.a.
0	-£10000	-£10000
1	£2000	£1818
2	£4000	£3305
3	£4000	£3005
4	£2500	£1708
5	£2500	£1552
		Total £11388

Discounting reduces the total return over the five year period from £15 000 to £11 388. It also increases the payback period from three years to five years, if we continue the assumption that returns are received at the end of each year. At the end of the fourth year the total discounted returns amount to only £9836, still £164 short of the initial payment of £10 000.

Net present value

The net present value (NPV) is the project's present value less the amount of its initial cost. If we continue the payback example the net present value for the five year life, applying a constant discount rate of 10 per cent is (£11 388 - £10 000) = £1388.

A project can be expected to increase the firm's profits if its net present value based on anticipated future earnings is positive, i.e. if the present value is greater than the expected cost. In cases where the firm has to choose between competing projects because it is unable to undertake all those available, the normal rule is to adopt those projects with the highest net present values up to the limit of available resources, provided the projects fulfil any other investment criteria set.

The NPV of any project offering a stream of future returns depends, of course, on the rate of discount chosen. Work out for yourself the present value of the payments anticipated in our example using a discount rate of 20 per cent. If your answer does not come to £8971 (each year's discounted value rounded to the nearest £1) check your calculations with the footnote. Remember that the discount factor is now 1.2 (for 20 per cent) and not 1.1.

With a present value of £8971 and a project cost of £10 000, the net present value is negative (-£1029). Thus if the cost of capital is 20 per cent rather than 10 per cent the project is not worth pursuing. Clearly the higher the rate of discount the lower will be the net present value. This can be illustrated with a simple graph as shown in Figure 4.5. This measures the rate of discount on the horizontal (x) axis and the NPV on the vertical (y) axis. The starting NPV is the undiscounted (or discounted at a 0 rate) difference between total returns

Internal rate of return

The internal rate of return (IRR) is the discount rate at which the NPV = 0, i.e. where present value is just equal to the project's cost. If you look at Figure 4.5 again you will see that this is where the NPV curve cuts the horizontal axis. The precise rate (taken from a computer program) is 15.28 per cent.

Business managers frequently refer to the IRR as the rate that the project earns for the firm, hence the term internal rate of return, i.e. the rate of return achieved if this sum is invested internally within the firm. Thinking of the investment in this way enables the manager to make a ready comparison with the cost of capital. If the IRR is greater than the cost of capital then the project can be expected to increase profits. If not, it is not worth proceeding with if profit is the yardstick used.

If several projects are competing for scarce resources the usual rule followed is to give greatest priority to the projects with the highest internal rates of return.

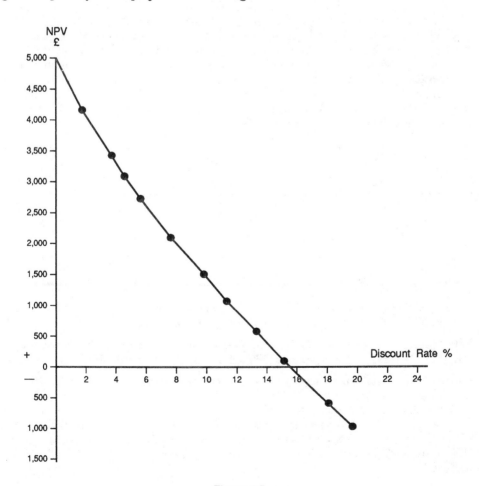

Figure 4.5

TEST YOUR UNDERSTANDING

19 Using an electronic calculator or, if possible, a computer program, calculate the net present value, (using a discount rate of 12 per cent) of the following project, which has a life of 5 years:

		£
Cost, all paid at the start of the period		25 000
Net returns at the end of:	year 1	5 000
	year 2	10 000
	year 3	7 500
	year 4	5 000
	year 5	3 500

20 Re-calculate the NPV for the project of question 3 for two other discount rates and use your figures to draw a graph of NPVs plotted against a range of discount values. Use your graph to estimate the project's internal rate of return.

Some issues of comparison

When making comparisons between two or more projects competing for a share of the available finance like should be compared with like as far as possible. Clearly, if there are big differences between project costs or between estimated project lives careful thought must be given to these and it must be decided whether a fair comparison is possible. There can also be differences even when project costs and lives are the same or reasonably close. Consider the following two investment projects. In this table the start of the project is shown as year 0 when the cost is shown as -£50 000. The returns are assumed to be received at the end of each year.

	A	B
Year	£000	£000
0	-50	-50
1	25	5
2	25	8
3	10	25
4	5	35

For project A the undiscounted NPV = £15 000; when the returns are discounted at 5 per cent the NPV is £9200, at 8 per cent NPV = £6200 and at 10 per cent NPV falls to £4300.

For project B the undiscounted NPV = £23 000; when the returns are discounted at 5 per cent the NPV is £12 400, at 8 per cent NPV = £7100 and at 10 per cent NPV falls to £3800.

If a firm is faced with the choice between these two projects and can only undertake one, which should it choose?

Notice that for the discount rates mentioned so far project B shows the higher NPV for rates up to and including 8 per cent but at 10 per cent project A has the higher NPV. This suggests that project A has the higher internal rate of return (IRR). In fact the IRR for A = 15.1 per cent while for B it is 12.63 per cent. This situation is illustrated in Figure 4.6

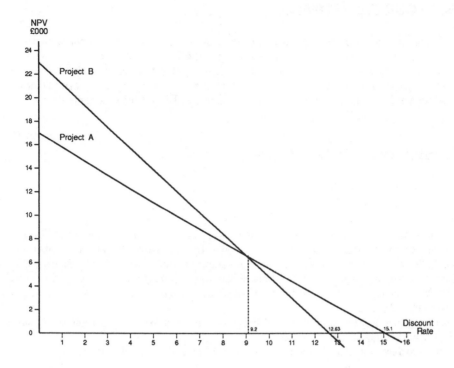

Figure 4.6

In the diagram you can see that the curve representing project B slopes much more steeply than that for project A yet both involved the same initial cost and both have the same length of time to run. What then is the difference?

Look again at the table of returns and the difference lies in the distribution of returns over the lifetime of the two projects. In the case of A most of the returns are achieved in the first two years whereas B only produces its large returns in the final two years. A's undiscounted payback period is two years while B only covers the initial cost in the fourth year. This means that B suffers severely from the higher rates of discount. The difference between $(1.15)^2$ and $(1.15)^4$ is nearly four times larger than that between $(1.05)^2$ and $(1.05)^4$. This means that the reduction in present value of a sum payable in four years compared with the same sum payable after two years is much greater if it is discounted at 15 per cent than at 5 per cent.

You should now be arriving at the answer to the question of which project should be chosen, on the basis of the most appropriate rate of discount and, if project A is selected, what the firm can do with the money returned in the early years. If the opportunity cost of capital to the firm is above 9.2 per cent there is no doubting the superiority of project A, as its IRR is higher and so is its NPV at discount rates above 9.2 per cent. In addition, the money returned in the first two years is likely to be reinvested at a high rate of return. If, however, the opportunity cost is below 9.2 per cent the answer is less simple and requires some further calculations. At low capital costs it could be that the firm would be better to undertake project B as this might provide a more profitable use for finance than any available for the money which would otherwise be repaid in the first two years.

Ranking projects only on the basis of their internal rates of return can, under some special circumstances when capital costs are low, lead to misjudgments. These can be avoided if care is taken to examine the full range of investment opportunities open to the firm.

TEST YOUR UNDERSTANDING

21 What factors do you think a firm should take into account when choosing a discount rate to use for investment appraisal purposes?
22 Set up an example of your own to illustrate the effects of raising the discount rate on projects which produce most of their returns late in a project's lifetime compared with similar projects whose returns are achieved in a project's early years.

Investment and uncertainty

Causes of uncertainty

Remember that any form of investment involves spending money now in the hope that this will bring in larger returns in the future. Immediately we recognise that we are looking to the future we have to accept some degree of uncertainty. No one can be certain what will happen tomorrow. The whole of business management has been described as the art of taking decisions under conditions of uncertainty. Many of these decisions involve investment.

Although we cannot remove uncertainty we can learn to live with it and the first stage is to try and understand it better.

For business investment there are two main causes of uncertainty.

* **Economic causes**
  These arise from a number of sources. Over some the firm may have some degree of control. Over others it will have no control but it can try to make informed forecasts and gain early information. The general economic climate is outside the control of any individual firm and all are affected by it to some extent. There are also likely to be associated markets which influence the firm's own product market(s). Trends in factor markets are also important. The firm needs to have some idea of probable future movements of interests rates as well as labour availability and costs. Trends in the firm's own product market(s) are, of course, of major importance if sensible predictions are to be made of future sales figures.

  The general conclusion, therefore, is that very careful market appraisal must come before all attempts at investment appraisal. If market appraisal is neglected accurate investment decisions will only be made by chance. Market research and future product demand estimation are examined more fully later in this course.

* **Political causes**
  Modern governments are expected to accept a large amount of responsibility for the economic well-being of the community. The belief that governments could and should influence the economic climate within which business operates is one of the legacies of Lord Keynes, the Cambridge economist of the 1930s, whose teaching held the promise of flattening the business cycle and eliminating large scale unemployment. Paradoxically, the mainly Monetarist governments of the large Western industrial nations of the 1980s, though rejecting much of Keynes' teaching, have retained his faith in the ability of governments to manage economic affairs. While claiming to restore free market forces these governments have intervened on some of the most important elements in business decision making, notably the cost of capital, while retaining and even strengthening, State control over another basic production factor, land and its uses. Future economists may well come to look upon the current obsession of social scientists, with their search for models to enable governments to build their versions of social Utopia, with the same degree of amazement and pity as modern

physical scientists regard the efforts of early alchemists to find the philosopher's stone that would turn base metal to gold. In the meantime, however, business managers have to live in a world where governments can manipulate currency exchange rates. These influence the purchasing power of money in world markets and the cost of basic materials. Governments can also manipulate interest rates, and, therefore, the cost of the capital needed to finance future development. This political influence over important basic business costs is, of course, in addition to the generally accepted power of government to levy taxes which further affect business costs.

Business managers not only have to try and foresee future movements in prices but also to predict government reactions to these movements, since, for example, government measures seeking to 'cure' price inflation may be more damaging to business decision making than the price inflation itself.

Coping with uncertainty

As already indicated, business managers are likely to seek to control those elements of uncertainty which appear to be within their influence - and to extend that influence wherever possible and to improve the processes of communication as well as the techniques of analysing information. Market research and large scale advertising are part of the effort to reduce economic market uncertainties. Similarly the chief executives of the major business companies go to considerable trouble to develop channels of communication and influence with leaders in the civil service and in politics, including both government and the opposition. After being taken by surprise by the Iranian Revolution in the 1970s managers of the major multinationals have taken care to improve their communication links in all the politically sensitive areas of the world, especially in areas where there are important economic resources.

However powerful the influence and painstaking the research the unforseen is still possible, even probable. Some provision for this has to be made in the investment appraisal process. One simple method is for senior managers to scale down all projections made by subordinate managers who have a vested interest in the acceptance of the projects they submit for approval. However, this soon becomes common knowledge and managers simply scale up their forecasts accordingly.

More scientific is the attempt to arrive at realistic estimates of future returns by applying probability factors to a range of possible outcomes. The most probable outcomes are thus weighted more heavily than the less probable but all possibilities do have to be considered. This also helps to focus attention on the areas of uncertainty and the developments most likely to produce changes in market conditions. It may suggest areas where more information or more concentrated marketing efforts are needed.

Other common techniques are to raise discount rates or target internal rates of return by a 'safety factor'. For example, if the cost of capital is expected to be, say, 15 per cent per year, a rate of, perhaps, 17 per cent is employed for discounting future returns. Your earlier examination of the effects of high discount rates on projects whose returns tend to come in the later years of a project's life will have shown you that the result of any increase in discount rates is to favour those projects which bring the most speedy returns and to penalise the longer term projects.

In a period of considerable uncertainty this is clearly a prudent course of action and is often reinforced by shortening the target payback period which projects must satisfy before they earn more detailed examination. In the early 1980s some large companies in the UK were insisting on payback periods as short as 12 months. This virtually ruled out all major investment projects. In a period of rising inflation, with all the political and market uncertainties this implies, it is clearly desirable to favour projects that promise early cash returns. However, the refusal to look at long term projects can damage both the firm and the economy as a whole. It is not a profitable course of action if inflation rates are falling and market conditions tending to stabilise. Failure to make long-term investments seems to be one of the reasons for the relative weakness of the British production system and for the tendency for consumer demand to be diverted into imports whenever total demand in the British economy starts to rise. We should always remember that not only is the business investment decision of crucial importance to the firm but also the collective investment decisions of business managers are of very great importance to the future development of the economy as a whole.

TEST YOUR UNDERSTANDING

23 Suggest two possible actions of a government that are likely to influence the investment decisions of business firms.
24 Why do business firms tend to look only to investment projects that produce substantial returns in their early years in periods of economic and political uncertainty?
25 The survey of business investment intentions regularly conducted by the Confederation of British Industry is often quoted as an important item of economic news. Why is such a survey believed to be of economic significance?

Financial functions in private sector organisations

The important part played by finance in business management has been a recurring theme throughout this book. In very general terms financial management covers every aspect of the financial affairs of the firm, from negotiating with the institutions of the finance market to investment appraisal and decision making. We can identify two broad groups of functions which roughly correspond with the two main divisions of accountancy in the private sector, i.e. financial and management accounting. These divisions are by no means rigid. They overlap to a considerable extent, particularly in the smaller or rapidly developing organisations.

Financial accounting in business

The word accounting has two broad meanings, each of which is important to business. In one sense it means keeping records, i.e. keeping account of money so that it can be seen what money the firm has and how it is being used. In another sense it means explaining and being accountable to others who have a right to know how the money entrusted to the organisation is being employed. The keeping and maintenance of accurate records are crucial in both cases. Money enters the firm through the provision of financial capital, through sales revenues and the disposal of physical assets. It leaves the firm in the form of payments to the providers of financial capital, through trading purchases and the acquisition of physical assets, so it is essential for full and accurate records to be kept of all the flows of money into and out of the organisation.

The existence of this constant money flow means that the organisation will have financial communication links with a range of other organisations, so all concerned must speak in a financial language that all can understand. Hence there is a high degree of uniformity in business accounting procedures, terms and practices. This applies to almost all parts of the modern business world. Consequently if you study accounting in the United Kingdom you will learn practices and terms that, with only fairly minor modification, are common to nearly every trading nation in the world.

Because the money used by the business comes from a number of different sources there are certain groups of people who have a right to receive financial information from the organisation. Where the organisation enjoys a structure created by the legislative and legal processes of the country, e.g. when it is a limited company set up in the United Kingdom under the Companies Acts, the right to financial information, the form it should take and rights to have representatives to check (audit) that information are also enshrined in the law, mostly in the Companies Acts and the body of company law built up around their foundation. The main groups of people with rights to financial information are:

- **The owners**
  In the case of the normal limited company the owners are the providers of share capital, i.e. the shareholders. The obligation to send annual accounts to all shareholders extends to public companies. The huge expense involved in printing and posting thousands of quite bulky company reports and accounts is leading to pressure to reduce the obligation to a simple financial summary unless shareholders specifically request the full accounts.

  The shareholders of limited companies gain some degree of additional protection in that the company accounts must be audited and certified to be a true and fair record of the company's financial situation by auditors who must be members of approved professional bodies. Auditors have to be appointed or re-appointed at the company's Annual General Meeting. This requirement does give some further assurance that the financial affairs of companies are prepared according to accepted accountancy conventions. Nevertheless, even this gives some scope for variation and ambiguity. Take over battles between public companies with each company supported by leading firms of accountants can nevertheless reveal very different ideas of what a company's financial position really is. In practice a great deal does have to be taken on trust, particularly as far as the valuation of a firm's physical assets is concerned. Few accountants are fully competent to check the value of highly specialised equipment, for example.

- **The tax authorities**
  In Britain there are two authorities with an interest in the financial affairs of the business. These are the Inland Revenue, concerned with income tax in the case of non-corporate organisations and corporation tax, in the case of limited companies, and H M Customs and Excise which is concerned with Value Added Tax (VAT), import duties, special taxes on alcohol, motor vehicles and oil, etc.

  Very small businesses, if they do not import, do not trade in goods subject to excise or other special taxes and, if their turnover is below levels specified in the Finance Acts, rarely need to become involved with H M Customs and Excise. All organisations operating for profit, however small and whatever their occupation, have to account to the Inland Revenue. This applies even to part-time operations. The Inland Revenue can assess a business, or indeed, an individual for tax on the basis of whatever income or profit it considers probable. The onus or burden of proving the true income or profit then lies with the firm or person concerned. This can be difficult, particularly if past years are involved, if adequate financial records have not been maintained. A tax inspector can base the assessment of profit or income on the evidence of a person's life style, so a desire to impress the neighbours with large cars and expensive holidays can make it difficult to convince a tax inspector that a firm has been running at a loss for some years! If full financial records are maintained according to normal accountancy conventions relations with the Inland Revenue are usually reasonably cordial. Tax inspectors seek to ensure that people pay their taxes according to the law as it stands and have no desire to see people paying more than they should. It is, of course, a legal offence to keep special (false) records for tax purposes.

- **Others with a special interest in the business**
  No one, other than an owner, part-owner, tax inspector, customs and excise officer or police officer (with a magistrate's warrant) has any right to inspect the financial

records of a non-corporate business organisation. On the other hand anyone owed money by the organisation or thinking of extending credit or lending money to it clearly has a legitimate interest in its financial condition. The difficulty of obtaining full and accurate information about a non-corporate firm's finances is one of a number of reasons why banks and other financial institutions tend to insist that business firms seeking to obtain finance on any scale do become limited companies. Banks normally know more about people's financial affairs than most so anyone contemplating the provision of credit to a business usually obtains a banker's credit reference as a minimum safeguard.

Once again there are more rights to information relating to limited companies. Private companies are required to file their annual accounts with the Companies Registry. Anyone can inspect these at the Registry on payment of a fee. However, many companies are dilatory in filing their accounts and the Registrar does not have sufficient resources to exercise strict control over this legal requirement. In fairness the fault often lies more with firms' accountants than with the firms themselves but, of course, there is no simple way of knowing precisely why any particular company is late. It is usually prudent, therefore, to assume that the real reason is that the finances are in a shaky state and the owners are not too anxious for this to become public knowledge. In any event failure to meet a basic legal obligation, such as ensuring that accounts are filed by the due date, is an indication of poor financial administration and a possible pointer to other defects in the management of the organisation.

Public companies are obliged to make their published accounts available to anyone who appears to have a legitimate interest. Since this could mean anyone thinking of buying the company's shares virtually anyone could ask for the final accounts. The company has the right to ask for a fee to cover the cost of postage etc. but most companies regard issuing their accounts as something of a shop window/public relations exercise.

One problem with ensuring that anyone with an interest in the financial affairs of a company can obtain sight of the final accounts is that some people's interest could be the desire to purchase or take over the company. Information contained in the published or filed accounts may then be used to value the company's shares and will assist a take over attempt. Awareness of the dangers of giving too much information in accounts ensures that most companies include only the information required by the Companies Acts and Stock Exchange regulations plus information not likely to prove helpful to a take over raider.

Financial accounting within a company requires accuracy, a good knowledge of the company's business so that physical assets are valued fairly, a knowledge of the law as it relates to business finance as well as familiarity with accountancy practices and conventions.

The accounting records

Business accounts serve a double purpose. They exist partly to assist the managers and owners of the enterprise to operate effectively and profitably and, as we have shown, to convey information to certain groups of people outside the business. The firm, therefore, needs internal accounting systems in order to keep track of the money flow which its activities generate. You saw earlier how the partner in an office supply firm felt she would have benefitted from instruction in keeping daily financial records before starting to run her own business. At the same time the firm, annually and often more frequently, has to account to shareholders, inland revenue and others for the income generated by the business during a given period and has to show its financial position at the end of the period. Accurate internal accounting procedures are needed not only to keep track of the money flow and ensure that bills are paid and collected, but also to be able to prepare the final accounts which show the financial position of the firm.

There are two important final accounts which all but the very smallest firms need to prepare. These are the **profit and loss account** and the **balance sheet**. The profit and loss account shows the revenue and cost flows during an accounting period and indicates the amount of profit or loss resulting from the firm's activities. The balance sheet shows the value of the firm's net assets on a stated date, together with a statement of the firm's liabilities (responsibilities) to the contributors of the finance used to acquire and generate the assets. In the case of very small firms the profit and loss account may be replaced by the simpler income and expenditure account, or, if the accounts are very simple and if most activities take place roughly concurrently with the money flows they generate, i.e. if no long term credit is given or taken and there are no significant stocks of goods, by a receipts and payments account. The differences between these records of financial flows arise chiefly from the treatment of the time lags between selling/buying goods and services, and receiving/paying money.

Copies of the profit and loss account and balance sheet for a listed public company are shown in Figures 4.7 and 4.8. Notice that in these published accounts very few details are given of either costs or revenues. Some companies give more details of sources of revenue by geographical and/or product divisions but it is rare for costs to further information to be given on production and distribution costs. The bare totals can often raise a number of questions. Notice in these accounts that whereas sales turnover rose nearly 83 per cent the cost of sales rose by under 42 per cent. However, distribution costs rose by over 75 per cent. Notes to these accounts and comments in the report indicate that efforts were being made to develop the company's import division and presumably its wholesale trade with other stores. This simple illustration shows how it is necessary to examine published accounts carefully and often to make further investigation in order to find out what a company is really doing.

TEST YOUR UNDERSTANDING

26 What are the dangers to a person starting a new business if that person has not received any accountancy training and has no assistance from anyone with financial training and experience?
27 Suggest reasons why company law makes it necessary for limited companies to have their accounts certified by a member of an approved professional accountancy body.

Management accounting in business

For many years it has been recognised that the accountant in business has responsibilities and opportunities going far beyond simply recording the financial consequences of other managers' actions. Management accountancy is expected to make a positive contribution to the profitability of the company in a number of ways. These may be broadly considered as the identification and control of costs, the handling of taxation and the management of finance.

Identification and control of costs

Management accountants were once known as cost accountants and costs continue to be one of their major concerns. One of the functions of the management accountant is to make other managers aware not only of the cost implications of their activities and

CONSOLIDATED PROFIT AND LOSS ACCOUNT
FOR THE FIFTY-TWO WEEKS ENDING 29TH JULY 1989

Notes		52 weeks ended 29th July 1989		53 weeks ended 30th July 1988	
		£'000	£'000	£'000	£'000
1	Turnover		15,689		8,590
	Cost of sales		10,129		7,174
	Gross profit		5,560		1,416
	Distribution costs	3,515		412	
	Administrative expenses	820		789	
			4,335		1,201
2	**Operating profit**		1,225		215
4	Interest receivable	999		306	
5	Interest payable	(166)		(18)	
			833		288
	Profit on ordinary activities before taxation		2,058		503
6	Taxati on profit on ordinary on activities		327		106
	Profit on ordinary activities after taxation		1,731		397
7	Extraordinary items		115		924
8	**Profit attributable to shareholders**		1,846		1,321
	Profit and loss account				
	Balance brought forward	851		555	
	Re-allocation of previously non-distributable reserve	–		235	
			851		790
			2,697		2,111
9	Dividends		886		1,260
	Balance carried forward		1,811		851
10	**Earnings per ordinary share**		3.52p		0.82p

Figure 4.7

CONSOLIDATED BALANCE SHEET
AT 29TH JULY 1989

Notes		29th July 1989		30th July 1988	
		£'000	£'000	£'000	£'000
	Fixed assets				
11	Tangible assets		**3,701**		389
	Listed investments		**36**		–
			3,737		389
	Current assets				
12	Stocks	**2,441**		825	
14	Debtors	**2,938**		2,545	
	Cash at bank and in hand	**8,364**		4,701	
		4,335		1,201	
	Creditors: Amounts falling due				
15	within one year	**6,568**		3,346	
	Net current assets		**7,175**		4,725
	Total assets less current liabilities		**10,912**		5,114
	Creditors: Amounts falling due				
16	after more than one year		**797**		21
			10,115		5,093
	Provision for liabilities and charges				
17	Deferred taxation		**504**		6
			1,846		1,321
	Capital and reserves				
18	Called up share capital		**3,138**		2,504
19	Share premium account		**5,318**		1,732
19	Goodwill reserve		**(656)**		–
	Profit and loss account		**1,811**		851
			9,611		5,087

Approved by the Board of Directors

PHILIP GREEN

DAVID ROSE

10th October 1989

Figure 4.8

proposals but also to show how costs may be reduced without harming essential activities. It is necessary to develop methods of costing the firm's production activities so that managers can know precisely what capital, labour and other costs have gone into each unit of product. Such information is essential if sensible decisions are to be taken over pricing the product and over choosing production levels. The management accountant should be able to calculate the unit and the marginal cost of each product, i.e. the average total cost and the cost of any increase in production from any given output level. The accountant may also be able to indicate how changes in production levels and methods might help to reduce costs.

As an aid to the clearer identification and control of costs the concept of cost centres has been developed. These help to cut across some of the departmental boundaries which otherwise conceal the full cost implications to the firm of decisions made in one part of the enterprise. It is essential that the person responsible for the cost centre has full control over and responsibility for the costs generated in the centre and which affect the activities of the centre. If any costs arise out of decisions made outside the centre then the whole concept breaks down because the head of the centre is having to accept costs which are outside his or her control. A production unit which had to accept charges for machine maintenance contracts negotiated by another department does not qualify as a cost centre.

In practice the costs of any given activity or form of production need to be related to the revenues generated, so that the concept of cost centres is tending to be replaced by that of profit centres. The profit centre idea also helps to bring home to managers the need to examine the implications for profit of any given activity or range of activities. If stress is on cost alone there is a danger that an opportunity is ignored because of its probable effect on costs. However, if the opportunity promises to add more to profit than to cost a different decision is likely to be taken. The profit centre approach encourages thinking in terms of the relationship between marginal costs and marginal revenue and to decisions that come closer to the profit maximising assumptions of traditional economics.

Cost accounting goes beyond just recording costs. It is often possible to make comparisons between activities and production methods and, perhaps, to estimate what particular processes should cost, or often their standard cost based on past experience and the work level that can be expected from experienced workers. If actual costs depart from expected or standard costs then the process can be looked at more closely.

Allocation of overheads

When firms produce a range of different products or perform a variety of different services, one of the problems of costing is the allocation of those costs which cannot be related to a single product or activity, but which are incurred on behalf of groups of products or for the organisation as a whole. The cost of a machine used for making one product and the wages of the machine operator are clearly costs incurred directly to produce that product. However, the cost of cleaning the factory as a whole, heating and lighting costs and the salaries of, for example, the finance director or personnel manager, who perform services for all departments and are described as overheads. They can present difficult issues of allocation to product costs. A common solution is to allocate overheads according to their relative contribution to sales revenue, but this ignores any actual differences arising from the nature of the activity or the length of time it has been established in the firm. New products tend to take up a disproportionate amount of overheads, which if reflected in their prices, would not allow them to be launched successfully in competitive markets. In practice allocation can be the result of subjective judgements of senior managements, modified by bargaining with specialist managers who naturally seek to make the lowest possible contribution. Since contribution to overheads can have a significant impact on the calculation of departmental or divisional profits a great deal of internal bargaining can sometimes take place and the results may be a truer reflection of the power structure within management than the actual cost of operations.

Budgets

The term 'budget' is used in business with some different shades of meaning. In a general sense a budget is a financial plan within which an organisation or part of an organisation is expected to operate. A budget may related to both revenue and expenditure, to expenditure alone or to an amount of money which a manager is permitted to spend for a stated purpose over a period. The chief buyer of a clothing chain, for example, may have a budget of two million pounds, meaning that the buyer is authorised to spend this amount on new stock during a stated period. When the term is used in relation to cost controls, however, the budget is a plan of anticipated costs for a given period. It is usually recommended that managers should participate in drawing up the budgets within which they are expected to operate so that they are realistic and understood. The underlying idea is that if all cost and revenue budgets are met then the firm as a whole will achieve its financial targets for the period.

If, during the period, departments or cost centres are not keeping within their budgets then it is necessary to find out why. It could be that assumptions on which the budget was based are no longer correct. Workers may have achieved a pay rise larger than anticipated at the time of drawing up the budget. Production required to meet demand may be greater or smaller than the levels previously assumed. The important thing is to find out why the budget is not being met and to modify other company practices or targets accordingly. If budgetary controls are not operating successfully it is important that an immediate assumption is not made that the cause of the failure to keep to budget is incompetence on the part of the manager. If competent managers feel threatened by a budgetary control system they will ensure that their own budgets have concealed safety features and the whole exercise becomes self-defeating.

TEST YOUR UNDERSTANDING

28 What are standard costs and how do they help the process of cost control?
29 What is the difference between unit and marginal cost? Suggest reasons why it is often more important to base production decisions on marginal than on unit costs.

Taxation and financial management

Taxation and financial management

One of the functions of the management accountant is to keep the total tax paid by the company as low as possible for any achieved level of profit. This frequently means organising expenditure so that the maximum allowances can be obtained against taxation. For large firms this can range from relatively trivial decisions, e.g. the most 'tax efficient' way to reward successful sales staff, to major decisions such as the location of production plants to obtain the maximum assistance from the European Community's Regional Fund.

It is unfortunately true that taxation distorts the activities, costs and revenues of most forms of business enterprise. For example it is usually cheaper to increase a manager's effective remuneration through benefits in kind, the most common being the company car, than through an equivalent increase in salary. This is partly because employers have to pay national insurance contributions (an employment tax) based on the total wage bill. Also, of course, large firms are able to negotiate substantial fleet discounts from motor vehicle suppliers so the cost of a vehicle to the firm is lower than the amount an individual owner would have to pay. This taxation/cost advantage remains even though employees now pay tax on the benefit derived from having a company car. The tax levied is much lower than the actual cost of owning and running an equivalent car privately.

Company accountants need to have a detailed knowledge of tax laws and regulations in order to guide their fellow managers and ensure that the company does not pay more tax than is necessary. It is not surprising that companies sometimes like to recruit former tax inspectors.

The management of finance

All areas covered in Unit 4 are concerned in some way with the management of finance. Here we simply summarise and add some comments on aspects of these. Management accountants should have a good knowledge of the financial system and the ways in which finance can be raised. They are the main link with the banks and other financial institutions whose support the company needs.

The accountant must also control company borrowing and ensure that it is in no danger of being forced to sell important assets to repay loans or meet heavy interest charges. The management accountant must be able to identify the company's safe gearing ratio, i.e. that ratio of its total debt to equity (gearing ratio), that it can support without financial risk should there be an unexpected rise in interest rates or fall in product demand. Highly geared companies are very vulnerable to the sudden onset of recession or steep rises in interest rates as suffered in the UK during 1988 and 1989. On the other hand under- gearing, i.e. rejection of borrowing and the building up of large reserves of cash, can mean that the company is missing profit-making opportunities and leaving itself vulnerable to take over by more aggressive management teams.

Management accounting also involves the allocation of finance to the company's internal divisions, e.g. appraisal of investment projects and analysis of the past performance of divisional managers. Financial investment, however, looks primarily to the future and not to the past, though this may be a useful guide to some aspects of the future. The allocation of finance within the company must accord with the strategic policy decisions of senior management.

For very large companies a major source of finance and (channel of use) during the 1980s was the disposal of subsidiary companies, and interests in associates and reinvestment by taking over other company groups. Investment during this period has tended to mean purchasing a company rather than building a new factory. It is doubtful, however, whether this tendency can survive a series of stock market crashes of the kind that afflicted world capital markets in October 1987 and October 1989. Again we must avoid the temptation of seeing the future simply in terms of a continuation of the past.

A less glamorous but nevertheless essential function of the management accountant is to ensure that money and credit, in particular, are effectively controlled within the company. If careful attention is paid to the flow of cash through the company, so that payments fall due as far as possible when the cash is available to meet them, then wasteful borrowing can be avoided. Credit is expensive and should not be used to cover slack administration. Credit control involves keeping careful checks on debtors and ensuring that incoming accounts are settled promptly within the terms of customer credit arrangements. Often this is a matter of accurate and prompt administration. A frequent cause of delayed payment is failure to provide accurate and intelligible accounts. Early computerised accounting systems caused many problems through their lack of detail and the work involved whenever amounts had to be questioned. There is no excuse for this today.

When bank credit is expensive some larger companies are tempted to make increased use of trade credit which they may see as 'free' or low cost involving no more than forfeiting an inadequate rate of cash discount. Nevertheless, when a company gains a reputation for taking extended credit the opportunity cost can rise steeply. Creditors soon recognise that settlement delays are costing them extra credit and administration charges and they take steps to ensure that these costs are reflected in prices. Companies with reputations as poor payers quickly lose bargaining power even in competitive markets. Firms are not anxious to compete for troublesome business. The loss of bargaining power can mean that the true cost of taking extended credit can be much higher than bank overdraft charges.

General financial management

Every business activity has a financial implication so that financial management enters virtually every corner of the business. The finance manager will be asked to report on the financial implications of proposed changes in product development and production method and may take the initiative in proposing changes which are likely to increase profits. Changes are not always popular with other managers so that diplomacy and communication skills may be as important as financial knowledge to successful financial management. It is also important to recognise that the long-term development and profitability of the company are not sacrificed for purely short-term profits. The finance manager is primarily a business manager before being a financier, and one important function may be to defend the long-term interests of the company in the face of shorter term considerations within financial institutions whose support the company needs.

TEST YOUR UNDERSTANDING

30 To what extent can the idea of 'tax efficiency' be in conflict with the interests of business efficiency?
31 'A stock market crash can increase the risk of business failures.' Why?
32 You notice in a set of company accounts that the total of debtors' balances has risen significantly. Should this cause you concern? What further information would you seek in order to find out if there is a problem?

Financial management in the public sector

Features of public sector finance

When contrasting their work with that of financial managers in the private sector, city treasurers point out that, whereas a company finance manager can do anything as long as it is not illegal, the local authority treasurer is bound strictly by the authority granted by Parliament and may not step beyond that authority however desirable for the community the desired action might be.

Nevertheless there are similarities in the work of the local authority finance manager and the finance managers working for private sector firms. There is a similar stress on cost identification and control and a similar need for the finance manager's guidance and advice concerning the financial implications of any proposed action by other decision makers within the local authority.

The most notable difference between private and public sector financial management is the absence in the public sector of any pressure to achieve a profit. Indeed there would be considerable resistance to any notion that profits should be generated by many social service activities. The absence of a profit motive, however, removes a powerful discipline for controlling costs and there are many tendencies within public sector organisations for costs to be unnecessarily high. Among these we may note the following:

- **Empire building**
  The pay of public sector managers has traditionally been linked to the size of the operation they manage. Grades almost always have a size qualification. There is thus a powerful motive to build up the size of the department managed and to exaggerate the amount of work performed. It is always difficult to know whether administrative work is the result of genuine demand for services or the result of managerial incompetence. It is possible for incompetent managers to increase work loads and staff levels and so reward themselves for their own inefficiency.

- **Protected employment conditions**
  It has long been virtually impossible to sack a worker in the public sector for incompetence, possibly because there is often no measure of competence against which judgements can be made. Dismissals usually occur solely on the grounds of illegal or immoral practices and there is an understandable reluctance to use these means unless there is very strong proof. Even redundancies and early retirements have been on a voluntary basis so that the people who tend to take advantage of these schemes are often those who can most easily find employment in the private sector. Trade unions are very powerful and have a reputation for protecting members with little regard to standards of service to the public. As salary structures are also usually very rigid there is little incentive for the competent who receive the same pay as the incompetent. Such conditions breed inefficiency.

- **Budgetary systems**
  Budgets in the public sector usually mean allocations of spending limits applicable for specific purposes for specific periods of time. Because unspent allocations cannot be carried forward to future periods or transferred to other purposes and because finance managers are known to cover overspending by some departments from underspending in others, most departments ensure that they spend the whole of their budgetary allocation and, where possible, overspend. Consequently there are many public sector stock rooms full of unused equipment and offices where equipment is brought up to date regardless of any need for replacement. Managers take pride in securing the latest possible equipment without regard to actual need.

- **Managers administer rather than manage**
  Public sector managers frequently lack the basic powers of management that managers in the private sector would regard as essential. Budgets, staffing levels, staff grades and salaries, equipment maintenance and a host of other activities are often beyond their control so that they cannot actually manage anything but only administer according to set rules. Without control over costs or revenues there are no incentives for efficiency - and often no definition of what is efficient.

Movement for reform in public sector finance

A growing recognition of these problems in the public sector has led to some pressure for reform. In place of profit there has been substituted a requirement that officials should seek 'value for money'. This has been accompanied by stricter controls over the allocation of money from public sector sources. According to comments made by serving officials in local authorities there is greater stress on managerial attitudes and practices in public sector finance. However, it will not be easy to change the entrenched habits of many people in the public sector.

Attempts to bring greater financial controls can bring their own dangers. Simply reducing the funds available to organisations from outside sources controlled by central government still leaves the allocation of funds internally to the decision makers within the institutions. These are frequently dominated by political attitudes and there is always the possibility that cuts will be made with the deliberate intention of provoking hostility to the central government. Even if these open political moves are resisted financial allocation is still influenced by managers' own beliefs and value judgements concerning the priorities of what is most in the public interest. In practice those sectors which have the political skills to manipulate the internal politics of the institution are likely to obtain the most funds. A powerful motive may be personal ambition, in spite of the genuine desires of finance managers to serve the best interests of the public.

Another recent trend has been to encourage public sector institutions to use their resources to generate income. Some indeed have become virtually self-financing, though closer inspection usually reveals that they have simply replaced patronage of the public purse with patronage by those business managers who are willing to divert shareholders' funds to projects which promote management status. Whether corporate business patronage is an effective route towards increased efficiency and greater public service is a question with no certain answer.

The attempt in the 1980s to make an increasing number of public sector institutions into quasi private sector bodies seeking to achieve a kind of financial equilibrium with a mixture of sales revenue, support from taxation and from business corporate patronage, is likely to have implications for the attitudes and objectives of these institutions that are, as yet, not fully understood. It will certainly bring more influences to bear on these bodies. It may make them even more confused over what their real objectives actually are and which sections of the public they are meant to be serving.

There are clearly no simple solutions to the problems of financing and financing control of public sector institutions. We should beware of all-purpose remedies such as 'privatisation' or 'democratisation' the meaning of which is rarely clear. Nevertheless the debate is healthy in that it forces us to ask basic questions about objectives, such as 'Do we want a police force to catch criminals or to reduce crime and stop people becoming criminals? 'and about the structure of institutions such as schools and colleges. This debate may lead to a better understanding of the issues and to better decisions about finance and financial control.

TEST YOUR UNDERSTANDING

33 How far, if at all, can the concept of profit be applied to educational institutions in the public sector?
34 What difficulties can you foresee in applying a concept such as 'value for money' to financial controls in the public sector?

NOTES TO QUESTIONS

Question 1
Lenders often require security for a loan to be provided by borrowers so that they gain the protection of possessing a physical asset which they can turn into cash, if necessary, in order to wipe out or reduce a debt which otherwise could not be recovered.

The principle is really the same as that employed by one of the oldest forms of borrowing - pawnbroking, where the borrower has to deposit an article of value which becomes the property of the lender if the loan and agreed interest are not repaid within the agreed period. In business finance it is not usually the physical property which is lodged. It would be difficult to deposit a factory or piece of land! However, what is usually deposited is the written title to the property, as without this document, sale is normally impossible. Another form of security might be a written undertaking by the borrower to take certain action or empower the lender to take certain action if the debt is not repaid as agreed. For example, power may be given to the lender to collect revenues or to take possession of stocks under certain circumstances.

There is nothing new in this principle of providing security. You may know the story of the Merchant of Venice, which illustrates another important commercial principle - that agreements must be reasonable if they are to obtain the full support of the law.

Question 2

It is an assumption of the law of contract that parties are of equal power and enter into contracts freely. Given this assumption then it is difficult for one party to complain about the terms of the agreement later. However, modern law recognises that private individuals are not equal to large, powerful business corporations either in knowledge or wealth. Consequently it is considered to be both socially and commercially desirable for ordinary individuals to have a certain amount of legal protection. This protection is not available to registered companies because, although it is realised that not all companies are large and wealthy, it is felt that a company should honour its agreements and should take care to obtain professional help in making contracts if its officers are in any doubt about their provisions.

Clearly a line has to be drawn somewhere and any distinction of this kind is bound to give rise to anomalies. The possible anomaly here is that sole proprietors and partners who make hire purchase or leasing agreements in their own names on behalf of their business organisations enjoy the statutory protection given to individuals, whereas the person trading as a limited company who makes the same kind of agreement does not have this protection.

It has to be admitted that this distinction is not always fully realised by borrowers and by some finance houses, especially where these are associated with equipment selling firms. Partners and sole proprietors who buy equipment on hire purchase or leasing terms would do well to check that the correct forms and procedures have been employed and to ensure that they obtain full legal protection.

Question 3

If possible you should obtain and consult any 'literature' you can obtain about the practice of factoring. In general, the benefits arise out of obtaining cash more quickly following the sale of goods than would otherwise be possible. In competitive markets it is often necessary to allow credit and when dealing with large firms the period of credit is often quite long. The money is usually safe. It will be paid but delay could mean that the seller has to borrow money from elsewhere or not have money available that could be put to profitable use. One possible remedy for this is to factor all debts and to arrange for the factor to take over the risk of non-payment. If the factor agrees to accept the seller as a client the seller obtains early cash and is relieved of the risk of bad debts. Clearly the factor has to be satisfied that the borrowing firm is dealing with highly reputable buyers before taking this kind of responsibility.

Question 4

Shares are usually regarded as the permanent capital of the company because even if they are redeemable, repayment is subject to conditions which reserve any option or choice for the company. The shareholder cannot ask for shares to be redeemed simply because he or she suddenly wants to convert them into cash.

At the same time shares are articles of value which can be sold. Shares in public companies which are constantly being traded on the main International Stock Exchange are virtually liquid assets as they can be sold immediately by telephone. Shares in smaller companies or private companies are much less liquid as buyers have to be found and private company shares cannot be advertised. A shareholder may have to find his or her own buyer for private company shares.

Question 5

A bond in company A can be regarded as being 'safer' than shares in the same company because bonds give rise to legally enforceable obligations to pay interest and repay borrowings regardless of profit, whereas shareholders stand at the very end of the line of any queue for repayment and dividends can only be legally paid from profits. However, a company which has difficulty paying a share dividend is also likely to have trouble honouring its bonds.

In another sense bonds are a lot less 'safe' than shares in that they provide much less security against financial losses caused by the depreciating value of money (inflation). A fixed rate of interest loses its real purchasing value when money is falling in purchasing power year by year.

You should always consider the standing of the company issuing the 'paper'. Shares in a large, first class-rated company which has 'trustee status', i.e. it has not failed to pay dividends for many years and trustees can legally invest trust fund money in them, are likely to be safer than bonds issued by a small company and backed with very little real security. In this connection you should beware 'junk bonds' used more in the USA than in the United Kingdom. These bonds can be almost worthless if the company ceases to be profitable. The worth of any promise depends on the ability of the person or organisation making the promise to keep it. I might sign a piece of paper promising to pay you £1 million in three days' time but you would be rather unwise to put much value on this!

Question 6

If you are fortunate and obtain the accounts of a company operating in many companies over a long period of time you will see evidence of many types of finance to meet its varying needs. In particular look for evidence of raising fixed interest loan stock or preference shares and note when and where this finance was raised. Ability to raise fixed interest or fixed dividend finance suggests that inflation was not seen as a major problem at that time. In periods of uncertainty you will find that companies of all kinds and sizes resort to short-term lending from banks. Note that although care has been taken in these tutorial notes to separate short- and long-term finance, in practice the distinction is not so clear cut. Short-term borrowing when constantly renewed becomes long term. However there is always the risk of non-renewal so that when conditions are favourable firms will seek to 'fund' at least part of their short-term debt by issuing long-dated bonds and/or additional shares.

Question 7

The National Savings Bank cannot be described as a full bank. It is a deposit bank only. To merit the description of a full bank in economic terms it should fulfil the three basic banking functions, i.e. the safe keeping, transfer and lending of money.

Question 8

Banks are commercial public companies and they also have a duty to generate profits for their shareholders. They must, therefore, reconcile the conflicting objectives of safety and profit. One of the bank's most profitable activities is the lending of money. The ability to lend deposits profitably also enables the banks to provide transfer and other services to depositors at low or nil cost. Banks now pay interest on current accounts. They can do this only because these deposits are put to work profitably.

At the same time banks recognise their duty to lend safely. They do this by seeking to obtain reasonable security for loans and by arranging their lending so that funds are constantly being returned. They can thus build up their own cash stocks very quickly by halting their lending and allowing returned funds to accumulate. From time to time, however, banks do forget to some extent their duty of care. The scale of Third World debt provisions made during the 1980s is likely to be a long-standing warning to the major banks that lending money can never be riskless.

Question 9

Banking has become very competitive in the 1980s. Many financial institutions compete for individual and business deposits and for a share in the traditional lending activities. Building societies, for example, even offer a traveller's cheque service. At the same time the trend towards 'one stop shopping' clearly evident in the retail trade, has also started to influence attitudes to banking. Organisations and individuals do not want to have to approach several financial institutions for different services. They are starting to expect their financial adviser to offer a complete package of services.

Nevertheless the benefits of specialisation are fundamental to all forms of business development. Banks generally are trying to reconcile the conflict between specialisation and personal service to the customer by turning the local branch into a kind of friendly doorway through which the customer can pass towards a whole range of specialised services.

Many of the financial services of the banks involve low opportunity costs because the bank is essentially selling spare capacity in the form of specialised skills and even equipment time. The fee earning services, therefore, can be very profitable. It should also be noted that most other financial institutions are moving along the same path. The major legal and accountancy firms are also trying to widen the range of their services and to do so without snapping the personal links with their clients.

Question 10

All full banks offer essentially the same services of safe-keeping, lending and transfer of money on behalf of customers. At the same time both branch and merchant banking are concerned with providing the fullest possible range of services to their customers. Their prosperity is always closely linked to the well being of their customers.

Nevertheless there are important differences. As the name suggests the branch, or high street banks, bring their day-to-day services as close as possible to their customers, so that a large branch network is considered to be essential to their activities. Merchant banks are not usually in such close daily contact with their customers as they do not fulfil daily routine services such as taking deposits or providing a cheque or cashpoint facility. The merchant bank depends on its ability to build up a close relationship of trust and mutual dependence between its own decision makers and senior managers of its clients. It is likely to have few or no branches but suitable staff will visit client premises as the need arises.

Merchant banking is much more entrepreneurial in its willingness to take risks in efforts to develop the profits of business clients and to share in those profits.

Some institutions which call themselves merchant banks offer only a limited number of services.

The branch banks operate in both the retail and wholesale markets. The large merchant banks tend to operate more in amounts that are more fairly described as wholesale.

Question 11

The major high street banks have become financial composites through the provision of a wide range of services that were previously perceived as separate specialised activities. In particular they have crossed the boundaries between the markets for short-term finance and those for long-term and permanent capital. Since 1986 several have moved into the capital market as both stockbrokers and market makers.

The explanation for this trend is similar to that offered in the notes to Question 3. In addition we should note the preference of large organisations for continued growth. In national oligopolistic markets the room for growth is limited. Further expansion requires extension both overseas and into new markets. British banks have always operated as multinational banks subject to political constraints imposed in foreign countries so that an effort to achieve fresh growth is likely to involve entry to new markets.

Question 12

Much international freight still travels by sea. Journey times are still likely to involve some weeks when account is taken of customs and other checks. Buyers do not usually wish to pay for goods until they have arrived and preferably not until they have had a chance to generate some sales from them. Exporters, on the other hand have had the costs of production, marketing and often of transport. They wish to obtain money as soon as the goods have been dispatched.

The bill of exchange, combined with banking services, offers one way to meet these conflicting needs. By releasing an accepted term bill to the exporter as soon as satisfactory export documents have been presented the bank enables the exporter to generate cash by discounting the bill. The importer does not have to pay any cash until the bill matures, i.e until the payment date arrives. The bank finances the transaction in a way which it is able to control and with a considerable degree of safety for itself.

Question 13

The conversion of short- into effective long-term finance can take place when firms become accustomed to the regular renewal of loan and/or overdraft facilities. They then either use this finance or use cash which would otherwise repay the loans, to develop long-term investment projects. They neglect to obtain long-term capital to cover this capital expenditure.

The dangers of this practice include becoming over-geared, i.e. over-dependent on borrowings, becoming vulnerable to a sudden downturn in economic conditions. If the banks then exercise their right not to renew a loan or to insist on reducing or clearing an overdraft they become very short of finance. A period when this is happening is not usually the best one to go to the capital market for long-term finance.

The practice can also be costly as short-term interest rates are much more volatile than long-term rates. Under a monetarist government interest rates can rise swiftly and a firm's interest costs can increase by large amounts in a short space of time. If the firm is forced to go to the capital market it will do so at a considerable disadvantage and at a time when capital costs are high.

Question 14

If the expansion of trade between members of the European Community continues firms are going to get used to the idea of a 'single European market' and will expect the financial market to operate on similar principles. They will wish to transfer funds quickly, simply and inexpensively between countries and to borrow funds as close as possible to the place where expenditure is being incurred. Firms will need 'single financial markets' for both short-, medium- and long-term finance. A British firm operating a distribution depot in Germany, for example, will wish to finance the building of the depot, the purchase of vehicles and its working capital from within Germany in ways which are familiar to the finance department in the UK, and will prefer to handle the administration of finance from the UK.

This kind of flexibility assumes that there will be no barriers to the transfer of funds between member countries and swift and inexpensive conversion between currencies. However, we might also expect growing demand for a single currency unit throughout member countries. For business firms this would be a major simplification. Unfortunately governments are likely to resist this pressure for reasons of national pride and the desire to run their own economies as they wish. Banks may also resist the pressure as it would remove much of their existing business and sources of revenue.

Question 15

The small business owner must consider the balance of benefit and disadvantage and, of course cost. The major question that must be asked is 'What is the alternative, if any?'

If there is no alternative the entrepreneur may well ask why. If the project is so risky that there is only one source of finance is it one that should be risked anyway? If there is an alternative of a loan at fixed or variable rates of interest then direct and possible hidden future costs must be considered. Given the experience of inflation suffered by investors in the 1970s it is possible that fixed interest loans are only available at very high rates and the business owner could be committed to paying these when competitors are obtaining much cheaper finance should market rates decline in the future. However, the course of future rates is always uncertain. If variable rates are chosen in the belief that future market trends will be towards cheaper money this may be a misreading of the economic signs. Rates may rise instead and at a time when sales revenues are declining.

The prospect of obtaining finance in return for a share of future profits (e.g. through equity) may thus look much more attractive. It appears that cost depends on ability to pay. If future profits rise everyone benefits. However, when the future comes, the business owner may be unhappy to see a large part of the fruits of all his or her enterprise, hard work and sacrifice going to institutions or individuals that did little to help other than provide money that the local bank might have been willing to offer anyway.

Raising finance through the issue of equity also involves the sacrifice of a measure of independence. If financial needs forced the issue of more than 50 per cent of total equity the owner has lost personal control and sacrificed the very independence that was the main motivation for starting the business in the first place. The successful owner is forced to ponder the fact that he or she is sacrificing hard-earned profit to make good the losses suffered by investors when they backed less successful entrepreneurs. The successful business owner is being asked to make good the results of the poor judgement of the investors!

There are undoubtedly occasions when equity is the correct source of finance for the small firm but it is not always the only or the most appropriate source for many people. Finding the best solution for this problem is as important as any other faced by the small business owner, who must recognise that his or her 'financial adviser' is not always offering truly impartial advice.

Question 16

The historic reason is that each one has been introduced to meet the needs of business organisations to have access to long-term capital at reasonable cost. As each market has become established the costs of entry have risen and a new market has been developed to fulfil the purpose of the original.

This raises the question, 'Why do costs rise so much and so quickly?' This is more difficult to answer. Inflation, particularly in monopolistic markets, seems to be a very fundamental tendency. Perhaps increasing competition in international financial markets will delay the anticipated escalation in costs of the relatively new Third Market.

However, it must also be admitted that there is also a strong demand to increase regulation and safety standards in financial markets. Some of the costs are incurred out of a desire (often reinforced by the law) to provide protection for investors. No capital market can operate effectively if investors do not feel that they can invest funds with a reasonable degree of safety. They do not expect completely riskless investment. They recognise normal business hazards but they will not tolerate losses caused by dishonesty and deliberate or careless fraud. As markets grow with success the costs of policing them increase as they inevitably attract their share of the rogues of the world. Attempts to persuade more 'small savers' to invest directly in the capital market have to be accompanied by proper regulation and safeguards. These are not cheap to operate and the costs have to be born by those who wish to obtain benefits from the market. It must be remembered that in finance, as in most other sectors, a cheap service can ultimately become extremely expensive to all concerned. It is usually better to pay a little more for better quality.

Question 17

In practice managers are far from indifferent as to the sources of their finance. While it is true that all finance has an opportunity cost there can be significant differences in the direct costs of raising funds.

Self-generated funds (retained profits) have considerable attractions for managers because:

- There are no market costs such as brokers' and underwriters' fees
- Managers do not have to undergo the scrutiny of external financiers wishing to analyse the reasons given for raising money. As long as the investment is not a financial disaster there is little prospect of external criticism.

In periods of inflation many managers may seek to raise fixed interest loans directly from financial institutions, thus avoiding market costs as before and also experiencing a falling real cost of servicing the debt as the value of money declines. However, after the experiences of the 1970s, British financial institutions have been reluctant to arrange fixed interest loans unless the rate of interest is very high. As most governments have subsequently claimed to be committed to reducing inflation firms do not wish to be committed to loans at high fixed rates over long periods, as interest rates may fall. Renewable short-term loans are a possible option. In these cases interest rates tend to keep in line with current market conditions but there is always the chance that renewal may be denied and then the firm has to repay the loan, possibly at a most inconvenient time.

Raising new equity through the capital market often involves very substantial market costs and exposes management to the detailed scrutiny of market financial analysts. In spite of this, however, a company whose shares are favoured by the market and which can offer a good chance of rising future profits may be able to issue new shares with a relatively low current yield. Consequently the cost to the firm can still be reasonably low. At the same time increasing the equity will reduce the firm's gearing ratio (the ratio of debt to equity) and enable it to borrow more short- term finance. Short-term borrowing is often the first stage in the process leading to an increase in equity. Consequently managers like to see their share price standing high in the market as this reduces the cost and generally eases the task of raising new finance.

How to raise finance is thus a matter of very great importance to business managers.

Question 18

Managers may feel that the scale of the project is likely to raise problems with which they do not feel equipped to deal. If the project involved a significant increase in the size of the labour force this could involve a new style of labour relations and might damage relationships with existing workers.

In the case of a small, family-controlled company raising a large amount of finance could involve a loss of independence as some degree of control and influence by one or more financial institutions might have to be accepted. This could also involve changes in the style of management and in relationships with workers that might not be acceptable to the present owners of the company.

In the case of larger companies a common reason for not pursuing an apparently attractive investment project is that it does not fit the strategic plans of the company. For example the company may wish to reduce its commitment to a particular market and to enter a new market where the immediate prospects are not as attractive but where the company believes its long-term future is likely to lie.

It is important to stress that investment appraisal is not simply a mathematical exercise but involves personal business judgements on the part of senior management in the light of their long term business objectives. The mathematical analysis is an aid to, not a substitute for, decision making.

Question 19

The following are the discounted values of the yearly returns:

		£
year 1		4464
year 2		7972
year 3		5339
year 4		3178
year 5		1986
	Total	22939

Since the initial cost was £25 000 the present value is lower than the cost and net present value for a discount rate of 12 per cent is thus negative, at -£2061. If you have used a computer program you may have a more accurate figure of -£2061.80.

Question 20

From a computer program and adopting a discount rate of 2 per cent the NPV is £4370; at a rate of 4 per cent it is £2871 and at 6 per cent it is £1490. The graph produced from these figures is shown in Figure 4.9. In this diagram you will see that NPV curve is 0 at a rate between 8 and 9 per cent. The internal rate of return, therefore, is between 8 per cent and 9 per cent. From the computer program it was found to be 8.35%. This is shown in Figure 4.9.

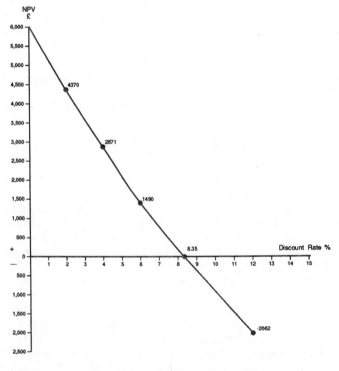

Figure 4.9

Question 21

The simple answer is that the firm should take into account the opportunity cost of capital. However, as we have already noticed, the opportunity cost is not always easy to calculate and not everyone will agree on what it is under any given set of circumstances. The basis for opportunity cost is the best available comparable alternative, e.g. another investment opportunity of equivalent cost, period length and degree of risk. In practice such an alternative may not exist.

A common approach by firms is simply to equate the discount rate to the estimated cost of capital required to finance the project. A target internal rate of return is frequently chosen on this reasoning, e.g. the finance manager calculates that capital required for 5 years costs, say, 16 per cent so, ignoring any safety margin the firm only considers projects with an IRR of more than 16 per cent.

There are dangers with this approach. For example, there may be other opportunities for investment open to the firm, with less risk, that would yield a return higher than 16 per cent so that undertaking projects at IRRs only a little higher than 16 per cent would not be making the most of the firm's profit opportunities. There is also the danger that projects financed from retained profit might be undertaken with a return based on comparison with the return achieved from a bank deposit account where the money has been held with the lost bank interest being seen as the cost of capital. However, this would be misleading because comparison is being made between a very safe, highly liquid bank deposit and a rather more risky and highly illiquid physical investment. If, later, you study financial management you are likely to meet this problem of choosing an appropriate discount rate again and will have to analyse the issues very carefully. At this stage it is sufficient to recognise that the problem exists and care should be taken in choosing the discount rate or target IRR.

Question 22

A set of simple figures showing returns over a four or five year period would be sufficient. In one table you need to put a high proportion of the returns in the first two years and in the contrasting table simply reverse the figures so that the high returns come late in the life of the project. If you apply a discount rate of around 5 per cent and then repeat the calculations with a rate of, say, 15 per cent, or 12 per cent, you will see the gap widening between the returns from the two projects. It should be clear from your example that the project with the delayed returns suffers most heavily as the discount rate rises.

Question 23

Any action of government that is likely to reduce the anticipated return from investment, increase the cost of capital, or simply create economic or political uncertainty is likely to influence the level of business investment. You should be able to think of a number of possible actions. Among the more common are:

- Actions likely to change the currency exchange rate because these affect the prices of imported materials and the world price of exports or competing imports and so affect both costs and returns
- Movements of interest rates which are influenced by governments
- Changes in the government's own spending because the government is a very large customer for business projects
- Changes in almost any tax because these affect product prices and consumer incomes, both of which affect product demand
- Any attempt to take direct control over prices or worker incomes or to impose any form of 'prices and incomes policy'
- Changes in relationships with other countries likely to affect conditions under which trade is conducted with these countries
- The government's own political strength or weakness because any possibility of a shift in government economic policy must influence demand and/or prices.

Question 24

The greater the degree of uncertainty the more difficult it is to predict future returns more than a few years ahead. If the uncertainty is very great then it may be difficult to look forward more than a year. Uncertainty also applies to interest rates which have an influence on the rates of discount to be applied to future returns. If safety factors are applied to both future returns and discount rates then returns anticipated more than a year or two ahead start to be heavily penalised. It is often said that uncertainty is the enemy of investment. It certainly kills long-term investment.

Question 25

The survey gives a good indication of the degree of confidence of business managers in the future prospects for growth in demand. Firms invest in order to increase their capacity to produce goods and services. They will take steps to increase production only if they believe they can sell the extra product profitably. If investment trends appear to be rising then confidence is high, firms are preparing to produce more and expecting profits and sales to rise. If investment trends are falling then confidence is low, and managers are expecting demand to be depressed and believe that sales and profits are likely to fall.

To some extent these expectations are self-fulfilling. If managers reduce investment they reduce the demand for capital goods and this helps to depress total demand. At the same time if they are not planning for expansion, employment opportunities stagnate and worker morale is likely to fall. They may spend less and demand falls further. In this way the whole economy can slide into depression and as sales start to fall investment falls further and the cycle is repeated.

Question 26

The immediate danger is that the person will underestimate the capital needed to finance the crucial first year of the business. There is a time lag between obtaining business and obtaining payment. Stocks have to be financed and rents paid and during this period ordinary living expenses have to be met. The business may be quite sound financially but lack of cash may force it to close.

There are further dangers in inadequate recording. These may make it difficult to collect payments or make payments when due. It may also be difficult to meet the requirements of H M Customs and Excise over VAT and the Inland Revenue over income tax.

Other dangers lie in not taking advantage of credit and not negotiating purchase terms.

Failure to notify the Inland Revenue that a business is being run for profit can also cause problems, both in agreeing the amount of tax due and actually paying tax on income which has long been spent.

Question 27

Limited companies have valuable privileges, including limited liability which protects shareholders from some of the worst consequences of financial disasters caused by managers acting on their behalf. In return there are obligations to ensure that the public interest is not abused. People trade with limited companies at their own risk but there is some protection in trying to ensure that the finances of the company are investigated regularly by a member of a professional body and the results of the investigation made available to the public. The requirement that a limited company's financial affairs should be scrutinised and certified by a properly qualified professional accountant is one small safeguard for the public that the privileges of company status are not being abused.

Question 28

The concept of standard cost can be applied to any identifiable operation from, say, changing a vehicle wheel to the manufacture of a complete motor vehicle. It represents the cost of the operation assuming normal working conditions and competent, trained workers and efficient, appropriate equipment. Where fixed costs and overheads have to be taken into account a standard output level has to be assumed. If actual output is different from the standard output then actual costs will also depart from the standard costs. If target profits are based on standard costs then actual profit is likely to be different from the target profit.

Standard costs are a useful aid to pricing and to cost control under conditions where demand is reasonably stable and can be estimated in advance, and where the firm has some degree of market control. It is less useful where demand is volatile and the firm is operating under highly competitive conditions. In these cases price is determined by market forces and the firm has to operate within this price constraint and may have to adapt production procedures to keep within allowable costs.

Question 29

Unit cost is simply the cost per unit, e.g. the average total cost, found by dividing total cost by the number of units produced.

Marginal cost is the cost incurred by producing one more unit, or the cost saved by producing one less unit. In most cases production levels move in steps greater than a single unit. Screws, for example, are not produced in ones but in thousands. In these cases marginal cost is found by dividing the change in total cost from one output step to the next by the size of the step, i.e. change in total cost divided by change in quantity.

If production is already taking place then fixed costs have been incurred. Machines have been acquired, premises obtained, workers and their managers hired and so on. To refuse an order because the revenue did not cover unit costs might be illogical because the revenue obtained might have contributed to the fixed costs which are not going to change whether the order is accepted or not. The important thing to decide is whether the additional revenue likely to be received will be more than the additional cost of meeting the order. If it is then the order should be accepted as long as this does not upset existing customers who may be paying a higher price for much the same product.

There are cases where marginal costs are very high. If, for example, increasing output from its existing level would involve purchasing an additional machine or taking on more labour, and if this additional capacity would not be fully employed by a possible order, then the firm would have to consider whether the high marginal cost would be justified. If there is little chance of the increased output being maintained or being pushed higher to make better use of the new production capacity then it may be wise to refuse an additional order.

In many cases, therefore, the output decision should be based on marginal cost in relation to marginal revenue. However, in the long run total revenues must be higher than total costs and this means that for production as a whole, in the long run, average revenues received must be higher than average costs incurred, otherwise the firm must eventually go out of business.

Question 30

Tax efficiency usually implies reducing a firm's liability to pay taxes, especially income or corporation tax. Business efficiency usually implies increasing the profitability of the business. The possibilities for conflict are thus immediate and clear. Reducing liability tax most often means incurring expenditure that does not necessarily contribute to profits but which does obtain exemptions from tax. The most common form of 'tax deductible' expenditure tends to be some form of investment in equipment, machinery etc. However, capital goods to aid production can also be goods that bolster the status of managers. Whereas a car may be an essential tool for a sales representative it is less essential for managers who spend 90 per cent of their time in the office. Company helicopters might, perhaps, be justified but it is difficult to see how helicopters taking senior managers to the Ryder Cup or the Glyndebourne Opera are really essential to the production activities of the enterprise.

Tax efficiency, therefore, tends to involve expenditure over and above what it strictly essential to the efficient production of profits. It can easily be in conflict with productive efficiency which puts strict limits on any spending not essential to profitable production.

Question 31

A sudden, severe fall in share prices has no immediate impact on companies because the capital they are already employing is not affected. However, it may have a number of dangerous consequences for business. Among these we may include:

- **A decline in public confidence in shares as an investment**
  This may make people less willing to entrust future savings in share purchase. Consequently business companies find it more difficult and expensive to raise finance in the future.

- **A fall in the market value of company capital**
  This makes it easier for companies to be taken over, usually by foreign firms not affected by the crash. This can divert managerial attention from their main function of producing goods or services for profit.

- **The value of people's savings falls**
  This applies even if they do not have many shares of their own, because all financial securities linked to stock exchange securities tend to suffer. People feel they are worse off and are less willing to spend. They are likely to try and restore the capital value of their savings by putting more of their income into less risky financial deposits such as building society accounts. If total personal consumption falls firms operate in a more difficult market and some may fail.

Question 32

Before deciding whether or not this rise is a matter of concern it would be necessary to examine other indicators of the company's trading record and efficiency. For example,

- Has sales turnover also risen? It could be that the new total is a smaller proportion of total sales than the old. This may be an indication of improved trading.
- Has there been any change in the direction of company trading? If there has been a move from home to export sales accounts can be expected to take longer to clear.
- Has the total of creditors' balances also risen? If there has been no increase in turnover but both debtor and creditor balances have risen this could be an indication of something wrong in the company's administration.
- Although not normally shown in the balance sheet the average length of time debts have been outstanding and the average size of debt, including whether there are one or two major items of debt would be instructive, and anyone with a legitimate interest in the financial health of the company would be entitled to ask for these facts. Unwillingness to disclose information would not be a good sign, suggesting that there was something to hide or that the administration was weak and itself lacked essential information.

Question 33

There is an understandable concern with the control of costs in public sector institutions. Where there is no profit objective there is a danger that managers establish their own objectives, most of which tend to escalate costs, and aim at organisational growth - which is the means of satisfying managerial, financial and status aspirations. Many of the control mechanisms imposed on public sector institutions tend to be distorted by managerial bureaucracy so that they become sources of extra cost instead of the reverse. The wasteful consequences of budgetary controls mentioned earlier are notorious.

It is not surprising, therefore, that a government which has an underlying political belief in the virtues of unregulated markets and of the profit motive, has sought to introduce the profit concept, if in modified form, to many public sector institutions, including schools, colleges and universities. The government can, after all, point to the success of the best independent schools which, if not actually profit seeking, are nevertheless obliged to achieve long-run, financial viability and, at the same time, offer education of a quality that can persuade parents to pay substantial fees for a service that could be obtained without charge in the State system.

However, the comparison is not altogether just. The main benefit that parents hope to buy through independent education is that of privilege both in access to higher education and in securing the more highly paid forms of employment. The style of education is geared to preparation for senior positions in business, the professions and the public service. This can be highly successful for a small proportion of the population, as long as it is a small proportion. An attempt to apply the same system to mass education is likely to founder precisely because the mass of the population cannot, by definition, be privileged. If an exclusive designer dress goes on general sale at British Home Stores it ceases to be an exclusive designer dress! Moreover most independent schools have long traditions of being semi-commercial institutions. Most have shareholders or others with a financial interest able to ensure that the schools have skilled financial advice, and operate on sound financial lines. This financial 'infrastructure' is mostly lacking throughout State education, except at higher education levels. To make it available for all schools assumes a supply of financial skill that is unlikely to be available at a price the institutions can afford to pay.

Any institution operating for profit to any degree must have control over revenues as well as costs. It must be able to make managerial choices between, say, offering a standard or sub-standard product at low price, and offering a high quality product at a high price. It must be able to make this kind of choice in accordance with the market and supply conditions it faces. Schools do not and are most unlikely to have the power to make such choices. They are charged with the responsibility of carrying out the educational wishes of Parliament and most crucial managerial choices are outside their statutory powers. A growing number of higher education institutions may be able to operate in a more profit-orientated climate but many may not and the excess and perversions of education seen in some American institutions, e.g. sports scholarships, offer a warning to those wishing to revolutionise the British educational system.

Another problem is the effect on courses offered. Many purely vocational courses could be highly profitable but what of pure science and arts studies. Institutions able to offer only vocational courses would be operating at a much lower educational level than, say, the ancient universities still able to offer a wide range of study. There would be a social and economic gulf between institutions offering education in its widest sense and preparing a chosen few for positions of wealth, power and privilege and those simply offering courses such as technical training for electronic technicians.

There are clearly considerable dangers in seeking to import the profit motive into education and indeed, into many other sectors of the public service. Yet the problems of ensuring adequate controls over costs and quality, and of establishing acceptable objectives, remain largely unsolved.

Question 34

The major problem of this concept is that of establishing precisely what constitutes 'value'. Should it be defined in terms of quantity or quality? How do you measure quality of services such as health, education, policing or social care? Is value for money achieved by ensuring that every person has the opportunity of a heart or liver transplant should this be needed or in ensuring that every old person has the chance to live his or her last few years in some dignity? We would probably wish to reply 'both', but does the community have sufficient resources to achieve every worthy objective? If these could be achieved in the health services what would be the implications of this for other public and private sector services? Economics teaches us that we cannot avoid having to make choices when we try to satisfy unlimited wants from scarce resources. Who makes the choice and on what basis? How do we decide between the claims of the young as against those of the old, of the mentally retarded as against those of the mentally gifted?

All communities, throughout history have had to make these choices. Often the choices made have looked strange, sometimes cruel and indefensible to later genera-tions. Are the choices we make likely to be judged any more kindly by future generations?

Close inspection of most public sector activities shows that even the most worthy are open to abuse. We value the ambulance service but know that, in some areas it has been treated as a taxi service, by people quite capable of making their own way to their local hospital. Hospital accident and emergency services have been abused by drunks and drug addicts. How do we distinguish between abuse and genuine need?

'Value for money' could simply be one of many slogans like 'to each according to need' which sound immensely attractive but which disintegrate as soon as we start to question what they actually mean and try to work out how they can be put to practical use.

5
Aspects of work and pay

The employer and the employee

This unit examines some of the economic issues related to people who are employed to work, i.e. people as factors of production, as resources needed by the economic organisation as a means of helping it achieve its objectives.

The employment contract

The employment contract is a legal agreement in which both sides accept certain conditions, some of which are specified and some of which are implied. In the UK since 1963 in Britain a written contract is legally necessary to which each worker must have access. Often employees are issued with a booklet setting out the main conditions of work as agreed with unions recognised by the employer. Most employees at managerial or professional level are likely to have individual contracts setting out the terms under they are employed. It is important to recognise this legal basis for employment because many actions on the part of both employer and employee can be judged to be breaking the contract and this can have important - and often financial - consequences for either party.

Under the employment contract the employer undertakes to provide work of the kind agreed, to provide suitable means for carrying out the work, to provide safe and healthy working conditions as required by law and to pay the worker according to the terms agreed between them.

For the employee's part there is an implied condition that he or she does possess the skills, training or abilities that were material to the agreement when it was made, e.g. someone recruited as an interpreter and who claimed to be able to speak fluent French would be breaking this condition if the employer later found that person incapable of conveying a simple message in French. The employee also undertakes to be present at the places and times agreed with the employer, to carry out agreed work tasks and to conform to the rules and management structure of the place of work.

In effect, therefore, the employer purchases the skills, knowledge, time and effort of the worker in return for financial payment and the opportunity to put those skills etc into practice. The worker obtains financial income and the chance to develop qualities that have a value in the labour market in return for sacrificing time and effort.

These are the general conditions underlying all employment contracts but in Britain at the present time they are likely to be modified by employment legislation, the volume of which has increased considerably since the early 1960s, and by agreements made between employers and trade unions or staff associations.

TEST YOUR UNDERSTANDING

1   The concept of **unfair dismissal** was introduced into British labour law in 1971. Explain in general terms what you think this means and what remedies you think a worker might have following unfair dismissal.

2   What matters do you think should be included in a formal contract of employment?

The labour market

The employment contract is not only a legal agreement, it is also a trading arrangement. The employer buys the work offered by the employee. Trading takes place in a market and markets are formed whenever there is an identifiable product, commodity or service which some people wish to sell and others desire to buy. In this case the service is labour, the readiness and ability to work. The sellers are the workers whose willingness to work in return for payment forms the supply force in the market. The buyers are the employers whose willingness to pay for work provides the demand force in the market. Within the market these forces of supply and demand are able to communicate with each other and interact so that the requirements of both sides can be met.

The employer's demand for labour

Employers want to employ workers as long as they believe that the cost of employment is less than the benefit gained from the work performed. The benefit is the contribution made towards achieving the employer's objectives and in the private sector of the economy the main objective is usually assumed to be profit. This provides the starting point for any kind of economic analysis of the demand for labour. Put in more formal economic terms this is the basis for what is commonly known as the **marginal productivity theory of the demand for labour**.

In economics **marginal** refers to a change at the edge. **Marginal product** is the change in total product resulting from a change in one of the factors contributing to production. Here we are considering labour so that the marginal product of labour is the change in total production brought about by a change in the number of workers employed. Mathematically a marginal value is always related to the smallest possible change, e.g. a one unit change in the influence (variable) producing the change in quantity of product. For simplicity we can regard a unit of labour as a single worker but this need not be the case. For example, employers may wish to examine the effect of increasing or decreasing work by a single hour; the hour then becomes the appropriate unit.

The marginal productivity theory simply states that employers will wish to continue to recruit labour up to the point where the addition of the last unit of labour increases the value of the total product achieved from employing labour by the amount that this last unit cost the employer. The value of the product is the revenue earned from its sale so the theory suggests that the employer will recruit workers as long as the cost of each additional worker does not exceed the increase in net revenue resulting from the addition to total production (often termed the marginal revenue product of labour) made possible by that worker's employment. You should remember that the cost of employing a worker is more than the wage that has to be paid to that worker. The employer also has to pay national insurance contributions and may have further expenses in providing various facilities or employees. If, to attract an additional worker, the employer has to offer a wage above the amount paid to existing workers it is likely that their wages will also have to be raised to avoid discontent and the threat of people leaving. Consequently the marginal cost of employing more workers tends to be higher than the wage actually paid to the worker.

The view that labour demand is derived from the relationship between the marginal revenue product and the marginal cost of labour rests on some important assumptions. These are that:

- The employer is pursuing an objective of profit maximisation so that labour is recruited only if it is expected to increase net profit.
- The employer is able to calculate marginal revenue products for individuals or for teams of workers.

If these are called into question then the whole basis for the marginal productivity theory collapses. If, for example, we believe that managers desire expansion and are able to pursue this at the expense of profit then employees may be recruited even though their marginal cost is higher than their marginal revenue product. It is not always easy to calculate the contribution made to revenue by any individual worker or group of workers. After all this depends to a great extent on the equipment provided by management and, indeed, on the quality of management. The problems are even greater when we consider the public sector, especially where public goods are provided and organisations do not make profits in the sense understood in the private sector. In the provision of public services such as health and education the number of workers employed often results from quite arbitrary decisions made by political institutions. For example, a decision to reduce average class sizes in schools would increase the demand for teachers. A decision to raise them will reduce demand.

The marginal productivity theory in its simple form appears to assume a very limited time scale in linking employer demand to the product of labour. Some workers are recruited for the contribution the employer hopes they will make in the future rather on their value to the firm in the week, month or year they are recruited. If this were not the case few non-technically qualified graduates would ever be employed! Because human feelings and relationships are involved in the employment contract some workers may also be employed because of their past contribution to the firm.

Although the marginal productivity theory may not always be applicable in its strictly literal sense it does serve to remind us that workers are employed ultimately for the contribution they make to their employer's objectives, whether these are financial or, in the public sector, established under the authority of Parliament.

The supply of labour

The supply of labour comes from individuals who choose to work. The total supply of labour in any one country depends on the size of the total population and the proportion of the working population 'working age', i.e. between the minimum school leaving age and the normal age of retirement. The proportion of those of working age who are actually employed in a 'gainful occupation', plus those registered as seeking work and claiming unemployment benefit, is termed the economic activity rate. This group is termed the workforce. The age structure of the resident population of the UK in 1977 and 1988 and the size and structure of the workforce in 1978 and 1988 are shown in Figures 5.1 and 5.2. Note particularly the numbers aged 0-14 and 65 and over, the numbers of females in employment and the numbers of self-employed.

The activity rate is affected by the numbers of those choosing to stay in full-time education, those choosing to retire from 'gainful' employment before the normal retirement ages, and those who decide not to seek gainful employment, are unable to find work and who do not register as unemployed or are not entitled to unemployment benefit. There is also a growing group of mainly young people engaged in work-related government training programmes. These are not really employed but neither are they unemployed.

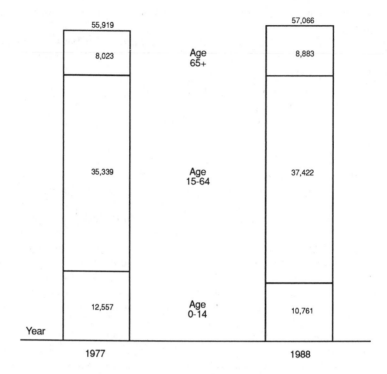

Figure 5.2   *The age distribution of the resident population
of the United Kingdom 1977 and 1988*

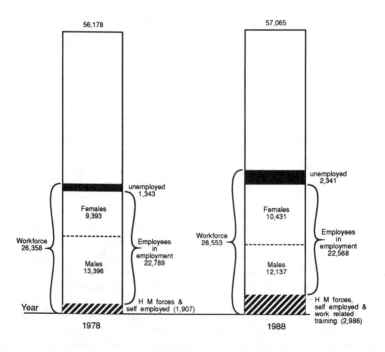

Figure 5.2   *The population and workforce of the United Kingdom*

Notice that there is a considerable element of 'choice' in the decision to work but, of course, individual choice is affected by a range of influences of which the most important is the need to earn an income in order to maintain whatever lifestyle is both desired and achievable. Another important influence is the prevailing social attitude to work. If the general pressure of opinion is in favour of having a job this may be very difficult to resist even if there is no real need to earn a financial income. Moreover, in most modern industrial societies, social status is linked to work and this adds further pressure to work. Changes in social attitudes can have a big impact on the size and structure of the workforce. The main trend between, say the 1950s and the 1980s has been the decision of a growing proportion of married women to pursue working careers. During the first half of the 1980s there emerged, in Britain, a trend towards earlier retirement, especially for men. However, a reduction in the number of young people entering the workforce at the end of the 1980s appears to be changing this trend and bringing back into employment a proportion of those who had previously chosen early retirement. However, many of these are re-entering the workforce as part-time workers in different employment sectors from those in which they spent their main working lives.

Economists frequently express this element of choice in terms of choosing between **income** (assumed to arise from work) and **leisure** (used in the sense of not engaged in gainful work and not necessarily implying idleness or even enjoyment). Most of us face the dilemma that in order to make use of leisure time we need income but in order to earn income we have to sacrifice leisure. Economists also tend to assume that, for most of us, the satisfaction gained from having an extra hour of leisure or an extra £10 of income depends on how much of these we already enjoy. Consequently if we have a relatively high income we will place high value on gaining some extra leisure but at a low income level we would be more ready to sacrifice leisure to gain additional income. Nevertheless this apparently reasonable assumption is complicated by the fact that many people appear to gain a number of important non-financial satisfactions from work, e.g. companionship, authority, status, and for some, the chance to engage in creative activity. A number of people, at all levels of employment, may even be so conditioned to work that they fear leisure.

The supply of labour to particular occupations, industries or sectors of employment is affected by pay levels, qualifications required, working conditions and any barriers imposed on entry to the work.

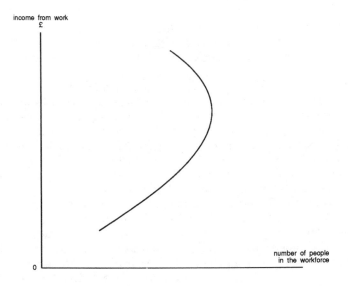

Figure 5.3 *A possible supply of labour curve*

TEST YOUR UNDERSTANDING

3 'Few people can work without equipment of some kind but to a large extent people and machines are in competition with each other for available work'. Explain and illustrate this statement with examples. What do you think are the main considerations taken into account by employers in their decision whether or not to replace workers with more advanced equipment?

4 How would you account for the change in the relative proportions of male and female workers indicated in Figure 5.2?

5 Look at Figure 5.3. This is the graph of a possible supply of labour curve. What does it indicate? To what extent do you think this graph reflects the desire to work of a large section of the workforce.

The financial rewards for work

In this section our main concern is with employees and their pay. Finance, of course, is a major motivation for the self-employed and the extent of their financial rewards must, of course, depend to a high degree on their skill and dedication. For employees, however, the decision what to pay and how to link the pay to the work contribution rests with the employer or the employer's managers. This raises some interesting issues, some of which are introduced here.

One of the major problems faced by the employer is how to relate the wage paid to the value of the work performed. There appears to be no ideal solution to this problem. Efforts have been made to devise payment systems that will encourage workers to increase their contribution to production but none is entirely successful. For simplicity we can distinguish two broad classes of payment system, those based on time and those based on the amount of production achieved.

Time rate systems

A time rate payment system rewards workers according to the time spent working and not directly according to the amount of production achieved. Payment may be per hour, day, week, month or year. You should distinguish between the basis and the frequency of payment. A person may be paid once a month but the amount of monthly payment may be calculated from the number of hours worked during the month - or on the number of hours contracted to be worked during the year, divided by twelve.

Once a time rate has been agreed there may be no apparent link between the pay and the quantity or quality of work performed. In fact, the link can never be completely broken. The value to the employer of the worker's performance is likely to be a major influence on the decision whether or not to employ that worker, the time rate to pay, the payment of future increased rates and, often, on opportunities for promotion to higher and better paid levels of employment and chances to enjoy any other available rewards (such as travel or use of company car) in addition to pay.

Superior status is still frequently attached to the term 'salary' as opposed to wage. In many firms in the UK, 'salaried staff' have privileges and even amenities denied to the rest of the workforce though the distinctions are now much eroded by legislation, by recognition of the importance of skilled manual workers, by new technology, and by social attitudes, reinforced by the examples of American and Japanese managements. Attitudes to salary differ between cultures. It is said that there is considerable competition in the USA. to feature in published lists of the top salary earners whereas in the UK many of the highest paid managers go to some trouble to avoid being identified.

Payment by results

To pay a person according to the amount of work performed would seem to be a fair method of payment. Closer examination, however, reveals some big problems. These include:

- Problems in calculating individual output.
- No two jobs are completely alike. Most workers are aware of cases where it is easier to achieve high output on one job than on another or with one machine rather than with another. Managers and supervisors can ensure that favoured workers get the jobs with the best chance of making high pay.
- Every time there is a change in production pattern rates have to be renegotiated - often a troublesome and costly process.
- Rates are supposed to be set objectively but some workers are better at manipulating work study procedures than others and it is not unknown for work study officers to be intimidated!
- When systems have been in force for some time anomalies arise and as these are corrected the systems become increasingly complex and difficult to understand. Mistakes are made in wages calculations and workers become cynical.
- Many workers have their own earnings targets. They work hard to 'make their pay' and then slacken off.
- Emphasis on quantity of work produced can have a bad effect on quality standards.
- Schemes intended to encourage production backfire when firms enter periods of difficult demand conditions.
- Workers generally prefer stable to fluctuating earnings even if the average of a fluctuating system is higher.
- High earnings become easier to achieve the longer a process is carried out. Consequently workers resist production changes that they suspect will tend to depress their earnings until new methods have been mastered.

Payment by results schemes tend to find favour in periods of high demand when technology is fairly stable. However, when markets are difficult and uncertain, when changes in production method are frequent and involve new technology they become increasingly troublesome and costly.

Among the more common schemes are those based on **piecework** (per item produced) and **time allowance** (tasks are given standard times and workers are paid extra for completing them in lower times).

Mixed time and results schemes

Measured day work is an attempt to get the best of time and results schemes. There are many different types of scheme but all offer additional payments for a work achievement above a target level within a given period of time. The worker gets reasonable stability of pay and there is less pressure to achieve high output. On the other hand the incentive element is reduced.

Profit related payments

The idea that workers, especially managers, should have an interest in the overall profitability of the firm, or of their part of the firm's activities, is an old one. Supporters of profit sharing suggest that it emphasises the interdependence between worker and management, and gives an incentive for all employees to reduce costs and promote profitability. On the other hand profit sharing can mean that workers' pay can vary for reasons quite outside their control. This is regarded as unfair and in difficult market conditions workers suspect that managers will underestimate profits to try and keep workers' pay low.

There are now considerable social pressures for workers to have regular, stable pay levels. Mortgage and other financial commitments depend on a stable level of pay. Consequently any profit related element can only form a small proportion of the total pay package for the vast majority of workers and in spite of some limited tax inducements, the main trends towards linking pay with profit have chiefly affected the top managers of large companies, whose basic salary is normally more than sufficient to guarantee freedom from most financial pressures. How far even these packages are genuine attempts to link pay with profit is doubtful. Earnings seem to rise readily when profits increase but fall little when they fall. Moreover a number of studies suggest that there is little close correlation between the pay levels of very senior managers of large companies and the profitability of these companies. For most employees the scope for extending profit related elements into pay seems to be very limited as a proportion large enough to have a significant effect on behaviour would make it very difficult for workers to assume the financial commitments now considered to be a normal part of ordinary life.

Payment in kind

This term is often used to refer to non-financial payments made to workers. They have a financial implication in that they save workers from incurring certain expenses. Such payments have a very long history. They formed an important part of the rewards to workers in pre-industrial society. Employers were often expected to feed, clothe and provide housing for their servants and for their families and, in most cases, to accept responsibility for looking after servants and their dependents. This kind of relationship was probably impossible to sustain when workforces grew in size as a result of industrialisation. It degenerated to a method of exploiting workers and defrauding them of their pay through corrupt 'tommy shops' where employees were forced to take overpriced goods instead of wages. Consequently, in the last century, Parliament introduced legislation forcing employers to pay wages in cash.

Changed social and economic conditions have brought a revival of payments in kind, though these are now heavily concentrated on the more highly paid employees. Among modern payments should be included the company car, more widespread in the UK than in any other industrial country, use of company credit cards for certain categories of spending, purchase of clothing for 'work', low cost home mortgages, assistance with travel costs, payment of telephone charges and 'scholarships' for employees' children in higher education.

There is no doubt that these payments have grown as a result of past periods of high income tax and of wage controls as means of rewarding more senior staff in ways that evaded wage controls and which were 'tax efficient' for both employer and employee. They have continued to survive because low rates of income tax are still a new experience in Britain and there are doubts about how long they will remain. Habit and the difficulty of changing established practices and the buying power of large employers enables certain benefits to be made available to employees, at a much lower cost to the employer e.g company cars are bought with substantial fleet discounts. Vehicle service agreements are negotiated at favourable rates and the additional tax paid by workers who receive company cars is still significantly lower than the costs faced by private car owners.

TEST YOUR UNDERSTANDING

6   Employers hire workers for their contribution to production. It seems reasonable, therefore, to base pay on the amount of this contribution. Why then are many

employers and employees opposed to payments by results schemes?

7 Suggest reasons why it is often difficult to compare the pay of workers employed on similar work in different firms.

Attitudes to work

Why work?

At first sight the answer to this question may seem a little obvious. Of course we work to earn money for without an income we have a rather precarious existence. However, is this the only or, indeed, the main reason why everyone works? Most of you can probably think of people who work but who have no very great need of the money they earn. You can probably think of others who have an income sufficient to satisfy their requirements but who are miserable because they are not working. Employers who have advertised jobs for older, retired workers report that they received large numbers of applicants, few of whom appeared to have any great financial need to work.

There is evidence, therefore, that money is not the only motive for working. Of course it could be argued that the desire to work is largely a matter of social conditioning. The person who has spent 30 to 40 years working regular hours in a regular place of work, and who has been subject to the discipline and structured nature of the working day, is clearly going to have as much difficulty adjusting to life outside work as the released, long-term prisoner or mental care patient. Is work then no more than a drug, necessary to sustain life in the addict?

Social attitude is certainly a very powerful force driving us to work. With the exception of the 'housewife' who has a well-established social position, unless we have worked or are working we tend not to have any recognised position in society. When two strangers meet for the first time it is almost standard 'ice breaking' procedure to find out the other's occupation or past occupation. This gives each a point of reference and a clear position in an ordered community. The idea that working involves 'going to work', to a set place of work for set hours each day, is very much a product of the first industrial revolution when the need to bring large numbers of previously undisciplined workers under a system of supervised control and to bring them to work on machines driven by a water or steam, brought about the factory system. This system is not an essential ingredient of work and is already changing, with growing numbers of people working at or from their homes, many 'telecommuting' with their employers under a modern outwork pattern of employment. This development is bringing back to the workforce many people with home commitments that would otherwise find it impossible to undertake regular employment. Not all of these are working for the sake of the money they earn. Clearly there are other forces involved and the fact that so many English family names have their origins in trades and occupations indicates how important a person's occupation has been in establishing people's identities in the community.

People have also been adept at developing ways to work even when they have belonged to groups for whom paid employment has been regarded as a mark of social inferiority. In Britain, many charitable and voluntary organisations have been developed and maintained through the efforts of married women from the middle classes for whom paid employment was socially unacceptable until around the 1960s. With the decline in numbers of this group the organisations have had to turn increasingly to paid workers and retired people. In earlier periods men in the higher social groups who had no inherited land to manage, bought commissions in the armed forces, or entered the Church or university teaching to provide themselves with occupations, although the financial rewards from these were usually small.

The fact that numbers of those with an evident desire but no pressing financial need to work undertook some kind of public service provides a possible clue to part of the reason why the need to work is so strong. No doubt there were those in the past who entered public service because this offered opportunities for corruptly acquiring large sums of money. Officers of the armed forces could become rich if they rose to high rank and were fortunate in battle but their chances of being killed or maimed were rather greater. There was clearly an attitude that associated work with service to the community when income was not of overriding importance. Today, when the public sector has become too large and important to depend on a small social class, those whose wish to serve or influence the community is more powerful than the need to earn an income tend to work for voluntary organisations of varying kinds.

Worker needs and satisfactions

Recognition that people seek satisfactions from work beyond income has led to a series of attempts to provide more 'scientific' psychological explanations. One of the best known of these has been Maslow's model of the hierarchy of needs. Maslow argued that human needs are on several levels. When the more basic levels are achieved with a reasonable degree of satisfaction, people move to higher levels. The bottom level, he believed, consists of the physiological needs such as food, drink, shelter and reproduction. The next level is the need for safety in the form of a secure, predictable environment. These two basic levels formed might broadly be termed the economic needs, which can be satisfied through income. At a slightly higher level comes love or social needs of friendship and social interaction, and at the next comes the desire for esteem, respect and responsibility - ego needs. Income is still relevant to these but only in its relationship with social status and the ability to have what might be termed 'a social life'. The social status attached to occupation and the standing of the employer could be just as important as income. At the top of the hierarchy is the desire for self-actualisation, the desire to satisfy more creative instincts and the development of individual potential.

The importance of this model, and its relevance to business organisations, lies in its suggestion that only when the primary levels are satisfied can the individual move up to the higher levels but when one level is achieved it ceases to be a motivating force, as the individual seeks satisfactions at the higher stage. If this model is thought to come close to reality then employers who offer high earnings but give little attention to the higher levels of need could have just as dissatisfied a labour force as those who provide what they feel is a creative and stimulating working environment - but with low pay.

Maslow's general beliefs have had a major influence on the thinking of those concerned with attitudes to work. D. McGregor, for example, in his book *The Human Side of Enterprise* (McGraw Hill, 1960) put forward an argument based on the two contrasting beliefs of management, Theory X (people have to be forced to work) and Theory Y (people want to work to achieve a range of objectives and these can be encouraged by progressive management). Not everyone has followed the Maslow path although nearly all subsequent writers and teachers have been influenced by his thinking. Some have developed rather different models. Among these is the duality theory of Herzberg who argued that **job satisfaction** and **job dissatisfaction** were two different concepts and that different features could promote job satisfaction (or its absence) and job dissatisfaction (or its absence). Factors promoting satisfaction he termed 'motivators' and these included recognition, achievement, opportunities for growth and advancement, responsibility and work itself. Those preventing dissatisfaction he called 'hygiene factors' and they included status, interpersonal relations, supervision, company policy and administration, personal life, job security, working conditions and pay.

Instrumental attitudes to work

A completely different view of worker attitudes to work was put forward by Goldthorpe and his colleagues, in a study of car assembly line workers in the 1960s. These were recognised to be a special case although Goldthorpe suggested that they might be typical of changing attitudes to work. These workers were essentially doing work which required little or no skill and which everyone knew to be extremely monotonous. However, the work was well paid, the pay being far above the levels that unskilled workers could expect in other industries and occupations. A high proportion of the workers studied appeared to have married women of a higher social standing than themselves so there were family expectations of living standards above those normally attainable by unskilled workers. By submitting to the monotony of work on a pre-automated car assembly line these workers were able to satisfy their families' life style aspirations but in doing so they looked outside work for virtually all their non-financial personal satisfactions. Unlike, say, miners in a mining village, there was no sense of social community among workers and they rarely had any contact with each other outside work. They worked purely for the money and used that money to buy the satisfactions they failed to obtain at work. This attitude has been termed 'instrumental' - work being simply the instrument to obtain the income needed to secure a desired life style.

Few people would now agree that this is a likely pattern for future working attitudes. We now recognise that pre-automated assembly line work and management bred some of the worst, and most damaging to business profits, examples of industrial conflict of modern times and when work becomes as repetitive and mechanical as it did in those factories it is a sure candidate for replacement by capital, in this case by automation and robots. The proportion of purely unskilled work to total labour has fallen steadily since the 1960s and the increasingly complexity of many work tasks has increased the amount of team effort required with the consequent opportunities for social communication within the workplace. The need to understand the social and psychological elements of work seem greater now than at almost any time in the past.

The implications and lessons of these different approaches to understanding human attitudes to work are a recognition that workers could achieve considerable satisfaction from their work, or they could become seriously dissatisfied and frustrated and that many of the features that lead either to satisfaction or dissatisfaction lie within the control of the employers.

TEST YOUR UNDERSTANDING

8   Suggest reasons for differences in the economic activity rates of females in different regions of the United Kingdom.
9   In the light of the theories introduced in this Unit discuss the view that 'teachers and lecturers cannot expect to receive as much pay as people in industry because their work is more creative and offers many non-financial rewards'.
10 Discuss with your fellow students the reasons that led you to enrol on the course you are now studying. To what extent do your findings support the view that income is not the only motive for work?

Conflict at work

Conflicts of interest

No matter what efforts an employer may make to enrich the work experience it is difficult to avoid the conclusion that there is a fundamental conflict of interest between the employer and the employed. In the last resort the employer is seeking to obtain the largest possible contribution to production at the lowest possible cost, while the workers wish to obtain the highest possible level of satisfaction from the financial and non-financial rewards of work for the lowest possible sacrifice in time, resources and effort. The employer will spend on improvements to working conditions as long as it seems probable that this spending is more than made good by the additional production achieved by workers. For this reason the so-called 'human relations' school of worker management based on the views of Maslow, McGregor and others in this general tradition, has been described as the 'contented cow' approach. Contented cows are believed to provide more milk than cows under stress. Workers who are largely satisfied with their work and its rewards are believed to be more productive than those who are dissatisfied. It is clearly in the employer's interest to reduce conflict at work as high levels of conflict can be very costly. Apart from the more obvious costs of industrial disruption in the form of strikes, go slows, working to rule and other forms of non-co-operation, there are heavy costs incurred from high rates of labour turnover and absenteeism, and disputes and arguments every time there is a change in production method. Disputes over the pay of individuals, poor quality of work and low levels of productivity generally associated with a workforce whose morale is low and whose attitudes are actively hostile to their managers are also costly.

Can conflict be constructive?

Some observers have argued that conflict can be constructive in that the effort to reconcile conflicting interests can lead to innovation, enterprise and the search for solutions which offer some rewards to all the parties involved. A similar idea emerges from the mathematical and statistical theory of games which shows that by no means all forms of competition or conflict involve 'zero sum' relationships. In a zero sum game one player's gain must be another's loss because the sum total of all gains must be equal to the total of all losses. Owner managers of small firms often tend to see worker pay in the context of a zero sum game with a pay rise won by a worker reducing the profit going to the employer's pocket. However, if the worker is helped to develop a more efficient method of working so that more production is achieved and the firm's revenue increased, this increase in revenue may be sufficient to provide a higher wage for the worker and more profit for the employer. Both gain as a result of the effort to satisfy their competing interests. In this light, therefore, wage bargaining can be a non zero sum game.

However, for conflict to be constructive in this sense there has to be agreement over the fundamental relationships of the parties involved. An argument between man and wife over arranging the family holiday can lead to a better thought out and more enjoyable holiday for the family provided the marriage is stable and not subject to any threat. If this is not the case a similar argument can lead to the breakdown of the marriage. Similarly, conflict between workers and employers can be constructive provided both sides desire the firm to remain in being and to be prosperous and provided they are in fundamental agreement about the role and functions of employers, managers and workers. If workers challenge the role of senior management, as agent of the share-holders to make the basic decisions concerning what is to be produced or challenge the right of shareholders to receive profit, then conflict is likely to be destructive and threaten the continued existence of the organisation.

Trade unions

Any long continuing conflict tends to become formalised, often ritualised with clearly understood rules and established institutions. People tend to try and create some kind of order in even the most chaotic situation. In the worker-employer conflict the individual worker is generally in the weaker position. The worker's basic economic need for income is greater than the employer's need for any one particular worker, except in cases where the worker has scarce skills which cannot easily be replaced. Since the early days of the first industrial revolution workers have sought to compensate for their weakness as individuals by combining together in trade unions. Because employers defeated early actions by unions by bringing in workers from outside the firm, often from outside the area, it has been important for unions to be organised both inside and outside the firm.

Union objectives and organisation

Unions are organisations of workers who have combined to pursue their common interests. Many unions are now so large and diversified that they include workers in a wide range of industries and occupations. Others are more specialised and contain workers in one occupation only. Some compete for members in the same occupation or firm. Modern unions owe their origins to the local societies of skilled craftsmen in the late eighteenth and early nineteenth centuries. Numbers of these merged and became national organisations with central headquarters in London from around the middle of the last century. Unionism spread to unskilled manual workers from around the 1880s and became a powerful force among the lower paid, clerical 'white collar' workers and the semi-professional and administrative workers employed in the public sector and some sectors, such as banking and insurance, dominated by large companies.

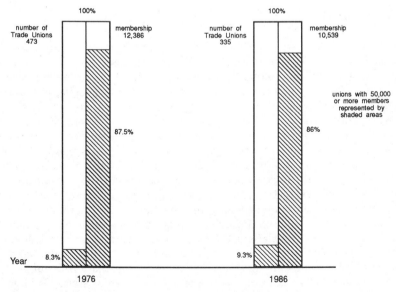

Notes: 1 The decline in numbers of unions and membership.
        2 The concentration of membership in a small proportion of large unions.
        3 In 1976 nearly 63% of members belonged to the 11 largest unions with 250 000 or more members. In 1986 this had fallen to around 55.5% of members in the 9 largest unions with 250 000 or more members.

Figure 5.4 *Trade Unions and membership 1976 and 1986*

Unions have always pursued a mixture of specific local objectives, such as pay and conditions in particular firms and broader, national objectives e.g. improving the position of working people in society as a whole. These wider objectives ensure that they are essentially political institutions and to further their political aims more effectively they played a dominant part in forming and financing the Labour Party at the beginning of this century.

Nevertheless they have always maintained a large degree of independence in order to concentrate on the interests of their own members and to resist subordinating their individuality to any form of strong centralised body. Their main central institution, the Trades Union Congress (TUC) does have a small full-time staff but it is little more than a very loose federation of those unions which choose to affiliate with it. Most of the manual and some of the 'professional' unions are affiliated but the TUC has very little power or influence as an organisation.

As shown in Figure 5.4 the larger unions contain the vast majority of members. These unions have a clear organisational structure with headquarters usually in London, and regional, district and local branch offices. Regional or district offices are normally staffed by full-time officials with normal administrative and clerical support. In some unions the full-time officials are elected and subject to regular re-election. In others they are recruited and appointed as in any other business activity. The senior, national officials with executive authority must now submit to regular elections.

Some of the largest unions have full-time or paid part-time officials at branch level but, in most, the branch is the link between the full-time structure and the local, voluntary structure which extends into the workplace. Most branches are based on local areas rather than on firms but many large firms now have their own branches. Where one large firm dominates an area the two are much the same. White collar and semi-professional unions are more likely to have workplace branches, probably because they have less difficulty than the manual unions in organising suitable meeting places within the workplace.

Workplace unions

All unions depend to a large extent on the voluntary work of employees within the workplace. In a large manufacturing establishment there are likely to be several recognised manual and non-manual unions and there has to be some kind of structured organisation of the representatives of each of these. The form this takes depends, of course, on the size of the establishment, the nature of the work carried out, the number of unions recognised and the relationships between unions and management. Manual worker union representatives are usually known as shop stewards and these often have formal, written recognition from management. In large factories there is likely to be a committee of the senior stewards of all the manual worker unions and a separate committee of non-manual worker senior representatives. The shop stewards committee would normally have a secretary and a chairman, frequently known as the convenor. Formal negotiations with management representatives would normally be conducted through these committees, often through a regular joint management-worker committee. Regular day-to-day negotiations relating to individual issues or problems arising from the normal daily friction of life in a working establishment are handled by shop stewards and departmental managers, often through the mediation of company personnel officers. In some companies one or two of the most senior stewards have become virtually full-time labour relations officers though trends in that direction have tended to be halted or reversed during the 1980s.

Because of the cumbersome nature of internal trade union structures and the element of competition between the larger manual worker general unions some employers have sought to make deals with just one union to have a one union firm or factory. The electricians' union gained a reputation of being the one most ready to make deals on this basis, leading to much publicised friction within the union movement and the expulsion of the electricians from the TUC. In fact attitudes of most of the union leaders have been modified by the economic, social and political developments of the 1980s and unions have started to look increasingly like other service organisations in the private sector of the economy. Most now recognise that they have to compete for members among workers, fewer of whom consider it essential to their interests to be in a union at all.

The future of unions

Most established organisations have a strong instinct for survival so that we would expect unions to adapt to changing conditions rather than disappear or remain as last defenders of a shrinking force of unskilled manual workers. The traditional role of the union in providing collective strength to the individually weak worker has been threatened by several developments over recent years. These include:

- **The extension of legal rights for workers**
  Workers had very few legal rights before 1963 when the Contracts of Employment Act was introduced. Since then they have gained legal rights relating to redundancy payments, unfair dismissal, sickness benefit, pensions, protection against race and sex discrimination, representation in relation to health and safety and, for women, job protection following pregnancy. From the Labour legislation of the 1980s they have gained some legal rights and protection against the power of trade unions themselves. It could be argued that the modern worker now has more need of legal services than of trade union solidarity. Indeed one of the main services now offered by unions is the provision of legal support in cases of dispute with employers.

- **Increasing proportion of skilled workers**
  Unions gain in support when the individual worker feels that there is no other effective defence against exploitation by employers. The modern worker is increasingly likely to have a skill that the employer does not wish to lose. This brings a greater degree of equality between worker and employer. The worker may feel greater protection in preserving and increasing personal skill capital and the transfer value it brings in the labour market than in preserving membership of a trade union especially if this is perceived as resisting the technical progress on which the worker's own future depends.

- **Changed attitudes of managers**
  The majority of workers in the private sector are now employed by one of the very large companies which tend to dominate some of the most important sectors of production. The managers, even senior managers of these companies, are employees the same as the rank and file workers and, in the current period of massive take overs through the capital market, they too share similar feelings of insecurity. They tend now to have a better understanding of the worker's need for legal rights and protection against arbitrary actions of superiors. These managers are also the products of political and social systems which are generally sympathetic to the concept of worker rights and less inclined to believe that owners of property can dispose of labour as they please. Managers are in closer contact with other workers than with anonymous shareholders. Few managers of modern large companies would tolerate the kind of autocratic actions considered acceptable among the industrial and commercial entrepreneurs of the first half of this century.

- **Labour laws of the 1980s**
  The broad movements of social, economic and legal trends outlined above are probably more significant than the detailed provisions of legislation deliberately designed to

weaken the powers and legal immunities of trade unions in their conflict with business management. Restrictive laws on strikes, pickets and even ballots have little effect if large numbers of people decide to ignore them. It is more significant that workers in general decided not to oppose the restrictions than that Parliament passed laws to introduce them. Parliament has passed ineffective legislation in the past. If a company's entire workforce decides to break the law it does not help the company to put the workforce into gaol, even supposing that the gaols were large enough and the police able and willing to arrest large numbers of workers. Some people might argue that failure to resist anti-union legislation was largely due to high unemployment in most of the 1980s. If this is correct then historical precedent would suggest that the laws are likely to be abandoned when unemployment falls and the political climate changes. However, it is by no means certain that trade unions will regain their old powers and immunities even under a government generally sympathetic to unions. Most union leaders appear to accept that public attitudes have changed and that unions must develop new roles for a changed economy.

- **Foreign-owned firms in the United Kingdom**
  Foreign-owned firms have gained a significant foothold in British industry and commerce. Some, mostly from the USA and Japan, have settled in Britain to secure an entry point to the European Community. Many of these firms have achieved success in very competitive markets and they are hostile to what they see as restrictive practices of organised labour, especially British labour organised in trade unions. In the difficult economic environment of the 1980s some of these firms were able to insist on the abandonment of much traditional British industrial relations practice, including the place given to unions as part of the price that has had to be paid for their entry to Britain instead of another part of the European Community. At the same time such firms usually have to ensure that their levels of pay and working conditions are superior to those found in comparable, unionised firms, to avoid antagonising workers. There is little incentive to introduce a trade union to a company whose workers enjoy benefits superior to those found elsewhere in the industry and locality.

Events in the 1980s, however, have shown that some of the most dissatisfied workers are those in the public sector and trade unions are still very powerful in this sector. This is an indication and a symptom of a much deeper problem of employment and pay in the public sector. The issue of public sector employment is a very wide and important one but it raises questions that are beyond the scope of this stage of study.

TEST YOUR UNDERSTANDING

11 Discuss the view that employers and workers must inevitably be in conflict. Do they share any common interests?

12 What role do you foresee for the trade unions in the industrial economy of the twenty-first century?

13 Some firms appear to welcome and support trade unions. Others appear to be hostile and, when possible, refuse to recognise them in the workplace. How do you account for these contrasting attitudes?

The management of labour

What is involved in labour management?

Although any firm which employs people is involved in labour management the larger the company the more extensive will be the range of activities which can be included within this general term. As a general outline we can say that an organisation with a large workforce is likely to have a specialised personnel department concerned with all or some of the following activities.

- Planning the structure of the workforce for the organisation's present and current needs in the light of its objectives.
- Recruiting workers likely to be needed from outside the organisation in the light of future plans.
- Arranging for training to fulfil the organisation's needs and policies
- Administering redundancy and dismissals made necessary as a result of the organisation's policies and occurring during the course of its activities.
- Administering any worker care and welfare policies pursued by the organisation.
- Managing the routine administration of employee records.
- Ensuring that managers and supervisors are aware of their powers and responsibilities to workers resulting from labour laws and the organisation's own labour policies.
- Handling labour disputes, including day-to-day communications with trade unions within the framework of the organisation's disputes procedures and agreements with trade unions.
- Ensuring that the wages and employee development policies of the organisation are adhered to throughout the organisation.
- Observing the development of labour management policies outside the organisation, advising senior management on labour management matters and sharing in the development and implementation of labour management policies within the organisation.

Planning for change

Management has already been defined in terms of taking decisions under conditions of uncertainty. This also applies to the management of labour. The senior management of the firm knows, or should know, what types and number of workers it needs to carry on its activities today. It also needs to estimate and plan for the workers it is likely to need tomorrow. This aspect of labour management is often known as **manpower planning**. 'Man', of course, is used here to refer to male and female workers. As market demand and production technology are constantly changing it is unlikely that today's workforce structure is going to match the organisation's requirements for tomorrow. The more accurate the predictions of future changes and the more ready the senior management to plan for changing needs the better the chance of being able to re-structure the workforce in a way acceptable to modern society.

It is not always desirable to wait until skilled people are urgently needed before seeking to recruit them. Skilled recruits may only be available by poaching from competitors. They will be expensive to hire and their former employers are unlikely to accept their loss without retaliation. If there are insufficient trained people available to fill all the vacancies some firms will have to go short and poaching recruits will simply mean that wages will rise with no guarantee that the poaching firm will be able to retain all its own employees.

Other options include re-training current employees, especially those likely to lose their jobs in the future, recruiting and training recruits from outside the organisation, including people working for other firms and, in some cases, the unemployed.

Recruitment

The personnel department will normally administer recruitment in consultation with and with the assistance of the departments actually requiring the new employees. It will also advise senior management on recruitment policies and methods and likely future needs as outlined above.

Training

This will also be administered by the personnel department and in many larger companies there is a separate department to handle training. The main areas for training include:

- Recruits who need some kind of induction training to familiarise them with the structure and ways of the organisation. If extended skill or other training is to be given this is arranged, often in conjunction with local educational institutions.
- Special training to meet changing organisational needs, often to ensure that workers can use new equipment or to acquire new skills required as the organisation adapts to changing markets or functions
- Management training which is now being given increased emphasis in many organisations. The main areas where management training is developing are: new recruits, many of whom need to have experience in as many departments as possible entering a specialised field; managers with, say, five or more years of experience who are to be prepared for more senior roles. This may involve arranging part-time courses for approved MBA or MSc qualifications or release for periods of full-time study at an approved business school.
- Courses for broadening the experience and knowledge of specialists, often as preparation for promotion or simply to try and break down the barriers that arise between specialists within the organisation. For example, engineers may be required to have training in marketing and finance in order to strengthen their understanding of the constraints under which production has to take place.

Redundancies and dismissals

One of the main responsibilities of the personnel department is to ensure that the organisation observes the legal requirements relating to this area. If there is any dispute, especially if a dispute is taken to an industrial tribunal, the department will be responsible for preparing the organisation's case and making sure that it is presented efficiently. Largely because of this many companies ensure that all redundancies and dismissals are handled through the personnel department. Before any form of 'severance' is confirmed it is necessary to check that the organisation's agreed procedures have been adhered to. The department will also be responsible for calculating the payment to be made to the redundant or dismissed workers.

In cases of large scale redundancy the department, out of humanity to long-serving employees and out of a desire for good public relations, may seek to obtain other work for the redundant workers. Sometimes quite elaborate arrangements have been made in collaboration with the Department of Employment.

Care and welfare

The extent of this work depends on company policies and, to some extent, on the scale of unemployment or labour shortages as these relate to the organisation. If workers are difficult to obtain the organisation may try to put present employees under an obligation to remain by benefits such as subsidised housing, assistance with holidays, private health care insurance or provision, etc. It will also seek to encourage recruits by assistance in finding houses, financial help with removal costs for a period afterwards. Some organisations have also tried to help workers prepare for retirement by organising courses, offering facilities in the development of new interests and providing financial advice.

Employee records

Given the fairly detailed legal framework within which recruitment and dismissals now have to be conducted it is essential to have accurate records of workers and of significant features of their conduct. Records are also desirable when considering employees for promotion or for re-training. The inclusion in the records of details of personal skills and interests can also be very useful as these may indicate suitability for re-training or for career development as the employment needs of the organisation change. Sometimes organisations go to some trouble and expense to recruit a new worker with specialised skills when they already employ a person with these skills. Fuller records would have saved expense and provided a development opportunity for the employee. Records are also necessary to enable forecasts to be made of future retirements and labour needs and to provide references after workers have left the organisation.

Management education

Every manager is a manager of labour. Every manager, therefore, needs to have some awareness of the law and the organisation's policies as they relate to employment. It is also desirable for managers to have some training in what the armed forces used to call 'man management', i.e. methods and techniques of leadership and of getting the best out of people. It is all too common for excellent workers to be promoted to managerial positions and to fail hopelessly as managers, often because they have not been aware of the skills involved when they become responsible for the work and conduct of other people. It is not the responsibility of the personnel department to overcome personality defects or to transform personalities. It can, however, help to ensure that managers are made aware of the personal skills involved in all forms of supervision and management. In order to do this it must have the support of senior management and the actual training should be carried out by non-employees of the organisation.

Labour disputes and trade union negotiations

In cases of major labour disputes or wage negotiations the personnel department is responsible for administration and ensuring that agreed procedures are followed. Agreements must, of course, be matters for senior management and unions though the personnel department can advise. However, a great deal of the time of many personnel departments is taken up with day-to-day communications with union representatives over a wide range of labour issues. Care is necessary to avoid becoming too close to the unions and appearing to take sides against departmental managers - even when the attitudes and behaviour of individual managers is known to cause problems. Personnel officers cannot afford to forget that labour is hired for its contribution to production or to achieving the objectives of the organisation. No organisation exists simply to provide employment or to fulfil the personal needs of individuals, and 'good labour relations' does not mean that the firm should lose sight of its economic functions. On the other hand employment does not mean dehumanisation and the personnel department does represent the interests of labour in the organisation.

Wages and employee development

All organisations should have a wages policy and a structure. Personnel departments are likely to be involved in establishing and modifying these. They will certainly be involved in administering them. They are also likely to be responsible for organising and implementing job evaluation exercises on which many wage structures are based.

Job evaluation is an attempt to classify systematically, without regard to the abilities of the people actually doing the jobs, a major part of the work performed in the organisation according to the aptitudes, skills, education, experience and responsibilities which each job requires. Jobs are graded according to the requirements of each and pay scales are formed to fit the grading system. The pay for each job depends on the grade awarded under the job evaluation exercise. Pay is thus intended to relate to the job rather than to the person doing the job. The person who considers that he or she is worth more pay than the amount related to the job may seek to gain employment at a higher grade. In practice, anomalies are almost bound to arise in any payment system and these increase as time passes. In most firms job evaluation is likely to have to be repeated at fairly frequent intervals and between reviews there are usually requests for re-grading, and disputes over grades, etc, requiring advice from the personnel department.

Providing employees with opportunities for development is another important aspect of the specialist's work. It is reasonable to ask how far a company should be responsible for developing the skills and abilities of its workforce when these almost always increase the marketability of the worker. If the worker leaves to go to another firm the organisation which has borne the cost of his or her training loses its benefits. Consequently employers tend to favour training that is job specific and which is likely to improve the quality and quantity of work produced by the worker, or which prepares the worker to take on more responsible work within the organisation. They are less eager to support the acquisition of qualifications that makes it easier for workers to move to other firms or industries. On the other hand, when firms are competing for the best workers, further training and education may be part of the reward package that such workers are seeking and employers not prepared to include this opportunity may not be able to recruit the best.

Policy making

The personnel department functions identified so far have been more administrative than managerial in the sense that they have been concerned more with implementing decisions made by others than with actually making the strategic decisions that affect the policy and behaviour of the organisation. This relatively subordinate role of personnel management has its origins in the history of business organisations and is also a reflection of the basic subordination of labour to capital in a capitalist economic system. The ultimate ownership and control of the business organisation rests with the owners of capital who hire labour and decide what share of the organisation's revenues are to be paid to labour. Even in the British public sector the ultimate power of decision making lies with the Treasury, the Prime Minister being the First Lord of the Treasury. If the Government is dismissed in an election or defeated by Parliament the British constitution simply replaces one First Lord of the Treasury with another. The dominance of capital remains. Consequently it is the accountant and the financial director who normally hold most organisational power in organisations in both the private and public sectors. In an interview with the author the a Deputy Treasurer of a major city made it clear that councillors discussed their plans with the Treasury officials before putting forward proposals in council. There appeared to be no central labour management department with anything like the power and status as that enjoyed by the City Treasurer's department.

The dominance of the financial function in the organisation has also been consolidated by the fact that finance and taxation became sufficiently complex and important to business survival to require specialists at a high level at an earlier stage of business development than personnel management. When financial specialists were required at senior managerial level they had to be recruited from qualified professional accountants so their status was assured. In contrast personnel management has had to struggle to gain semi-professional standing. The comedy personnel manager of the post-war Peter Sellers film *I'm all right Jack* was not so far removed from the truth in a good many industrial companies of the period.

It was the entry of statute law into modern labour relations that made it essential for all but small firms to employ trained personnel specialists. This started with the Contracts of Employment Act in 1963 and continued with legislation on redundancy payments, wage controls, productivity bargaining, equal pay and race discrimination. The highly controversial and largely unsuccessful attempt to introduce American-style legally enforceable contracts with the Industrial Relations Act of 1971 left a more long lasting legacy in the concept of unfair dismissal and the right of a worker to challenge dismissal on grounds other than breach of contract. Something of a legislative climax was reached with the Employment Protection Act of 1975. The Conservative Government of the 1980s modified employment protection laws mainly for the smallest firms but the developments of the 1960s and 1970s, as they affect individual worker rights, have remained intact. They have been strengthened by a series of laws designed to give individuals rights to challenge union power and to bring the conduct of industrial disputes within fairly strict legal constraints, the breach of which can be extremely expensive.

It is only a short step from monitoring actions to ensure that they conform to legal requirements to influencing decisions and policies to modify behaviour so that breaking the law becomes much less likely. Moreover, the claim by governments that much legislation was merely codifying and extending existing 'good employment practices' meant these became more influential, as an increasing number of companies wished to be seen to conform to these practices. Personnel management gained in status and managerial influence. This process was further assisted by the mergers that have become constant throughout the past thirty or more years. Groups found themselves with a maze of different personnel and wages structures and wished to bring greater uniformity and consistency, partly for administrative tidiness and partly to stop trade unions from playing one company's structure against another's to try and secure wider acceptance of the best elements of each.

In many organisations personnel directors have gained status and influence but rarely, if ever, are they able to challenge the established dominance of the financial director. I cannot think of one major public company whose managing director has risen to the top through the personnel department. Most have risen through production, finance or marketing.

TEST YOUR UNDERSTANDING

14 Identify the main personnel areas (e.g. recruitment, redundancy) in which managerial decisions are constrained by legal requirements.

15 The personnel manager of a private sector, industrial company notices that over half

of its most highly skilled workers are due to reach retirement age within the next five years. Discuss the policy options the manager can propose to senior management.

16 Identify the main forms of discrimination practised in modern commerce and industry in the United Kingdom. Is it possible to eliminate discrimination by Parliamentary statutes?

NOTES TO QUESTIONS

Question 1

Workers who are dismissed have two possible legal remedies. They may seek to show that the employer was in breach of their specific contract of employment (wrongful dismissal) in which case they can sue for financial damages and costs resulting from that breach. Alternatively they may seek to show that the employer 'unfairly' dismissed them for reasons that are in breach of general legal safeguards established by Parliament, or without a fair, and reasonable reason or in a manner that was unreasonable and in breach of those codes of practice which have become virtually a part of normal labour law. Thus, for example, an employer who dismissed a worker because of dislike of a particular hairstyle would probably be guilty of unfair dismissal, whereas dismissal because an employee refused a request to cover hair likely to be a danger when working close to moving machines or who refused to cover or modify a style likely to cause offence to customers, would usually be found to be fair.

The concept is an important one because it prevents an employer depriving a worker of the means of earning a living because of a personal whim, or prejudice or dislike of behaviour which has no relevance to work. It also prevents an employer from intimidating workers who wish to support a trade union.

The normal remedy for a worker would be to take the case to an industrial tribunal, a kind of semi-formal labour court where disputes are examined by members representing employers and workers under a legally qualified chairperson. If the worker is a member of a trade union the union would normally take up the case and advise and assist the worker during the hearing.

If the Tribunal finds in the worker's favour employers cannot be forced to reinstate a dismissed worker, but if they do not do so financial compensation will be awarded. There is an appeal procedure if employer or employee feels that the Tribunal's decision is unjust.

Question 2

The following are some of the issues which are commonly found in contracts of employment:

- An outline description of the job to which the worker is appointed.
- Pay, starting pay, frequency of payment.
- Hours of work, entitlement to holidays.
- Entitlement to sickness benefits.
- Entitlement to pension benefits and outline of any contributions required from the worker.
- Disciplinary procedures and rights of appeal against disciplinary measures.
- Rights to join a trade union and to engage in trade union activity.
- Procedure and rights of both parties to terminate the contract.
- Constraints relating to working against the employer's interest for a period after leaving the employer's service.
- Procedure for settling disputes arising from the contract or its interpretation.

Where numbers of workers are employed for similar work it is usual for a general contract to be written in the form of a booklet called 'Conditions of Employment' or something similar. If such a booklet is not issued to all workers they must have access to copies on request.

Question 3

Almost all kinds of work involve the use of equipment of some kind. The hairdresser needs at least a pair of scissors, the poet a pen and paper, the footballer a ball, field and goalposts. The amount of work a person can do is often increased if more equipment is used. The hairdresser can work more effectively with specialised seating, washing and drying equipment, even the poet might be helped by a word processor and the footballer can train more effectively with the help of additional equipment.

Employers can frequently choose between various possible combinations of labour and equipment to carry out certain work. An extreme example might be digging a ditch which could be done with say, twenty labourers using picks and shovels or by one worker with a mechanical digger. Because employers can make this kind of choice between different combinations of labour and capital equipment it is fair to see workers and machines as competing with each other to some extent.

Through much of the past century industrial development has followed the path of replacing labour with ever more complex equipment. Consequently there is a danger of assuming that machines are superior to people and that increasing efficiency must always mean introducing more advanced machinery.

This is not always the case. If we make the reasonable assumption that the employer wishes to minimise the total cost of any given work process then the chosen combination should be the one that performs the work at the least cost. In this case the important factors will be:

- The scale of operations. It is likely to be wasteful and costly to purchase a machine capable of making 1000 units of a product per day if the firm can only sell 100 units per day. A moving production line serviced by robots may be a suitable process for the family saloon in mass demand but is unlikely to be the least cost method of producing a luxury limousine.
- The unit cost of labour compared with the unit cost of equipment in relation to the marginal product of labour and the marginal product of the equipment. If it is cheaper to obtain an additional increment of product by employing extra equipment instead of extra labour the employer will purchase equipment in preference to hiring workers. Only when the cost is the same between additional workers and equipment will the employer be indifferent as to whether one or the other is acquired.
- The relative reliability of equipment and workers. Unscheduled stoppages are expensive in modern business. If the employer fears that equipment will break down then labour may be preferred; if there is a greater fear of workers striking then equipment is likely to be preferred.

In economic terms this is the rational approach and assumes that the basic objective of the employer is to maximise profits. In practice some employers may have a personal preference for machines, others for people, and where there is doubt about true costs or about future conditions these preferences can determine the actual choices made.

Question 4

Figure 5.2 shows that whereas the number of male workers in employment fell between 1978 and 1988, the number of female employees in employment rose by a little over 11 per cent in this period. During this time the total workforce rose by around 8 per cent.

Economists tend to look for explanations for this kind of trend by analysing the supply and demand factors. When we do this we find strong influences on both demand and supply. Clearly, once started these forces interact with each other but it seems likely that the demand pressures may have started the process.

The main demand influences favouring a growth in female employment include:

- Growth in those sectors of activity which have traditionally been sources of female employment. These include the various social services, such as health and education, the communications services, travel and hotels and general administration - office work of all kinds.

- Shortages of male workers with the required skills, especially skills in the services growth areas.
- In the early years female workers were encouraged because they were cheaper. To some extent they still are, because relatively fewer female workers are able to obtain early promotion or to afford the time and finance necessary to acquire special work skills commanding premium pay rates.
- Females tend to be more flexible in working hours, more willing to work part-time and to have a higher rate of turnover so that employers may feel that they are less at risk of taking on a heavy and expensive burden if they employ a woman in preference to a man.
- Changes in social attitudes have made it much more acceptable to employ women in responsible jobs and often they adapt more easily into new work situations.

The main supply factors would probably include:

- Those same changes in social attitudes have encouraged women to work and discouraged them from staying at home.
- Housework has been largely mechanised and no longer provides a full time occupation.
- Convenience foods have made it easier to cope with feeding a family.
- There has been a steady growth of women entering further and higher education to provide an expanding and increasingly highly skilled and qualified female workforce.
- Families are now planned to a much greater extent than in the past.
- It has become socially acceptable for men to play a part in housework, in looking after babies and very young children and generally assisting women who wish to work.
- Families have become smaller and there has been an expansion in pre-school facilities for children thus encouraging more women to enter or re-enter the labour market.

Question 5

The graph suggests that as income from work rises from very low levels more people are attracted to the workforce but as income rises further some workers prefer to spend their increased income by taking more leisure so that above a certain level rising incomes from work result in less work being offered to the labour market.

This view can be supported through the normal ideas of diminishing marginal utility. As people gain more income they value further income less, until the stage is reached when further leisure is valued more highly than increased income. At this stage people take advantage of rising earnings from existing work, choosing not to work or to work less. After all there is no point in earning a high income if there is no time to enjoy and spend it.

On the other hand there can be a preference for income for its own sake rather than just as a means of spending. High income from work brings status and a number of 'perks' at work so that people may work more if they think there is a chance to improve incomes to a significant degree.

For many people work itself has a utility. People work for more reasons than simply to earn a living. Increased income can become a justification or excuse for devotion to work, whereas in reality, it is work itself that is the main attraction. In these cases income could vary considerably without any significant change in the quantity of work offered.

There is still some controversy surrounding attitudes to work and leisure and about the correct shape of labour supply curves. Economic analysis on its own cannot settle this debate. There is still a need for more information.

Question 6

Employers hire workers for their contribution to production. It seems reasonable, therefore, to base pay on the amount of this contribution. Why then are many employers and employees opposed to payments by results schemes?

No doubt many workers object to payment by results schemes because they think that life is more comfortable under a payment system that is not linked with results. Few of us welcome the prospect of having to work harder for our money.

On the other hand many workers do have real fears that schemes can be unjust, hard to understand and liable to lead to a reduction in pay for causes outside the individual worker's control. There is often suspicion of employers and a belief that errors 'in the office' will be difficult to detect and more difficult to correct.

The most serious worry concerns dislike of fluctuating earnings. Most of us live in a society where we have to face regular financial obligations of mortgage payments, local taxes, fuel and insurance bills which we need to know can be paid from a regular salary. The chance that pay could fall below a necessary minimum is feared more than the chance to earn more is welcomed.

Many employers have also become disillusioned with payments by results systems. Setting up and maintaining a system can be expensive. It involves the employment of time study personnel and takes up significant time in entering the information on which pay is calculated. Mistakes occur and cause additional work and friction with workers. Disputes over payments become a source of ammunition for shop stewards keen to establish territory and a leadership role in the workshop. There is also evidence that they do not achieve their function of boosting production in that experienced workers know how to use the system for their own ends. They learn to build in spare capacity so that they can achieve their desired earnings levels without much difficulty and then pursue their own objectives. It is in this way that workers often achieve regular earnings and avoid unplanned fluctuations.

Employers also face problems when their main problem is not to maximise production but to increase flexibility to meet customer demands. They may then want shorter production runs with more changes in design and production method. These changes are resisted by workers who prefer to avoid changes that threaten their ability to earn their desired pay levels.When 'results' means quantity there is often a sacrifice of quality, so that more has to be spent on inspection and quality control. This can also generate friction between inspectors and workers who feel that over-fussy inspections and controls reduce their earnings.

Attempts to overcome these problems often lead to complex schemes that are not understood by workers and therefore provide little incentive for work improvement.

There is no perfect payment system nor any system that can act as a substitute for efficient management and control methods.

Question 7

Pay comparisons are often misleading even when the work appears to be similar. Conditions of work, including hours of work, fringe benefits and payments in kind are all likely to be different. No two jobs are ever completely the same. The skills required and the difficulties of work can be different in ways that may seem trivial to observers but very important to those involved. Payments in kind and fringe benefits have been spreading and are no longer confined to senior managers. Even the provision of a car park can have an effect on net pay. Car parking is often given high priority in the list of concerns faced by company personnel managers. Workers denied parking not only have to pay for space in public car parks but also run greater risks of having vehicles damaged and stolen. There is also a status element in having access to company parking space.

The important issue to the worker is the purchasing power of the actual take home pay and this varies in different areas of the country. Workers able to live in pleasant surroundings close to work do not face the travel costs of those who have to travel long distances and, of course, the hours they sacrifice to be able to work are fewer. Living costs vary from area to area and these differences are not always reflected in area allowances.

When all the factors are taken into account most people recognise that comparisons based simply on gross pay can give a completely false impression of relative real earnings for different groups of workers.

Question 8

With some local exceptions female activity rates are generally higher in the Southern regions of the UK than in the Northern, in Scotland, Northern Ireland and Wales. This means that the proportion of females of working age who are 'gainfully employed', as defined by economists, is higher in the Southern half of the country than elsewhere. Whenever economists seek to analyse possible reasons for a difference in market behaviour (here we are concerned with the labour market) of this nature they like to examine factors affecting demand and those influencing supply.

In the past two decades the level of economic activity in the South has been consistently higher than in the North so the total demand for labour is greater in the South. Since there are significant economic and social obstacles for the mass migration of male labour from North to South, the unsatisfied demand has been transferred to females. Once the pattern of female employment became established this changed attitudes of both employers and workers.

Moreover the structure of industry and commerce favours female employment in the Southern half of the country. There is a high proportion of employment in the service industries, especially financial, educational and administrative services. These have a long tradition of employing female labour and have been much quicker than the heavier manufacturing firms of the North in adapting their recruitment and labour management policies to the need to attract women workers.

Economists frequently assume that supply responds to shifts in demand in most markets and then, in turn gives a further impetus to any long run changes in the pattern of demand. Conditions in the South have tended to make it possible for more women to enter employment and look for long-term careers rather than just temporary pre-marriage jobs. Among the factors affecting the supply of female workers we can recognise:

- A higher proportion of women in the South stay longer in full-time education and so are able to pursue careers in such sectors as the civil service, teaching, the financial services and in the newer knowledge-based industries such as electronics and computer software development.
- Commuter transport services tend to be quite highly developed in the South so that men and women are willing and able to travel to work over distances that would be regarded as impossible in the Northern regions.
- Housing and other basic living costs tend to be higher in the South making it almost obligatory for families to have more than one income in order to achieve comfortable living standards. Although this pattern is spreading throughout the country it is not widely accepted in the Northern and Celtic regions of the country.
- There is more part-time work available in the South because a smaller proportion of the work is dependent on factory production schedules. This tends to suit women who wish to combine work with looking after young children.
- Social attitudes have responded to the changed conditions in the economic labour market and most social changes tend to start in and around a country's capital city, especially when this is the commercial and cultural centre of the country. Once attitudes have changed the pervading social pressures tend to impel women towards work, whereas in some other regions of the country there is still social hostility to the idea of women with young children seeking to continue a demanding career.
- The alternative to work is often not very attractive for women living in the commuter belt around London. Men who travel to work to central London from the outer suburbs can be away from home for eleven or more hours each working day. A wife staying at

home can lead a very lonely and empty life and it is not surprising that large numbers prefer to use their time more constructively and profitably. In many Northern and Celtic regions homes are often much nearer to the main centres of work and to schools. It is common for fathers and children to return home for a midday meal. The whole lifestyle is different and less dependent on two incomes.

Question 9

It is common for employers and other observers to take the view that high pay is needed to compensate for poor working conditions. In fact this view comes directly from Adam Smith's suggestion that additional pay was needed to induce workers to undertake the less attractive work. In contrast those whose work was judged by society to be attractive did not need to be attracted into it by high pay. They would be willing to work for lower financial rewards because of the non-financial rewards the work appeared to offer.

However, if we take as a starting point Maslow's concept of the hierarchy of needs then we have to recognise that people are only motivated by the desire to fill the higher levels of need such as esteem, respect, responsibility and self-actualisation once their more basic economic needs have been satisfied. If these basic needs remain unsatisfied then they become important in the eyes of the worker who cannot afford to be attracted by the non-economic aspects of work. Putting this in a more down to earth way it seems reasonable to think that even the most brilliant scientific researcher is going to have difficulty concentrating on research if distracted by worries over how to pay the month's mortgage or if filled with guilt because the family's living standards are below their reasonable expectations.

If there is any substance in the Maslow model and the views of his many followers industrial employers should pay more attention to the non-financial rewards of their better paid workers and be less willing to give yet higher incomes. The mainly public sector employers of teachers, lecturers and others, on the other hand, should ensure that the economic/financial aspirations of their workers are met because only then will the workers be motivated by the non-financial rewards.

Question 10

It is you who must write the notes to this question to which there are at least two aspects. First the underlying reasons for studying. In most cases there will be a vocational motive. You hope to gain a degree and anticipate that, as a graduate, more career doors will be unlocked for you than if you do not have a degree. You have chosen to study a business related degree, perhaps because you believe that a career in commerce or industry will satisfy your financial and non-financial needs more completely than a career in another field. If you examine your motives and those of your colleagues you should recognise some of the pressures and ambitions that lie behind your decision, unless, of course, you are simply meeting the expectations of parents or others who have influenced your educational development.

There is, however, another aspect to the question. What are your attitudes to study itself? Do you regard study as work? If so do you see it simply as a means to an end - the end being gaining a degree which will help you to obtain employment at the level you desire. Do you get any other form of satisfaction from study? Do you think it likely that you will pursue any aspect of your studies when these seek to be directly relevant to your employment?

There are not right or wrong answers to questions like these but the way you face them and the kind of answers you give and receive may help you to think a little more clearly about your expectations from your future career and life itself.

Question 11

There is a fundamental conflict between the interests of employer and employee. The employer seeks to obtain maximum return from the labour employed at the lowest practicable cost. The employer measures the product of labour and the contribution this makes to the objectives of the organisation and sets this against the total cost of employing the labour. The employee seeks to obtain the maximum reward from working at the lowest practicable sacrifice of time, resources and effort. The employee measures the extent of the sacrifice that is made in order to work and compares this with the net financial return plus any non-financial satisfactions from working.

The worker feels aggrieved if those making the most sacrifice do not appear to receive the greatest reward. The employer is suffering a potential loss if the rewards are not being made to those making the greatest contribution to the firm's objectives.

However, the conflict between employer and employee need not be seen as a zero sum game. The employee's gain is not necessarily the employer's loss. Both may gain if the employer can devise a reward structure that provides incentives for the worker to contribute as much as possible to the organisational objectives and, in doing so, add to the financial and non-financial satisfactions from work.

There are also some common interests between the employer and employee. Both desire the successful survival of the organisation. Satisfaction of individual need becomes more uncertain if the organisation ceases to exist. Both may be able to move to different organisations but this will almost always involve a cost and a risk that the move will be less than satisfactory. In many cases it will be in the employer's interest to encourage the individual worker to develop personal capital and skills. The more proficient the worker the greater the potential value to the employer. The worker will expect to receive greater rewards from the increased proficiency but the contribution this makes to the firm's finances may justify providing these increased rewards. Again this raises the possibility that both may gain. The employer can become dependent on the worker's skill but the worker may be equally dependent on the firm to provide the kind of working environment in which that skill can be exercised and attract a value in the labour market.

Question 12

Crystal ball gazing is often a rather unrewarding exercise but an attempt to predict future trends of any institution helps to clarify its current role and functions so that these can be related to possible future changes in the structure of the economy and community. Trade unions developed in the nineteenth century to

- counterbalance the weakness of the individual worker in conflict with a more powerful employer through the strength of group solidarity
- resist changes that threatened the livelihood of skilled workers and to ensure that these were able to defend their interests when changes became inevitable
- advance the interests of labour in its inevitable economic conflict with the owners of capital.

It can be argued that each of these functions has now been weakened. The case for this view rests on the following developments. Individual workers have gained greater legal safeguards and rights and an increasing number of highly skilled workers are essential to employers' activities. The average level of education has risen among workers in all sectors of employment. The more highly educated the worker the less likely is the worker to fear and resist change because this is seen to bring benefits as well as threats to security. Rising average incomes and the spread of pension arrangements in the community have started to bridge the gap between the owners of capital and labour. A growing proportion of the capital in the country originates in the savings accumulated from incomes from employment and from pension contributions out of employment income. This capital is administered by financial institutions but is owned by or held in trust for employees - the sellers of labour. The old division between capital and labour may now be replaced by that between young workers with mortgages who are net borrowers and the older and retired workers with few debts and significant savings (mostly from pension schemes) who are net savers or are living on incomes from accumulated savings.

However, these changes do not necessarily mean that trade unions no longer have functions to perform, rather that their traditional roles need to be modified. For example, to take advantage of legal rights workers need to know those rights and be able to afford legal representation. Workers can still suffer from change if they are not trained to adapt to it and are not helped to obtain compensation when necessary. Modern workers also need protection and representation to ensure that they receive the best possible pension provisions and to prevent employers from exploiting and weakening pension funds. All these needs can be supplied by trade unions if they themselves adapt and develop the skills necessary to provide the services now required.

Question 13

It is probably fair to say that most employers would much prefer to operate without the constraints imposed by trade unions. However, if they are in the workplace and have shown that they have some power then the employers or their senior management will seek to gain some influence and control over them and try to achieve attitudes where workers will not see management as being hostile to the functions and aspirations of unions in the workplace. Managers cannot manage any organisation if they are in open conflict with workers all the time. They have to achieve a method of living with them and of gaining their support and loyalty.

Some managers also believe that by involving worker representatives in some of the processes of management they educate them to the problems and complexities of management and thus gain greater understanding and sympathy. Moreover, when a shop steward has been part of a team involved in, say, restructuring job specifications and pay differentials, that steward has to accept a degree of personal responsibility for its decisions and will have to help to defend them in the face of inevitable protests from individual workers who feel that they have been unfairly treated. By extending the functions of worker representatives managers can weaken their power to oppose management decisions.

Many managers also recognise that using the structure of workplace unionism they gain a ready-made communications channel to pass information to and receive information from: the workforce. If the unions did not do it for them managers would have to set up and administer their communication and negotiation structures. There is no guarantee that the management organised structure would be more efficient than the one developed by the unions.

Nevertheless some firms are widely recognised to be anti-union and will try to avoid having to recognise any union in the workplace. Some are foreign-owned companies which have succeeded in avoiding unions in their own countries. Such companies may go to great lengths to avoid recognising unions. Often they have the ultimate sanction of being prepared to move to another country if their freedom from unionism is threatened. No union wants to gain a public image of driving companies and jobs out of the country so this possibility is likely to be a serious barrier to open conflict.

On the other hand, to avoid pressure to recognise unions the companies will generally have to provide pay and working conditions at least as good and often better than those prevailing in equivalent unionised firms. They will usually have to create and maintain an effective representational structure, probably more effective than one depending on unions whose administration within the workplace is often extremely amateur. Many do not appear to have even the most basic records such as an up-to-date list of members. They were released from this as a matter of day-to-day necessity when employers agreed to deduct union subscriptions from wages. You may see this as a further example where employer 'co-operation' has helped to weaken the structure and power of workplace unionism. Shop stewards who, in the past, had to collect weekly union dues from members at least knew the identity of every member and could not avoid two-way communication. Shop stewards today have to make a sustained effort to achieve the same degree of communication - and by no means all have the inclination and skill to make that effort.

Question 14

Legal constraints affect a very wide range of labour issues in contemporary Britain. Some of the main areas are:

- With very few exceptions, advertising, selection and initial wage must not be affected by discrimination on the grounds of race or sex. In most occupations the applicant has the legal right not to disclose criminal convictions suffered more than five years earlier.
- During employment the same legal bars apply against discrimination and pay must be on an equal basis between men and women for equal work - a phrase whose meaning has been extended as a result of decisions made by European Community courts.
- Conditions of work are influenced by health and safety legislation which is often very specific and detailed. This type of legislation has a very long history. In modern times it goes back to the Factory and Mines Acts of the last century. Certain potentially dangerous machines have to be regularly inspected and safety clothing must be worn for some types of work.
- Trade union activity is restricted in a few occupations, mainly the Armed Forces and some locations considered to be essential to national security. Pay bargaining procedures in some parts of public sector employment are subject to legal conditions and constraints.
- Workers have statutory rights to certain holidays (bank holidays) and, with some exceptions, mainly affecting part-time workers and those employed in very small firms, women have jobs protected during pregnancy.
- In some occupations, where there are public safety considerations, such as driving some kinds of transport, hours of work are restricted and there are minimum rest periods.
- Redundancy and dismissal are subject to clear laws and there are clearly defined rights of compensation.
- Pension arrangements are also subject to statutory regulations

Question 15

One option is to do nothing and wait until each retires and then seek to recruit a replacement. However, if this is the position in one firm it is likely to apply to others. These workers already in short supply may than be almost unobtainable and the firm could suffer severely as a result. Some action is desirable.

The personnel manager could consult production and technical specialists with a view to seeing whether there are likely to be technical developments to produce a machine or process that could make the specialist skill obsolete or required on a smaller scale. If there is such a possibility, preparations should be made to begin introducing the new technology. Some new specialist workers may be needed and these may have to be recruited and trained by the time the first of the older workers retires.

If the skill seems likely to remain an important one for the foreseeable future steps should be taken to ensure that replacements are ready for the retiring workers. These steps could include re-training or training workers already employed by the firm. Suitable workers would have to be located and replaced either by other workers or machines.

The firm could start to recruit younger specialists from outside the firm and when these became available the old workers could be encouraged to retire or to take part-time work prior to retirement.

The firm could recruit new workers and use aptitude tests to see if they could be trained in the required skills. Selected candidates would then commence training.

If the special skill was related to one product only, consideration might be given to stopping production of this product or at least examining its contribution to profits and calculating how much additional cost would be worthwhile incurring to maintain production.

Question 16

Although sex and race discrimination are illegal in the UK there is little doubt that they still continue, sometimes unconsciously as people are unaware that they are discriminating. If women and ethnic minorities know that they are not welcome in some firms or occupations only the boldest will seek to enter, especially if they are not occupations of high prestige or status. In some cases the practice is conscious and exercised deviously using barriers of qualification or skill, knowing that these are unlikely to be possessed by applicants. The reason may be personal feeling but is more likely to be caution and the wish to avoid assumed hostility from established groups of workers. It is easier to discriminate than to go to the trouble, expense and risk of seeking to test or change the attitudes of long-established groups of workers.

Although most publicised cases of discrimination concern recruitment (or its absence) there may be even more discrimination in promoting workers. Managers still frequently assume that groups of older, male workers will be hostile to being managed or supervised by a woman or by a person of a minority race. This fear may be unjustified, especially if the pioneers are chosen with care. The Chairman of Shell has pointed to the success of that company's first lady manager of an operating company in a country not noted for its respect for female rights.

Uncommon now in Great Britain but more serious in Northern Ireland is discrimination on grounds of religion. In this issue it is not difficult to sympathise with managers who may literally be putting their own and other lives in danger by resisting discrimination. There is no simple solution to this problem until the wider conflict is resolved. An emerging issue is that of the potential growth of Islamic militancy with demands going beyond equality of treatment to the right to practise discrimination against non-Islamic groups.

One further form of discrimination that has so far received little attention in the UK, although in the USA it is banned in some States, is age discrimination. In many occupations further progress and/or recruitment are virtually impossible for men or women over the age of 50 and in some cases over 40. During the period of high unemployment in the 1980s this was not only practised without question but also institutionalised through State encouraged early retirement schemes. The return of full employment in some occupations and regions and the emergence of shortages of workers in a few has led some people to question the desirability of this form of discrimination. The assumption of physical and mental decay in all those over 50 unless they are lawyers, politicians or priests has little support in logic or fact. It has led to a considerable waste of scarce economic resources (the workers discriminated against). There are signs that this final form of discrimination is likely to receive more attention, especially now that a significant proportion of the total population of the UK is over the age of 50. From around 2010 the proportion of people between the ages of 16 and 50 is likely to fall and the community will not be able to afford to maintain the high proportion of dependants, many of whom are well able to contribute to production, though not necessarily in the careers they pursued when younger.

It has already been implied that some forms of discrimination continue in spite of laws making them illegal. Because of this some people argue that laws are ineffective and may even provoke hostility and prejudice. This is unlikely. There is a great deal less race and sex discrimination today than in the early 1960s and changes in the law have certainly played a part in changing behaviour. Many laws aimed at producing social reform have been disliked and evaded in their early days but most have played an important part in changing attitudes and behaviour. Political leaders have a role to play in leading public opinion and they can do this to some extent by changing laws. Most people do not want to break the law and if a law makes certain kinds of behaviour illegal and if the majority of people in the higher social groups support the law, these practices tend to become socially disreputable and so less widely practised. Broadly then, if the law and what is sometimes termed 'informed public opinion' are in agreement then the law is likely to change behaviour in time. If, however, this agreement is absent, as with say, gambling in Britain in the 1950s and the alcohol prohibition laws in the USA in the 1930s, then illegality will prevail, and crime will increase until the law is changed.

6
Purchasing and the firm

The purchasing function

Purchasing in different sectors

Purchasing is the term given to the business activity of legally acquiring the equipment, materials, supplies and services required by a private or public sector organisation for carrying out its activities. In this wide sense purchasing is concerned with methods of obtaining the use of equipment other than buying, e.g. hiring, leasing and contracting. Examination of the financial implications of various possible methods of obtaining goods and services is clearly an important part of the purchasing department's functions and it has to work closely with financial departments.

Purchasing, of course, is something that all firms do. It becomes a specialised branch of management when the volume and diversity of goods and services purchased leads to the possibility of waste and inefficiency and when the cost of a specialised department is paid for from the cost savings achieved by the co-ordination and purchasing skills it brings.

The following different classes of purchasers have been identified. Each has slightly different objectives and operates in a slightly different way.

- **Industrial purchasers**
  These operate in organisations which have profit or clear financial objectives to meet. In these cases the required equipment, materials, etc. have been determined by other managers, especially production managers, to fulfil specific purposes. The function of the purchasing officer is to obtain the required goods and services to the best advantage of the organisation. Clearly the purchasing officer will point out any apparent anomalies that are raising purchasing costs, or point to changes in practice that could reduce costs. To take a very simple example, if one department only was using different office printing and copying equipment from all the others, preventing the purchaser from taking advantage of bulk purchase discounts and other special terms, the purchasing department would wish to examine whether this department could come into line with the others. However, if there were special reasons which were of more importance than the cost savings being sacrificed the needs of the department would prevail. Specialist purchasers, who themselves are in danger of being too much influenced by other firms' sales people, need to keep in close touch with the operating departments who actually use the goods they purchase. On the other hand they also have to be aware of personal prejudices. Claims that some materials are of superior (or inferior) quality may not be supported by records of breakdowns or complaints.

- **Intermediate purchasers**
  These operate in firms which buy goods for re-sale. Importers, stockists and distribu-

tors, including retailers, are examples. These are looked upon as different from industrial purchasers because there is a much closer link with marketing. The main consideration in buying is not the usefulness of the purchase to the organisation but how readily and profitably it can be re-sold. In many sectors of retailing buying and marketing are virtually the same activity. The buyer can only go out to buy after an extensive study of market trends and conditions and the buyer's skills depend heavily on knowledge of the market place. A simple example known to all of us is greengrocery. The greengrocer's skill lies in buying fresh produce at prices the local market will pay. This requires buying just enough produce to sell it fresh each day with enough variety to maintain the interest of customers. No one wants to buy rotting fruit and vegetables. The actual sale of the goods purchased is known as merchandising, i.e. the skill of display, presentation, advertising and promotion to sell the goods that have been purchased. If the buyer misjudges market trends then no amount of merchandising skill is likely to redeem an almost certain disaster.It is sometimes suggested that the buyers in some trades, particularly the fashion trades, such as women's fashions, have tremendous power. There is some truth in this. If the buyers in all the main national retail and wholesale stores in the UK (and today this number is very small) decide that certain trends in, say, colour, skirt lengths etc. will be dominant in the forthcoming season and they buy accordingly, it is going to be difficult for women who do not go along with the trend to find anything new and fashionable to wear. On the other hand, if the majority of women do not really like the current year's dominant fashion trends they are likely to buy fewer new clothes than usual. Given the financial structure of modern retailing with its high fixed costs, even a small percentage fall in sales is likely to lead to a proportionally much larger fall in profits. It is the buyers who are most likely to be blamed for the financial disaster. There is no shortage of volunteers to replace unsuccessful fashion buyers! If the UK stores are out of line with trends in other countries there will be major changes in their senior management.

Buyers, like their colleagues in industrial marketing, have to be aware of general economic trends and have to make judgements about the future course of these trends. If, for example, the majority of households are likely to be stretching their incomes to meet high mortgage interest payments there is likely to be little opportunity for women to replace their wardrobes to conform to a major change in fashion. However, if after a year or two's relative depression and low levels of retail spending there is a fall in mortgage costs or rise in disposable incomes, then buyers may judge the time favourable to encourage a fashion shift. Modern buying is carried out on a world stage and decisions are likely to depend on marketing judgements. For example, if disposable incomes are expected to be low buyers may seek lower priced goods made in low cost countries. If disposable incomes rise they may prefer higher quality and higher priced goods from different countries. In virtually every respect buying decisions will be based on marketing considerations.

- **Institutional purchasers**
  This is the term given to those in the public sector, operating in organisations financed and controlled by central or local government and having functions to perform that are prescribed by Parliament, sometimes modified by the decisions of local authorities. The basic objectives of efficient purchasing are likely to be much the same as those of industrial purchasers, but often the financial pressures may be subordinated to some degree by political considerations. For example, purchasers may be under instructions to support UK manufacturers and to order from UK suppliers in preference to foreign competitors, unless there is a significant price or other difference making it undesirable to do so. Again, for political reasons, some organisations may refuse to purchase goods from certain countries whose political systems they oppose. For many years most public sector purchasers were required to deal only with contractors who were deemed to pay fair wages' and to conduct their labour

relations according to 'acceptable' standards. In recent years institutions have been encouraged to put financial considerations above purely political considerations.

Probably more serious and difficult to detect is the tendency for some managers in the public sector to seek to satisfy their own status ambitions by purchasing the latest and most advanced equipment without regard to actual need or cost. One of the functions of a centralised, specialist purchasing department is to identify and eliminate this practice, but in institutions which have no profit measure and often no way at all of measuring efficiency, the elimination of wasteful expenditure can be very difficult. Careers in the public sector are frequently based on the way money is **spent**. They rarely depend on success in **saving** money. This is a constant problem of public sector activities, aggravated by modern tendencies to increase the average size of public sector institutions. It is possible that undetected waste in a significant number of large institutions more than destroys the savings achieved by scale economies when they are created from a series of smaller organisations.

Purchasing objectives

In any organisation the purchasing manager's aim is to ensure maximum efficiency in purchasing. This involves obtaining the equipment, materials and services actually needed to carry out the functions of the operating departments, to obtain these at the lowest cost consistent with such features as quality, reliability of delivery and maintenance. A specialised knowledge of many sectors of supply is required as purchasing officers cannot rely on the objectivity of advice from the operating departments, any more than on the claims of suppliers. Specialised knowledge is also needed to ensure that short term cost savings are not achieved at the expense of long term losses. There has been a tendency in recent years for suppliers of electronic office equipment to reduce initial capital costs to the lowest possible level and to charge high prices for the materials required to keep equipment in operation. They judge, generally correctly, that more careful scrutiny is given to the initial expenditure than to the routine replacement of essential parts and the provision of operating materials. It is often more difficult to keep check on annual expenditure flows for materials than on initial capital costs. Clearly, however, it is the purchasing department's responsibility to examine these issues and to calculate costs over the full estimated life of equipment, taking into account realistic levels of use and handling by, often, unskilled staff.

Purchasing materials supplies often involves negotiating bulk contracts and here again the lure of attractive discounts has to be balanced against costs of storage, risks of deterioration and 'shrinkage'. Office staff tend to use paper more lavishly and wastefully if they can see that there are ample supplies. On the other hand keeping stocks low can cause expensive delays and upset customers if supply breakdowns cause delivery dates to be broken. If stocks of materials are deliberately kept low care has to be taken to ensure that suppliers are chosen with reliability of delivery well in mind.

Purchasing costs must also be considered against the overall financial position of the organisation, taking into account taxation, cash flows and discounted values of future payments, as explained in Unit 4. When all these factors are taken into account outright purchase of equipment may be regarded with less favour than leasing or hiring. Outright purchase may appear to be the cheapest option but this could raise the firm's borrowings at a time when interest rates are high and when there are more profitable uses for borrowed finance. Leasing, for example allows the cost to be spread over the working life of the equipment so that its costs are met out of the additional revenues it generates. Leasing or hiring may also make it easier and less costly to keep equipment up-to-date at a time of rapid technology changes and, in some cases, where the finance house is linked to the equipment supplier, the threat of withholding payments may ensure that maintenance is provided efficiently.

Ensuring that quality standards are maintained is a constant problem, particularly where long term contracts are involved. If suppliers have been forced into accepting very low prices they may be expected to try and restore profit margins by reducing quality standards. If profit margins are very low they will not be too concerned if contracts are not renewed. Very large customers may, therefore, come to regret using their buying power too forcefully. They could be left with very large sums to pay in compensation for defective products. They will have to pay these if smaller suppliers whose components or materials caused the problems go into liquidation through lack of funds. Most large companies insure for product liability but their future premiums tend to rise after a substantial claim and there is no competition from insurers to take over a 'bad risk'. Some companies prefer to accept some responsibility for quality control for essential components, checking on control methods and making their own physical inspections. Purchasing involves rather more than familiarity with suppliers' catalogues. Where the purchasing organisation has sufficient buying power in the market to exert a major influence on purchase price and quality standards it should have a detailed knowledge of the supplier's cost structure and production methods, to ensure that the price the supplier receives is sufficient to achieve the standards required.

An efficient purchasing department must not only possess a wide range of knowledge, experience and skills, it must also maintain continuous contacts with other specialists within its organisation and be aware of or have access, to information on production methods and trends, and marketing and financial trends.

In some organisations the purchasing department has gained a more important managerial role. It is the purchasing officer who normally is the first to become aware when there are changes in the markets where the firm is a buyer. These changes may affect the firm's production conditions so that the purchasing manager is able to make recommendations about possible changes in production method or development, in order to take advantage of or avoid unpleasant consequences of changes in commodity or components markets. In short the modern, specialised purchasing department is able to contribute the department's knowledge of supply markets to the sum of information on which significant managerial decisions are based.

TEST YOUR UNDERSTANDING

1   Outline the considerations to be taken into account when it is proposed to change to a new supplier from one known to the organisation for some years.
2   Explain why it is important for the purchasing department to co-operate with production and marketing departments.

Purchasing and uncertainty

Market power and long-term contracts

One of the major sources of uncertainty for any business organisation is the state of the markets for the materials, commodities and components required for production. If the firm is large enough it may have enough buying power in the market to ensure that it is able to exercise some control over the prices and conditions under which it buys. The purchasing department may then develop a thorough knowledge of the market conditions under which its suppliers operate and gain sufficient knowledge of their production costs to be able to calculate the prices which efficient suppliers would be able to charge, and still make a reasonable rate of profit. The purchasing department can then invite tenders from a list of suitable suppliers and accept those from firms which it feels confident can ensure satisfactory supplying standards of delivery, price and quality. In many cases roughly similar results can be obtained by negotiation without going through the formal process of inviting tenders.

In less inflationary times it is fairly common for firms to negotiate long term agreements under which orders to a minimum level are promised in return for fixed prices over an agreed period. This helps to reduce the level of market uncertainty for both suppliers and buyers. On the other hand it also reduces the degree of flexibility and there is a danger that the firms start to take each other for granted and allowing service standards to slip. There is the further danger that the purchasing department loses touch with rapidly changing conditions in materials markets so that ground is lost to competitors. Where rapid changes are expected, and where prices are subject to inflationary pressures, long term purchase agreements are unlikely to be suitable. Sellers will try to build in such safeguards that the advantage of having firm prices over a reasonable period of time is lost. When suppliers are dependent on materials from foreign countries there is the added problem of fluctuating exchange rates and the supplier may wish to peg prices to a more stable foreign currency or, in some cases, to one of the 'basket' currencies such as the Special Drawing Rights (SDRs) of the International Monetary Fund or the European Currency Unit (ECU) of the European Monetary System.

The futures (or terminal) markets

Through much of the 1980s the commodity markets, in which prices have a long history of being volatile, have had to face the added uncertainties of fluctuating currency values. Firms relying directly or indirectly on imported commodities need to have a sound working knowledge of these markets.

In those markets where it is possible to grade the commodity accurately and, therefore, where it can be sold by description in the knowledge that the delivered commodity conforms exactly to the description, trading can take place on the basis of both immediate and forward delivery. Trading for immediately delivery is known as **spot** trading and prices are spot prices. Payment is made on the basis of the price agreed and is due either immediately or at the end of the current period of account. Most markets have an account system.

Trading may also take place for delivery at a stated time in the future but at a price agreed at the time the deal is made. The agreed price will, of course, be based on the traders' estimates of the way spot prices are likely to move in the period up to the delivery date. For example on the London Commodity exchange on November 23 1989 tin was being traded at prices from 6770 to 6780 US$ per tonne. On the same day trading for delivery in three months' time was based on prices from 6910 to 6915 US$ per tonne. Traders clearly expected the price of tin to rise over the period. On the same day, however, the three month price of nickel was lower, at 9350 US$ to 9375 US$, than the spot price of 8850 US$ to 8875 US$. When forward deals are made the prices agreed must be held and delivery made as agreed. In most markets an immediate deposit of 10 per cent of the total bargain price is paid.

It is not always convenient to make firm agreements several months in advance. Not only does a substantial payment have to be made immediately but market prices may not move as predicted. The purchasing manager who was committed on this basis could be at a disadvantage against a competitor firm which decided to buy in the market closer to the time when stocks were required. One way of retaining flexibility while avoiding the risk of loss through unexpected price movements is to deal in **futures**. For example, an importer might have purchased a large quantity of a metal, or a commodity such as cocoa or coffee, from overseas producers and be expecting delivery in, say, several months' time. Buyers would be unwilling to commit themselves to firm orders and prices until nearer the time of arrival. If the price were to fall in the meantime the importer would suffer a substantial loss. One way to guard against such a loss would be for the importer to enter the market to sell futures. This is the commodity traded at a middle quality standard on the clear understanding that the trading deal will be reversed before actual delivery is due. Thus the importer will buy back the futures in, say, three months' time when the imported commodity is due to arrive. If the price does, in fact, fall the importer will be able to buy back the futures at a price lower than the selling price. The profit made on the futures will offset the lower than expected price obtained when the actual commodity arrives for sale in the UK. The importer, of course, has to pay brokers' charges on the futures transactions but these are regarded as a form of insurance against the risk of loss from the unexpected price change. Another part of the price is that of foregoing any chance of profit from an unanticipated price rise. This is also acceptable because the importer is a trader, not a speculator, and understands the dangers of speculating on future price movements. The process of sacrificing the chance of profit in order to secure safeguards against risks, especially risks from price changes, is known as **hedging**.

On the other hand the trader, or the manufacturer in metals or any other business seeking to hedge against price movement risks could not deal in futures unless the market did contain speculators willing to take these same risks in the hope of making a profit. The person who bought the importer's futures and then sold them back took a risk and could only make a profit if the price **rose higher than the agreed futures price**. Since this price was established by market forces the speculator must either be consistently lucky or have a detailed, accurate and up-to-date knowledge of the market. Any gambler who believes that luck is consistent is well advised to reserve a sheltered space under a railway arch. Futures speculation is no pastime for amateurs or for those who are prepared to trust their money to others whose business is gambling. Anyone who knows how to make a large and steady profit from a London market is unlikely to share that knowledge with the general public!

TEST YOUR UNDERSTANDING

3   What are the main sources of uncertainty faced by the purchasing manager?
4   Why and how may an engineering manufacturer deal in commodity futures?

Purchasing organisation

Like all the other managerial functions the organisation and structure of the purchasing department depends on the size of the organisation and the nature of its activities. What may be right for one firm at one time may be quite wrong for another or even the same firm at a different time.

One of the most familiar debates surrounding the organisation of purchasing concerns the extent to which buying should be centralised. Centralisation permits the purchasing manager to keep a check on what and how much is ordered, to ensure conformity where this does not conflict with the genuine needs of individual depart-ments or establishments and to ensure that the firm's buying power is used to its maximum effect. Centralisation also makes it easier to keep a check on delivery dates and to control payments.

However, where a firm has establishments in a number of locations allowing some localised buying helps the firm to create local goodwill and the reductions in delay and administration can make good some or all of the reductions in discounts. The longer the chain of administration the more errors and delays are likely to occur, frequently leading local establishments to over order to guard against deficiencies in supply. Since they do not know which purchases are going to be affected they tend to create the largest possible reserves over the widest possible range of goods. The waste that can be generated by over centralised purchasing can be avoided by allowing a reasonable degree of discretion and by monitoring expenditure and stock levels, making comparisons between establishments where this is practicable.

There is clearly no common rule that all firms should follow. The main consideration is what system or mix of systems best achieves total purchasing economies, bearing in mind bulk discounts, distribution, warehousing and administration costs. Where cost centres are established their managers are likely to take a renewed interest in the economics of purchasing. Some may feel that they can achieve lower costs if they gain more discretion over purchases and stock control. In contrast purchasing managers can also feel that if too much local discretion is permitted their own role is threatened or diminished, and they may find it difficult to change from a position of control to one of acting as monitor and adviser. These are organisational issues that have to be resolved by the senior managements of individual firms.

In recent years a number of local authorities have set up central purchasing departments though these tend to be mainly administrative and less active in initiating buying than the purchasing departments of large firms.

Stock control

The importance of stock control

As firms have grown bigger, and their activities more varied and complex, the work of ensuring that stocks are kept at the necessary level to avoid the two extreme problems of delays from shortages and waste from overstocking has become more specialised. In addition it is necessary to plan the timing of purchases to minimise the firm's borrowings. It is costly to have a large bank overdraft one month and a substantial balance the next when better planning of cash flow could keep a small, steady positive balance. It is also desirable to ensure that there is no danger of being taken by surprise by production or marketing changes when the firm is left with large, unusable stocks of materials with little re-sale value.

Any modern stock control system should ideally keep a running total of the physical stock of all goods held but this does not eliminate the need for regular physical checks on the quantity of stock actually held. Some errors are inevitable and there has to be a check on losses by theft and pilfering. It is also desirable to check that a computer system is not being manipulated to the profit of someone who understands the system better than the purchasing manager. Modern computer crime takes many forms. Where systems are working effectively, however, computers will record all outflows of stock, whether by sale or otherwise, and will automatically adjust stock totals. They will also signal when stock has reached re-order levels or when regular replenishment is failing to keep stock within chosen levels.

Most stock control systems adopt a format where the aim is to keep stock levels within a stated maximum and minimum. Between these there will be an order level set according to the anticipated or agreed time gap between order and delivery and the rate at which stocks are used. The aim will be to re-order so that stock will be delivered just as the level reaches the minimum. This minimum is set at a level to allow a reserve in case of unexpected delays or unusually rapid use. Where there are predictable seasonal variations in use systems can easily be modified to allow for these.

Some firms, which are able to plan production according to regular patterns, pursue a policy known as 'Just in Time' whereby delivery is arranged to take place just before stocks run out. This is intended to reduce the costs of storage and risk of 'shrinkage' to their lowest possible levels. The risks involved in such a policy are obvious and firms confident enough to take them are likely to have substantial buying power so that suppliers can be made subject to severe financial penalties and loss of valuable contracts if they fail to honour agreed delivery times.

Stock valuations

In most cases stocks do have to be maintained and these have to be valued for the normal purposes of accounting and financial control. If prices never varied during the normal time interval when stocks were being held valuation would present no serious problems. However, when purchase prices do vary because of market shifts, or, more commonly, because of general inflation, business profits can be substantially affected by the method chosen to value stocks held by the firm. Three common methods are usually known as **Lifo**, **Fifo** and **Avco**.

Lifo stands for 'last in first out'. For valuation purposes this means that stocks are valued and profits calculated on the assumption that the items used were the ones most recently purchased. Inland revenue authorities may object to this practice if they feel that it is understating true profits - by overvaluing stock purchase costs and undervaluing the value of remaining stocks held. Much depends on the type of activity, the length of time stock is being held and the current rate of inflation. Tax authorities, of course, may introduce their own rules for taking inflation into account.

Fifo stands for 'first in first out'. This means that there is an assumption that the stocks used were those bought first. If prices are rising this practice produces a larger operating profit and a larger figure for existing stock values.

Avco stands for 'average costs out'. The figures used for profit calculation and stock valuation are those based on a weighted average of stocks purchased during the period. The following example illustrates the effect of choosing these different methods of valuation.

Date of purchase	Tonnes purchased	Price per tonne (£)	Cost (£)
January 2	10	50	500
March 1	15	53	795
June 1	10	55	550
December 1	15	58	870
		Average	Total
Total	50	54.3	2715

Suppose that by the end of December 30 tonnes had been used to produce a sales revenue of £1650.

If the Lifo method is used then calculations are based on the assumption that the 40 tonnes consists of the 15 December purchase + the 10 bought in June + 5 of those bought in March so that the total cost would be £870 + £550 + £265 = £1685. This valuation would produce a loss of £35 and remaining stocks (20 tonnes) are valued at £530 + £500 = £1030.

If the Fifo method is used it is assumed that the stocks from the beginning of the year are used first to produce a figure for cost of £500 + £795 + £275 = £1570. This suggests a profit of £1650 - £1570 = £80 and a valuation of remaining stocks of £870 + £275 = £1145.

The Avco method produces a material cost of 30 x £54.3 = £1629, a profit of £1650 - £1629 = £21 and a remaining stock valuation of 20 x £54.3 = £1086.

Costs other than material costs are ignored in this simple example. Notice that each method produces a different profit and a different valuation of stocks at the end of the year.

In deciding whether or not to agree to a firm's use of one or other of these methods an auditor would have to consider whether it gave a true and fair picture of its true financial position. A firm would be expected to keep to one method and not to keep changing it to produce whatever result it wished.

TEST YOUR UNDERSTANDING

5 Centralised buying and the use of its market power has always been recognised as a feature of the specialist multiple retail (chain) store. When multiple trading started to extend to department stores and hypermarkets (superstores) buying became more complex and mixed. Suggest reasons for this.
6 Why is stock control such an important part of the modern purchasing function?
7 Under what circumstances would you argue that Lifo was the fairest basis for stock valuation?
8 Outline what you think are the main benefits and dangers of computerisation to the purchasing manager.

NOTES TO QUESTIONS

Question 1

The more obvious considerations will be those of price, delivery and quality of the goods or services bought. Presumably the proposal will not be entertained unless there is a promised improvement in at least one of these, with no deterioration in the other two. However, there are likely to be additional factors to bear in mind. These include:

- The contacts that have been built up over years between the staffs in the two organisations. These contacts are likely to mean that shortcuts can be taken when necessary, that the supplier is likely to make a special effort to avoid letting down people who may be regarded as friends rather than just business acquaintances.
- The suppliers' knowledge of the buyer's business. The supplier will know the probable needs of the buyer and is able to plan accordingly. If errors or omissions are made in ordering the supplier will usually know who to speak to make corrections or to check the accuracy of an order quickly and without fuss. If there are likely to be market changes affecting the buyer the supplier will usually give advance warning.
- The effect on the supplier's business. The purchasing manager may wish to give some thought to any especially favourable terms being offered by the prospective new supplier. These may simply result from a competitive market and the old supplier may have been guilty of taking the buyer for granted for too long. On the other hand the new supplier may be deliberately seeking to destroy the old supplier in order to reduce market competition and gain market power. In the meantime generous terms represent the price to be paid now to gain future market strength when costs may be recouped without fear of moving to competitors.

Changing a long-established source of supply is not a matter to be taken lightly. The benefits can often be less than expected. This does not mean that such links should never be broken. Competition is always a spur to efficiency and quality of service. Moreover news soon spreads in the business environment. Knowledge that the firm has dropped a long-standing supplier because of failure to withstand market competition can have a revitalising effect on other suppliers.

Question 2

The purchasing manager must be able to anticipate the requirements of production departments in order to ensure that the goods and services will be available. If changes are being made or considered the purchasing department needs to be able to work out the implications for supplies and will usually need some time to investigate a new market and make arrangements for new sources of supply. The purchaser is at a serious disadvantage if materials are wanted quickly.

Purchasing managers need to know what changes are contemplated so that they can inform their colleagues if there are likely to be any serious problems, such as uncertainty of delivery or price of essential commodities or components. More positively they may be able to initiate changes made desirable by developments in their supply markets. The purchasing manager able to predict changes in price trends may be able to set in motion changes in production that will enable the firm to gain a competitive advantage when the change takes place.

In short the purchasing department needs to be aware of developments in marketing and production and to ensure that production and marketing managers are aware of developments or possible future developments in the firm's sources of supply. The more the various specialists integrate their specialised knowledge the less the uncertainty that firm has to face.

Question 3
The main sources of uncertainty affecting purchasing are:

- The firm's own product market. The materials buyer must give firm orders and order in advance of production and sale but cannot know for certain how well the product will sell.
- The firm's own marketing decisions. Decisions to change direction, to enter new and withdraw from old markets, or to give more - or less - emphasis to certain markets all have implications for the buyer.
- Production decisions always have direct effects on purchasing. Changes in production method, in the mix of commodities, in the timing of different batches of product, all affect the purchasing department.
- Changes in the markets in which goods and services are purchased have to be allowed for and these can alter the purchaser's buying strategy.
- Changes in the cost of finance can have very important consequences for buying policy. Any rise in interest rates will put pressure on the firm to keep stocks as low as possible and will force companies to put pressure on suppliers to reduce prices. If the rise in finance costs is taking place against an uncertain market environment it may be preferable to risk a delay in production to keep stocks low and reduce storage and handling costs. Under different financial and market conditions a higher level of material stocks may seem a small price to be paid for ensuring continuity of production.
- Where goods are purchased directly from overseas suppliers attention has to be paid to the political, economic and financial situation in the countries concerned. Political change can take place very swiftly and can have major consequences for trade and the flow of goods and services. Changes can close or open markets. Almost all change brings risks and opportunities. Purchasers have to be as alive to these as readily as marketing managers.

Question 4
Most engineering manufacturers use metals of some kind. Relatively few goods are made purely from plastics. Prices of most metals, especially the non-ferrous metals, copper, lead, zinc, tin, aluminium and nickel fluctuate constantly and sometimes unexpectedly. Engineering manufacturers are specialists in using metals and cannot be expected to develop a detailed, specialised knowledge of the conditions in all the countries which are significant suppliers of the metals they use. Profit margins in engineering manufacturing are not usually very large. Most markets are competitive and manufacturers can suffer a major profit collapse if they are surprised by unexpected prices in metals essential to their forms of production.

Many engineers, therefore, can benefit from hedging this risk of price movement. If they do so they are simply practising a form of specialisation - passing the price change risk to a market specialist - the expert futures dealer.

The manufacturer is most at risk from an unexpected price rise when production quantities and final product prices have already been decided. This risk can be hedged by buying futures in the relevant metal market within the London Metal Exchange. The engineer will, of course, deal with a broker but instruct the broker to buy futures for a quantity roughly equivalent to the amount the firm is expected to purchase in the future period of, say, three months. If the price rises more than the amount anticipated in the futures price the manufacturer will be able to sell back the futures at a profit to offset the extra cost of buying the metal actually required. If the price falls the manufacturer will lose money on the futures deal but this will be offset by the extra profit earned because the actual metal will be purchased at a lower than estimated cost. The manufacturer hedges against the risk of loss at the price of forfeiting the chance of profit and paying the dealing charges.

Question 5

The older style multiple, often known as a chain store, concentrated on a single line of goods such as ladies' shoes. Even the grocery chains were normally limited to packaged groceries, rarely straying into the more difficult products such as meat and vegetables. Much of the success of these stores was linked to their market power and ability to centralise the buying function to obtain maximum benefit from bulk buying discounts and from scale economies in marketing and distribution.

In contrast the older, independent department stores had taken pride in the range of goods sold and buying had been very closely linked to selling. Buyers were recruited from successful sales staff and most buyers continued to be employed as managers of the selling departments. Operating in many different markets the department stores had rarely enjoyed substantial market power in more than a few.

As the older independent department stores either closed or were taken over by multiple groups the issue of purchasing became very important. The multiple's instinct was to centralise, to limit the range of products and to concentrate on bulk purchase of goods that could be sold throughout the country at predictable quantity levels. However, this policy tended to make the department stores unsatisfying for customers who saw little point in going to a large city centre shop which appeared to offer nothing better than the goods in the local shops. The department stores have not really developed a completely satisfactory formula to overcome this difference in attitude and they have not been among the most successful sectors of retailing in the 1980s. Some have sought refuge in franchising, i.e. renting space to specialist distributors or manufacturers of goods such as clothing, and restricting their own trading to a restricted range of goods. To do this seems to be abdicating their role as retailers to become little more than retail property companies.

The hypermarket or superstore entered retailing as a kind of streamlined version of the department store but with its roots firmly in the world of the grocery based supermarket. The stress on self-service trading has meant that it has never been strong on the non-portable, high value household goods while on electrical products it has had to face competition from the discount stores which have never sought to attain the range of the hypermarket. As the number of separate stores in a hypermarket multiple tends to be relatively small it has been easier for these to combine both centralised and non-centralised purchasing, using whichever method appears most suitable for the product. On the whole, however, the stress has been strongly towards centralisation, making it difficult for the separate stores to develop their own individuality or to develop any kind of strong regional personality.

Even in hypermarkets the information on which buyers act is all gained from sales data. There is little or no personal contact between buyers and shoppers. Sales data provide information on what the customer is buying, or not buying. It gives no information about what would have been bought had it been available. First hand contact with the market and its trends seems to be lacking.

Question 6
Stock control is important for several reasons of which the most important are:

- **The cost of holding stocks**
  Given the high cost of borrowed funds it is wasteful and damaging to retain stocks at a level higher than is essential. On the other hand it is equally, if not more, damaging for shortages of any stocks to cause production delays. To ensure that stocks are just sufficient to keep production running smoothly without incurring high storage costs requires careful and intelligent control methods.

- **The cost of stock administration**
  The larger and more varied the stock held the greater the cost of administration and security. The more attractive the stock the greater the danger of theft and the more likely it is for errors to be made in both ordering and stock distribution.

- **Savings from reconciling purchasing and revenue flows**
  Stock control also includes fitting orders to the organisation's cash flow to minimise borrowing and so reducing costs.

- **The need to avoid holding unusable stock**
  Another part of stock control is to ensure that purchasing takes into account likely changes in production and marketing trends so that the company is not left with large quantities of unwanted stocks.

Question 7
In a period of rapid price rises a case can be made for Lifo on the grounds that the true opportunity cost of stocks used is the latest replacement cost, so that valuing materials used at this replacement cost removes from profit any monetary element caused purely by inflation. Goods are sold at current prices and the materials used will have to be replaced at current prices so that, to include in profit the rise in monetary value of materials which has resulted from holding them over a period of rising prices gives a false picture of the true profit earned from trading.

However, to value stocks at the original purchase price when their real value, in monetary terms, is higher does seem to be building in to the balance sheet an element of concealed profit and it is more difficult to defend this - although it may be argued that there is no guarantee that the stocks will all be used and if they had to be sold as scrap the old cost would be nearer the true position.

The benefit to the company of reducing recorded profit is only significant when there are substantial price rises during the period materials are held in stock. If prices are constant there is no difference to profit or stock values whatever the method used. If prices are falling then Lifo could be overstating profit and overvaluing stocks because the current cost of replacing stock is falling and the balance sheet value of stocks would be greater than their re-sale value.

This kind of problem illustrates some of the financial difficulties created by periods of rapidly changing prices, particularly by a period of rapid inflation.

Question 8
Computerisation enables the purchasing manager to have daily stock totals for all stocks held by the organisation. These figures will be compiled automatically whenever stock enters or leaves the control area. Information on invoices or retail sales tickets will be fed to stock data programs in the normal process of trade. Consequently separate stock records do not have to be made or adjusted. The total administrative load to the organisation is much reduced and the information fed to the purchasing department is completely up-to-date.

Computer programs will also signal to the purchasing officer when re-order levels are reached, and may even trigger an automated ordering system unless overridden by the purchasing office.

By removing much of the routine work of administration the purchasing manager is freed to concentrate on the more positive managerial functions of investigating supply markets, checking that supply terms and prices are the best available and ensuring that marketing and production managers are aware of developments and trends in the materials and components markets.

However, there are dangers. The way in which stock information is compiled, its detail and the fact that it is constantly kept up-to-date, can convey an impression of accuracy that may be misleading. All systems are open to error and abuse. Computers present challenges to thieves and often change the nature of crime but they do not prevent theft and pilferage. If programs contain a built in margin for unexplained stock 'shrinkage' this will become known and employees will ensure that the shrinkage does actually take place - and probably be exceeded. The only sure way of knowing actual stock levels is by physical inspection and physical checks are still necessary. However, where stock information is based on laser scanning of bar codes the risks of error are reduced and actual shrinkage is then mostly caused by breakages and theft which should be easier to control.

Computers are liable to break down, so that backup copies of records need to be made and kept. Costs caused by computer breakdown can be much greater than most people realise until they suffer them. Programs may also contain errors and these can be troublesome.

If too much reliance is placed on computer records managers may not be alert to changes in trends or to changes in supply markets until they actually feed into the records. Computerisation means that managers have to be more, not less alert to market shifts.

In general computer maintained records are a great aid to purchasing management but have to be understood and used intelligently if they are to reach their full potential.

7
The elements of marketing

What is marketing?

It is important to recognise that marketing is not selling. A clear distinction has to be made between the **strategic** activity of marketing and the **tactical** activity of selling. Marketing is concerned with helping to plan the long-term objectives of the organisation. Selling is one of the ways in which the organisation seeks to achieve those objectives. A good salesperson does not necessarily make a successful marketing person. A good marketing manager is not necessarily very successful at selling. The two activities complement each other. They do not require the same set of qualities though both need to recognise the importance to the firm of the buyers in the market place and to accept that the firm can only survive if its products are acceptable to the market.

Marketing embraces the following major functions:

- **Identifying the product strengths and weaknesses of the organisation**
  This is as important for a service organisation as it is for a manufacturer. The strengths will influence product promotion in the market. The marketing manager has a responsibility to ensure that senior management is aware of the weaknesses so that it can decide whether or not to try and remedy them or try to avoid exposing them.

- **Identifying market features and trends and their implications for the organisation**
  This involves continuing research into market conditions, identifying the main influences on the market, predicting future trends and their implications for product development within the organisation. Recommendations have to be made concerning the future of existing products, any desired modifications and, of course, the development of new products.

- **Forecasting future demand for the organisation's product range**
  Assuming that senior management has made broad production decisions in the light of anticipated trends, the marketing department needs to try and forecast future demand at a range of possible prices so that the profit implications can be examined and future production capacity planned. This will only be accurate if future market movements have been anticipated correctly.

- **Devising strategies for achieving sales objectives**
  This requires decisions on price, distribution method, target population, advertising, promotion techniques and other elements in what is commonly termed the **marketing mix**.

- **Co-operation with sales management**
  In smaller organisations the marketing manager is likely to be responsible for selec-

tion, training and control of the sales force and selling activities. In larger organisations there is more likely to be a specialised sales manager who must, nevertheless, integrate closely with marketing policies and strategies and be able to assist in putting these into practice.

These functions will now be examined in more detail. By this time, however, it should already be clear that the marketing role within the firm, whatever its sector of activity, is of prime importance. No organisation can dispute that it can continue to exist only if it is able to satisfy market demand, whether that demand is expressed through purchasing decisions in a market place subject to the price system, or through the political machinery of the State, in the public sector. In the past it was common practice to regard firms as being either production or market orientated. If production orientated it subordinated the selling function to the desires and requirements of the producers. In such a firm there was no place for marketing as we have defined and explained it. If any firm of this kind still survives in any of the major industrial, market economies, its future is bleak in the extreme. The general assumption is made here that market orientation, the recognition that the market determines production, is a survival condition for the modern organisation in both the private and public sectors of the economy.

This assumption not ignore the arguments of those who follow the teaching of Professor Galbraith whose writing has had a considerable influence on economic thought in the past twenty-five years or so. Galbraith believed that the large multinational companies were powerful enough to impose their will on the market. The companies were accused of using modern communication techniques to persuade the public to buy the goods that were profitable to produce. This is putting a new and somewhat sinister twist on the term 'production orientated firm'. We cannot, of course, deny that there is always a strong element of persuasion in any kind of selling but bankruptcy courts and employment agencies have been thronged with ex-sales and marketing people who only wished that Professor Galbraith had been right. Sooner or later the power of market demand re-asserts itself.

TEST YOUR UNDERSTANDING

1   Canned pet food has become a major consumer market since the early 1950s. Before then the majority of cat and dog owners fed their pets on cheap fresh food and household scraps. How far does the development of this oligopolistic market support Professor Galbraith's view that producers manipulate consumer demand to satisfy their own profit objectives?
2   'Anyone can sell the best product on the market. It takes really effective marketing to sell the worst.' Discuss this comment attributed to the general manager of a life assurance company.

Identifying and adapting to change

If you look at the five marketing functions identified earlier you will see that the first three are concerned with forecasting future developments and their implications for the company and its strategic objectives, while the last two are concerned with formulating and implementing the strategies and tactics needed to achieve those objectives. This unit looks at the predictive functions, and the strategic and tactical implementation functions are considered in the next.

Company analysis

You have noted that one of the functions of the marketing department is to identify the product strengths and weaknesses of the organisation. It is important that this exercise is carried out in full recognition of the main trends of change that can be identified in the general market environment in which the organisation operates. Failure to recognise the implications of major technological changes in sufficient time to adapt and move with them has brought about, or contributed to, the collapse of many organisations. The firm which, for over half a century, had supplied metal pen nibs to the majority of schools in England failed to recognise the threat posed by cheap ball point pens until it was too late. Many small distributors of radio valves disappeared when transistors were introduced. The two firms which had long shared most of the market for weighing equipment in Britain could not survive the introduction of electronic weighing without having to surrender their independence. You can probably think of many other examples. Firms must be ready to adapt not only to the market as it exists but also to the changes likely to take place in the future. Marketing can help this process by carrying out a systematic analysis of the strengths and weaknesses of the organisation in the light of the threats and opportunities arising out of changes in the technological and market environment.

This is sometimes referred to as **SWOT** analysis, i.e. the analysis of the organisation's: **Strengths**, **Weaknesses**, **Opportunities**, **Threats**. In the light of this analysis the organisation will hope to develop a 'strategic fit' between its strengths and market opportunities and, of course, to remove the weaknesses and survive the threats.

Strengths and weaknesses in this context are referred to in relation to current and anticipated market trends and not intrinsic features of management. A strength one year may become a weakness a few years' later. For example, an accountancy firm may be particularly strong on taxation planning and negotiation but if tax laws are simplified and tax rates reduced these qualities may not be required to the same extent. The need may move, say, to company liquidations and receiverships where the firm may be much less strong. Since a major shift in market trends is likely to have implications for the employment of fixed production factors such as machines or highly specialised staff, the company may need to plan ahead in accordance with market forecasts, in order to be ready for the changed need when it arrives.

As already indicated, shifts in market trends produce both opportunities and threats. The shift opens up the chance to develop new products and services, and the company able to provide these during the early growth stage of the new trend is in the best position to exploit what may be a temporary monopoly if competitors are not ready for the change. If the company is one of those which had not forecast and prepared for the shift it may be forced either to watch a more enterprising competitor prosper, or to pay inflated prices for the machines or staff needed to enable it to adapt production to the change.

Market research

It should now be clear that predicting future market trends is a major part of the marketing department's contribution to the overall management of the organisation. In this unit a distinction is being made between general market research, designed to identify the way a market is likely to develop, and the estimation of future demand for specific products. Clearly the two processes cannot be rigidly separated as information required for one is likely to be relevant to the other, but as an aid to understanding the functions of marketing it is useful to distinguish between them.

All organisations are likely to be operating in a fairly clearly defined market sector but the boundaries of that sector may be shifting. For example, a polytechnic or university is serving that section of the population which wishes to obtain higher education. For several generations, ignoring the temporary disruption of war, it has been assumed that this section of the population was almost completely dominated by the 17-20 year-old age group, with a few exceptions. Today, however, demographic change, the technology revolution and major social changes suggest that this traditional section is likely to form a smaller proportion of a total student population, which will include a significant proportion of mature adults seeking to re-train or to prepare themselves for a mid-career change of occupation. This change in market, if it is indeed taking place, implies major changes in the nature of the product and method of production. An increasing proportion of students are likely to be part-time or to mingle part- and full-time study. There is likely to be pressure to complete courses in shorter periods, to tailor courses to particular occupations or career requirements and so on. Different kinds of teaching staff and teaching methods are likely to be needed. Organisations may have to change so that students can continue with a particular course while moving from one area to another, perhaps from one country to another.

Almost every product and service you can bring to mind has faced or is facing major market changes likely to affect the range of product produced, the methods of production and the people who organise and carry out production.

Sources of information

It is necessary to distinguish between secondary and primary sources of market information. The secondary sources are existing publications while primary sources are those which have to be tapped in order to produce information which is not available in any existing published form.

Among the main published sources are those prepared by the national government. In Britain, official statistics are compiled and published by the Central Statistical Office (CSO) and most of these are published through Her Majesty's Stationery Office and sold through the book trade, including the Government bookshops. From these can be extracted data relating to changes in the size and age structure of the population, its geographical distribution, income trends, household sizes, leisure habits, expenditure patterns and so on. You should spend some time in the statistical section of a good reference library and gain an idea of the enormous quantity and range of information available in CSO publications.

Other information is prepared and published by trade associations, specialist publishers and, of course, by specialist market research organisations, some of which conduct regular surveys into trends and developments in specific branches of commerce and industry.

Most organisations are likely to need information that is not available in published sources, however, specialised. This must be gained by going out into the market place and finding out how people react or are likely to react to specific products. Of course, it is rarely possible to interrogate an entire target population. Other methods have to be used. One of the most common is to conduct a sample survey. Choosing a sample to provide a reliable indication of the behaviour of the population from which it is selected is a skilled operation as is the control of the survey which must be carefully managed and monitored. Surveys are expensive and only available to large firms or to trade associations.

Other methods of gaining primary market information include experiments where members of the target population are exposed to simulations to find out their reactions to reasonably realistic market situations. The organisation's own records can also provide source material if these are examined systematically.

Some important market predictions are made by observing trends in the most advanced countries and examining the implications of similar trends being experienced in other countries whose incomes and living standards are rising. Account must, of course, be taken of known cultural and social differences. Large multinational companies are in a favoured position to identify these developments and they are also likely to take part in transferring the trends.

Product demand estimation

In the light of its predictions of future market trends the organisation has to take strategic decisions as to which products it is going to develop and how to modify its production plans. Consideration must then be given to specific products and decisions made concerning product design, price," selling and distribution method and the quantity to be produced. These decisions depend on the marketing department's success in predicting likely future demand at a range of prices and subject to certain assumptions regarding advertising, production promotion and distribution method.

At this stage it is useful to remember what is involved in a general demand function, i.e. the list of influences on the demand for any particular product. In general terms we can say that:

$$Q_x \quad = \quad f(P_o, P_a, Y_d, A, N, T, M, E, Z) \quad \text{where:}$$

Q_x = the quantity demanded of the 'good' X
P_o = the price of X (the good's own price)
P_a = the prices of other good
Y_d = the level of disposable income of the target population
A = the marketing effort, including advertising devoted to the product
N = the size of the market, i.e. number of potential buyers
T = taste for the product as determined by social attitudes
M = the availability, including cost, of money and credit
E = expectations of the future, including actions of competitors, future price and income movements
Z = any influences specific to the product X

Accurate demand estimation has to try to turn this general demand function into a specific demand equation for the product. This involves putting values on the co-efficients that help to make up the complete equation so that, for an equation such as:

$$Q_x \quad = \quad aP_o + bP_a + cY_d + ... + nZ$$

the marketing department has to try and estimate values for a, b, c, etc. to indicate the relative importance of each of these influences in determining the quantity demanded at any given time. Those of you who are also studying microeconomic theory will recognise that this involves estimating the values of price, cross price, income, advertising and other possible elasticities of demand for the product.

Demand estimation, of course, involves predicting probable demand in the future, so not only must the relative importance of these influences be estimated but also predictions must be made concerning the movement of these variables, for example, likely trends in disposable income, market size and shifts in social attitudes.

When looking at this list of demand influences it may have occurred to you that some of them are within the control of the organisation and some are not. For those outside its control the organisation can only seek to predict future movements. For those within its control it must try to answer a series of 'what if?' questions and to test out likely consequences of various strategic combinations of say, price, advertising and distribution. Not only must the organisation try to predict the reactions of potential buyers but also those of rival suppliers to the various possible strategic sets.

In these functions marketing relies heavily on computer models. Modern marketing managers have to be computer literate and familiar with such aids to computer market analysis as spreadsheets. At the same time we have to remember that computer models are only an aid to analysis. They are as accurate as the information on which they are built. The quality of market research and demand estimation is a major factor in successful marketing. It must also be constantly remembered that market research is really only a highly refined form of crystal ball gazing. No one can be completely certain what the future will bring. The element of uncertainty and surprise can never be entirely eliminated from the marketing function. This is one reason why it is probably the most absorbing of all the specialised functions of business management.

No amount of experimenting and surveying can be a completely sure guide to the way the product will actually perform in the market place. Nevertheless to put the product into full production is an expensive process and if it fails the resulting financial losses can be very heavy. In many cases, therefore, the firm decides to put the product into limited production and to **test market** it over a limited area through a selected range of stores. The test marketing continues over a pre-determined time and the sales figures over that time are carefully analysed. If they conform to the desired growth pattern the product will be put into full production and launched, making any modifications to the product, packaging or design that seem desirable as a result of the text. If the growth pattern suggests that sales are unlikely to reach the targets necessary to achieve desired profits, the product will be dropped and the costs incurred written off.

Market research specialists point out that products that have been test marketed have a higher success rate than those that have not but, of course, this may simply indicate that firms able to afford test marketing are likely to be more careful in their market research, product design etc. anyway. There is no doubt that this kind of 'dress rehearsal' can provide valuable information that will help to make the full launch a success and sales departments are likely to have more confidence in a product that has already proved itself in test marketing. On the other hand it does delay and increase the expense of the launch and can give rival suppliers information that may help them to bring forward their own rival products, so that the product may face stronger competition than it did under test. There can never be a perfect solution to the problems of predicting future product performance.

TEST YOUR UNDERSTANDING

3   If you were asked to question a random sample of potential customers for a particular type of family saloon car would it be satisfactory to go into the local High Street on a Monday morning and question the first twenty people you met? Explain the reasons for your answer.
4   Why do market research firms go to the expense of employing interviewers when they could send questionnaire forms through the post?
5   What do you think are the main influences on the demand for personal microcomputers?

Marketing strategies

However successful a company may be it cannot rest on its laurels and assume that profits can be maintained and improved without reviewing its objectives, its performance and developing strategies to achieve or continue to achieve its objectives. Failure to do so could mean that the company fails to adapt to changing market conditions and suddenly finds itself with collapsing sales and profits. Clearly if sales or profit targets are not being met and are not keeping pace with the perceived performance of market rivals then the need for reviewing products and their marketing is an obvious matter of urgency. Less apparent is the need for continual review when products are selling well and profitably.

The product life cycle

No company can assume that the past and present will be projected into the future. We saw in the previous unit that the future, even the unexpected, had to be prepared for. All products, other than those that fail to become established in the market, pass through what is known as the product life cycle. The stages of this cycle are fairly well defined and understood. What is less clear and likely to be different for different products is the length of time any one product is likely to spend at each stage of the cycle. The normal pattern of the cycle is shown in Figure 7.1.

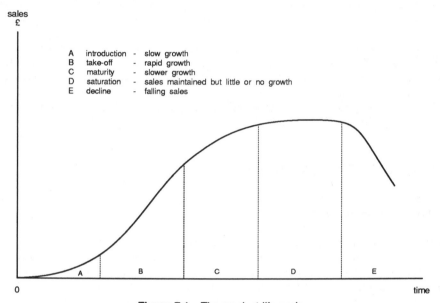

A	introduction	-	slow growth
B	take-off	-	rapid growth
C	maturity	-	slower growth
D	saturation	-	sales maintained but little or no growth
E	decline	-	falling sales

Figure 7.1 *The product life cycle*

This shows the general shape of the product life cycle curve, indicating that there are five stages to the cycle. Although different writers tend to apply slightly different terms to the stages there is general agreement about the features of each stage. Initially the product is likely to grow slowly as it gradually becomes known in the market and the 'pioneers' among consumers start to take it up. If it gains acceptance this initial stage is followed by rapid growth. However, as the market moves towards saturation, and as competing products appear, the rapid growth stage gives way to a period of slower growth. The growth rate is likely to fall until sales reach a plateau and there is little or no further growth. Eventually the final stage is reached and sales start to decline. If this decline continues the stage will be reached where production ceases to become profitable.

Although no one disputes the broad course of the product life cycle the practical use of the concept is limited because it has proved impossible to predict either the absolute or the relative lengths of each stage in the cycle. There appears to be no way to predict the probable length of stages C and D even after stages A and B have been experienced. Fashion products can be expected to pass through all stages quickly, often within a year. Others can continue in the maturity and saturation stages for extended periods of several decades. Some familiar breakfast cereals, a number of leading confectionery brands and bottled sauces were already well-established in the 1930s. The ability to survive for half a century does not, of course, mean that the product can survive another 50 years. Sooner or later the final stage will be reached unless it can be given a new lease of life by some kind of modification. It must also, of course, be remembered that the majority of new products never get beyond stage A and are withdrawn without having made significant inroads into the market.

If the product life cycle model does not help a firm to predict future sales nor give any indication how the more profitable stages can be prolonged, neither does it indicate anything about the product's share of total market sales. A firm might be content with extending and maintaining stages C or D, and be satisfied with the resulting profits, without recognising that the product is losing market share. If this loss is not reversed stage E will appear suddenly and be extremely difficult to reverse. Smiths potato crisps maintained total sales volume for a period in the 1960s when the manufacturer failed to recognise the major market growth and change resulting from the entry of Imperial Group to the market. Smiths only began to recover after takeover by a larger, international food group, which introduced new production and marketing techniques to challenge Imperial.

The main usefulness of the model is to provide a warning to firms that product lives are mortal and that if the firm is to continue to enjoy growing sales and profits it must develop new or modified products even as it is experiencing the benefits of growth of existing products. The implications for the marketing department are clear. It must be ready with strategies to ensure that sales and profit growth can be maintained or improved and not wait for crises to develop when product sales start to decline.

Some broad marketing strategies

The main approaches that may be taken to maintain, improve or restore sales growth are likely to include the following:

- **Increase the effectiveness of sales and distribution methods**
  The effectiveness of existing advertising, pricing and distribution channels need to be kept under review. These can become stale after a time and a change of advertising agency or distribution network can sometimes revitalise sales. However, care should be taken to ensure that these changes do not also provide openings for competitors and they should not be seen as substitutes for more penetrating changes of strategy. When the established British and American motor vehicle distributors downgraded large numbers of their local distributors in the 1960s and 1970s they created openings for importers of German and Japanese cars, the strength of whose challenge was not understood at the time by the firms then dominating the market.

- **Modify existing products**
  The great majority of 'new' products are really modifications of old ones and are introduced to incorporate new features, or to adapt to changed social and market conditions, or to fill gaps in a product range which are being exploited by rival producers. For example, washing powders have been adapted to wash with cold water, recognising that the modern generation no longer associates washing with boiling water and clouds of steam. One of the most remarkable marketing modifications of a product was the reputed re-packaging and re-launching of baking powder (the demand for which fell away with the introduction, first of self-raising flour and then of cake mixes and the general decline of home cooking) as a refrigerator deodoriser!

- **Extending market areas**
  If the home country market appears to have reached saturation level fresh growth can be achieved by entering new markets, particularly countries whose income levels are rising and where tastes can be expected to change accordingly. In the 1980s continental ski clothing and equipment suppliers moved into the British market where winter holidays were gaining rapidly in popularity. In the same period British tobacco and baby food companies increased their marketing efforts in developing countries where

changing living standards and income levels were leading to the adoption of what were there perceived as European life styles. British tobacco and baby food companies were looking for ways to make good the decline in sales due to anti-smoking trends and falling birth rates in the home markets.

- **New product development**
  Perhaps surprisingly this is a strategy that has not always been very successful, especially with large companies. Product diversification, especially when pursued almost as an act of desperation in the face of a long-term trend of falling demand,can lead companies into new market areas which they do not fully understand. During the 1970s Imperial Group (formerly Imperial Tobacco) pursued an extensive diversification strategy and this so weakened the company that it became a prey to Hanson, which sold off most of its diversified product divisions and concentrated on its older core activities. On the other hand the potato crisp producers of the 1960s became the snack food producers of the 1970s and 80s and in doing so created the multi-billion pound market of today. The most successful form of product diversification appears to be to extend, develop and transform an existing product range, as in the case of the growing range of canned pet foods. Least successful are attempts by companies to move into what is, for them, entirely new product markets. The famous attempt of a successful computer entrepreneur to develop an electric car now stands as a warning to producers not to rush into product areas which are entirely outside their previous experience.

TEST YOUR UNDERSTANDING

6 Suggest reasons for the extended product life cycle of the main brands of breakfast cereal. Do you detect indications that some of these may be approaching the final stage of the cycle?
7 Some representations of the product life cycle contain a stage before the one represented by A in Figure 7.1. What stage do you think this might be?

Implementing strategy and the marketing mix

Successful marketing management, involving the successful implementation of strategies, combines two related elements. These are the identification and selection of target markets and the adoption of a suitable marketing mix as defined later in this section.

Target Markets

The consumer market is far too wide a term to be of any practical use to a marketing department. If market research has been carried out thoroughly it should be possible to define potential markets with a fair degree of accuracy, to establish the characteristics of these, and decide which segments are likely to prove the most suitable for achievement of the strategic objectives. It is usual today to divide any given product market into fairly well defined sub-markets, known as market segments. For example, there is a market for private cars but within this there are segments relating to company cars, to 'main' family cars, to family second cars and to cars owned and driven by the younger members of the family. Each of these market segments has its own particular characteristics and each can be further subdivided. The company car segment is made up of cars available in a pool for use by defined groups of employees, cars allowed to individual employees for company business and for family use. This last segment can be further subdivided into 'executive' cars and cars for use by others, such as middle management and sales or technical staff.

There are many ways of defining market segments, and companies will choose whatever method best suits their products and marketing methods. Almost all methods, however, will be associated with price differences. People are likely to be prepared to spend more on a main family car than on a second car. Firms sending senior staff on overseas visits will be less price conscious and more concerned with times and facilities than individual tourists. Virtually every market will contain groups which are less concerned with price than others. This is not just a matter of income differences, though these, of course, are important, but it also results from differing attitudes to the product. An older person, for example, whose main household companion is a dog, is likely to wish to spend more on feeding this companion than will a younger family where the dog has to compete within the household budget with the demands of several children and the upkeep of a house. In this case the gross family income may be a poor guide to willingness to spend on pet food.

A company introducing a new product may have as its main target the largest and potentially the most profitable market segment but be unwilling to launch the product immediately into this segment because of production and other costs. Initially it may seek to gain acceptance of the product in that (smaller) segment which is prepared to pay an above average price and which is more concerned with an image of affluent or luxury consumption than with price. Introduction at the 'top end' of the market has a number of advantages. Initial production is on a smaller scale so the financial risks of the new product launch are reduced. People with more money available for consumption are usually more willing to experiment with new products. To be seen as one of the first to discover something new may carry desired social prestige. Most important of all it is much easier to widen the appeal of a product which has been perceived as a 'luxury' product than it is to raise the status of a product which has been perceived as 'cheap'. Most widely accepted products (both goods and services) have made the progression from initial association with luxury to mass demand. Packaged holiday tours, bingo, snooker, cigarettes, coffee and even tea have made this progression at various times in the past. You can probably think of many other examples. Consequently, moving from one segment to another, or broadening-modifying the product range to cover more segments as the product gains acceptance in one, may be part of the overall, long-term marketing strategy.

The marketing mix

Having identified and selected the desired target market segment(s) the marketing department has to choose its package of marketing instruments in order to implement its strategy. This package relates to those influences on demand over which the company has some degree of control. They are the **product price**, the **product features** as presented to the market, the **promotional** and advertising methods and levels to be employed and the **channels of distribution** to be employed. This last is sometimes referred to as **place**, so that you can remember these four elements of the **marketing mix** as the four **p**s.

The term 'mix' is important because all four elements have to be fully integrated to make a harmonious marketing pattern. The elements must not clash otherwise the image that is to be projected will be shattered and cannot be expected to make a successful impact on the target market. If, for example, the product is to be launched with an image of high quality, to appeal to the market segment prepared to pay above average prices, then the price must be at the top end of market expectations. At the same time the product must convey the impression of quality and, preferably, be of above average quality. This quality must be reflected in the packaging. Buyers do not believe that a product is of high quality if it is distributed in inferior packaging. For some products labels can be important. This applies particularly to those which stand alongside competing brands on superstore shelves. The distinctive bottle shape and label of Croft Original Sherry played a significant part in its marketing success. The marketing campaigns which helped to establish this product as a brand leader contain some valuable lessons in effective marketing. The luxury image was carried through the price - at the upper end of the market range, the packaging through the bottle shape and label, which were similar to an older brand of Croft port which already had a reputation of quality. These elements were reinforced by a series of television advertisements featuring Bertie Wooster and Jeeves, to convey a further impression of quality and luxury in a humorous and light hearted way, while satirising the snob element of sherry drinking. This product, when launched, was new in the sense that it introduced a sweet sherry that looked like a dry sherry. Market research had established that most British people preferred a sweet sherry but had been brought up to believe that it was 'socially correct' to ask for, and be seen to be drinking ,a dry sherry. Before the launch of this product sweet sherries marketed in Britain were dark coloured and dry sherries were pale coloured. By choosing Croft Original, people could enjoy the kind of sherry they liked without social discrimination! Moreover, as sweet sherry had long been regarded as inferior to dry, the whole marketing stress on luxury and quality was designed to overturn this view for the Croft brand, while reinforcing it for the older (dark coloured) rivals. The whole well researched and managed marketing campaign was extremely successful and repays close study by any serious student of marketing.

Although all the elements in the marketing mix must make a coherent pattern and while attention must be paid to each, different companies tend to rely on the individual elements to different degrees. This can be accounted for to some extent by the differing characteristics of different products but also by the different approaches and past experiences of the companies themselves. While not wishing, at this stage, to go into too much detail it is useful to examine very briefly some attitudes to the various elements in the marketing mix.

Product characteristics and quality

For consumer non-durables, such as foods, most producers seek to identify those features which attract consumers, to emphasise these and to remove or disguise any features that are believed to repel consumers. Much use, therefore, is made of artificial colourings and flavourings though today, this is be balanced against concerns over possible health hazards associated with some of the 'additives'. For non-durables the question of reliability and proven quality becomes rather more important. In the early 1960s some British motor trade manufacturers took the deliberate decision to reduce expenditure on quality testing, judging it to be less expensive and as effective to deal generously with consumer complaints as and when they arose. They failed to foresee the long-term damage to the reputation of British motor manufacturers caused by this policy. They also probably underestimated the readiness of disgruntled buyers to complain, the cost and inconvenience of having faults rectified and overestimated the ability of retailers to handle customer complaints in ways that left customers satisfied. In contrast to this, Japanese motor manufacturers, conscious of the old image of Japanese goods as cheap imitations of European products, were anxious to ensure that their cars would quickly gain a reputation of reliability and value for money in European markets. In support of this deliberate marketing strategy they paid very great attention to quality control and product inspections so that, in this market at least, it is the Japanese products that are gaining a reputation for high quality while British products are finding it difficult to overcome the much less enviable reputation earned in the 1960s and 1970s.

All virtues, of course, can be taken to excess. It is not always desirable that products should be of the highest quality. If, for example, the manufacturers of children's shoes insisted on the highest standards of durability, their products would become more expensive and parents would be tempted to keep children wearing shoes that have been outgrown, causing serious damage to children's feet. Quality in this product would be associated more with ensuring that shoes were available in a full range of fittings, that they were made sufficiently robust to last for the length of time that a child could be expected to remain at one size and that shoes were sold by trained retail staff, aware of the dangers to the young of wearing ill fitting products.

Price

The price of any successful product must be acceptable to buyers and be sufficient to meet supply costs and provide reasonable profits to suppliers. There is a long running debate among economists over the principles and procedures employed by those firms which have sufficient market power to be able to choose prices for their products. It is sometimes argued that prices are determined by production costs and that producers use other marketing methods to create the level of market demand to ensure that they attain their profit targets.

In fact no producer can ignore the relationship between demand and price but, as shown in Unit 7, price is only one of the influences on demand and its importance relative to the other influences varies from one product to another. The strength of the price influence can be measured by estimating the product's **price elasticity of demand**. This is a measure of a good's sensitiveness to price changes found by dividing the **proportional change in quantity demanded** by the **proportional change in price**. It is important to understand the difference between proportional and absolute change. For instance, if a firm increases a product's price from £10 to £11 the absolute change is £1 but the proportional change is 1/10. If the price of another product priced at £5 is increased to £6 the absolute increase is also £1 but, in this case, the proportional increase is 1/5. A £1 change from £5 is proportionally twice as great as a £1 change from £10.

If the result dividing the proportional change in quantity by the proportional change in price is greater than one, e.g. if the quantity change is proportionally greater than the price change, then demand for the good is said to be **price elastic**. If the result is less than one, i.e. if the quantity change is proportionally less than the price change then we say that demand for the good is **price inelastic**. If the proportional changes are the same the value for price elasticity of demand is, of course, one and demand for the good is said to have unitary price elasticity. Because the changes are usually in opposite directions - a **price rise** normally brings about a **fall** in quantity demanded - the measure should be preceded by a negative sign but this is ignored when deciding whether demand is price elastic or inelastic.

The more elastic the demand for any good the more likely is it that companies will stress price advantages in their marketing mix. The demand for individual brands is normally more price elastic than that for the product as a class, but this still does not mean that companies will engage in price competition. Where a high proportion of supply is dominated by a few large companies, especially where these companies sell under several different brand names, a price reduction for any one brand is likely to lead to a similar reduction in the prices of other brands, with the result that there is no significant change in the market share of each of the main brands but all suppliers enjoy less revenue. As their costs will have stayed unchanged this means that the profits of individual suppliers will fall.

Thus, when the demand for products is price inelastic, or when market supply is dominated by a few large firms the price to the final customer is often given a fairly low priority in the marketing mix and other, non-price elements are given more emphasis.

TEST YOUR UNDERSTANDING

8   Describe the various market segments which you believe exist in the market for rail passenger travel.
9   What changes have taken place in the characteristics of the demand for wine over the past two decades or so? How do you think these changes are likely to have affected strategies for marketing wine?
10 For which, if any, of the following products is demand price elastic? What further information would you need before recommending a supplier to base marketing strategy on price advantage?

Product A, for which demand rose 15 per cent after a price reduction from £5 to £4 per unit.
Product B, for which a price rise of 10 per cent resulted in an increase in quantity sold per week from 2000 units to 2500 units.
Product C, for which a price rise of one twentieth failed to change monthly sales revenue.

Advertising and product promotion

Managerial attitudes to advertising

The cost of advertising is one of the costs of business activity. If a firm is seeking to maximise profits then we would expect it to spend on advertising up to the point where the net additional revenue resulting from advertising just equalled the last item of advertising expenditure. This is simply an application to advertising of the normal rule, that profits are maximised when marginal revenue is equal to marginal cost.

In practice there is little evidence that firms do consciously seek to achieve profit maximising levels of advertising. Indeed not all advertising is linked to a specific sales effort, so that it is often extremely difficult to measure the results of any given item or set of items of advertising expenditure. In the absence of any clear cut yardstick of spending it has been found that firms use a variety of methods of determining their advertising budgets.

Percentage of sales revenue

This is a simple, easy to calculate and understand method of deciding how much to spend on advertising. It also, on the face of it, links expenditure to the level of sales and it appears to suggest that the more successful the advertising the more money will be devoted to it. However, closer examination also suggests that this approach is not entirely logical. If sales start to fall then the firm will advertise **less** even though a decline in sales might be taken as evidence that **more**, rather than **less**, marketing effort was desirable. Similarly, if sales are rising the firm will advertise more, in defiance of the normal concept of diminishing marginal returns. Recognising that sales are normally considered to be the result rather than the cause of advertising some firms base their budgets on anticipated rather than past revenue, but there is no guarantee that anticipations will be achieved or that, if achieved, they can be attributed to the chosen advertising spending.

Managerial bargaining

It can be argued that once the firm has achieved a minimum level of profit, sufficient to meet the expectations of shareholders and the institutions of the finance market, the various specialist managers will seek to maximise their various spending budgets in order to increase their own status and rewards within the organisation. This view suggests that the marketing or sales manager will seek the largest possible advertising budget in negotiation with the finance manager and other, competing managers of spending departments. If this is the approach then spending is not directly linked either to sales or to profits though presumably the sales manager will have to try and justify his claim to finance allocation on the basis of benefits to the firm. To what extent such claims are likely to be based on evidence that any given level of expenditure will produce a foreseeable increase in profit is rather doubtful. It seems more probable that managerial utility is identified with the size of the spending budget achieved and that budget allocations are the result of inter managerial bargaining.

Parity with competition

There is some academic support for the view that changes in market shares of sales can be linked to changes in the market shares of advertising. If, for example, firm A manages to increase its share of total market advertising by, say, 10 per cent, it can expect to increase its share of total market sales, if not by 10 per cent, then by a significant proportion of 10 per cent. However, this assumes that competing firms do not either increase their own advertising by an amount sufficient to restore the former position or reply to firm A's advertising initiative by some other strategy such as a price cut, or by increased incentives to distributors.

Observation of consumer markets in which advertising is a major element in the marketing mix of all the major suppliers, suggests that any attempt by one firm to increase its share of market advertising will be met by a corresponding increase on the part of all the others, so that the original position is roughly restored. Firms appear to react to individual advertising initiatives in much the same way as they react to price initiatives, e.g. any attempt to steal an advantage is quickly countered while a move that appears to leave the individual firm exposed (a price rise, or cut in advertising spending) will not be copied unless it is taken as part of an agreed, negotiated (collusive) strategy. Firms certainly watch each other's marketing moves extremely closely and respond to any move thought likely to influence market sales shares. This is evident from observing the advertising of major consumer product firms in oligopolistic markets.

Responding to the moves of market rivals by 'tit for tat' movements in advertising implies a clear danger that advertising expenditure is subject to a 'ratchet effect', in that spending tends to rise but not fall. In some cases advertising appears to have become a defensive strategy intended not only to maintain market share in the face of constant pressure from market rivals but also to erect a barrier against potential new entrants to the market. Any new entrant to the market would have to match existing suppliers' heavy spending on advertising. Assuming that the existing suppliers already promote a range of brands of varying prices and appeals, to cover all segments of the market, the chance of a new entrant picking up a significant share of sales simply by offering an extra brand is small if the newcomer has no genuine innovation to offer.

Advertising to achieve specific objectives

This assumes that it is possible to make some estimate of the effect of a particular kind of advertising campaign. This is feasible where a particular sales approach is used to sell a product over a specified period. If, for example, a college wishes to recruit a target number of new students to a particular course it may have calculated from previous experience that a given number of local press advertisements will produce n enquiries of which, say, 20 per cent will become fee paying recruits to the course. Thus, on the basis of past trends the college should be able to calculate the number of advertisements needed to produce a given number of recruits. A similar approach can be adopted to mail order shots made to sell specific products. One weakness of this approach is the implication that any given level of advertising expenditure will produce a particular ratio of sales and new turnover so that insufficient thought is given to the quality of the product and of the advertising. The more carefully designed and targeted the advertising the more effective it is likely to be. The better the product the more effective the advertising is likely to become as the reputation of the product spreads. No amount of advertising will maintain long-term sales of a bad product once its poor reputation has become well-established.

Further aspects of advertising

Many observers have argued that the modern advertising industry offers substantial advantages to large firms and helps them to preserve their market power, thus becoming a powerful barrier against the entry of new competition to many markets. In support of this view we can point to:

* **The economies of scale in advertising**
  There are two aspects to the cost of advertising. One is the total or absolute cost of a given campaign. To launch a new consumer product with any hope of achieving support from the major retail superstores or national chain stores a firm is likely to have to commit itself to an advertising budget measured in millions as opposed to thousands of pounds. Only very large firms can contemplate a major campaign on this scale. A firm only able to afford a modest budget is unlikely to achieve national sales unless it can achieve marketing support from another direction. The other aspect of advertising cost is what can be termed 'exposure cost', i.e. the average cost of a campaign per person exposed to the advertising message. If a campaign costs £200 000 and its message reaches 400 000 people then the exposure cost is 50p per person. In contrast, a local campaign costing £5000 might reach only 5000 people and thus have an exposure cost of double that amount. In practice most advertisers are concerned not just with exposure to people in general but to those likely to be interested in the product advertised, who have the means to buy it and who could, therefore, be considered to be potential buyers of the product. A great deal of effort is now put into the task of identifying these potential buyers and in targeting the advertising directly to them. Much modern market research is concerned with identifying different segments of the market and discovering their characteristics, interests and what motivates them to buy one product rather than another. There is a greater recognition of the difference between advertising and effective advertising. Side by side with exposure cost advertisers set response rates. The most important cost, therefore, may not be either the total nor the exposure but the cost per response. It must, of course, be recognised that not all responses are converted into sales but a low conversion rate may have far wider causes than ineffective advertising. The product itself may be at fault, or the distribution channel, or simply the handling of those who do respond. However, without response there are unlikely to be any sales and response rate is one of the most useful measures of the effectiveness of any advertising campaign directed towards specific sales objectives. Once again large firms tend to have an advantage in commissioning or obtaining the benefits of market research. This can be costly but the cost can be recovered in savings on the actual cost of advertising and in obtaining more effective advertising. This is the reason why there is a value in lists of people who can be assumed to have an interest in a particular product. Many people have become

aware of the practice of selling lists through receiving direct mail from investment brokers after buying shares in a privatisation issue. You will notice that most of the high cost television advertising, particularly that showing at peak viewing times, is for general consumer products such as soap powders, the lower priced family cars, convenience and pet foods in which most households can be assumed to have an interest. The development of international markets in a growing number of consumer goods is giving further help to large firms able to afford a high cost campaign. Anyone who has lived or travelled in several countries in Western Europe or North America will have noticed that some advertising films are shown in different countries with very little modification beyond changing the language where necessary. If you observe some of the advertising for the most common products you will see that 'acted sketches' often tend to give way to silent scenes with 'voice overs' or to cartoon sketches. One reason for this is to make it easier to modify the film for use in different countries. Voice overs and cartoon scripts can be changed from one language to another more effectively than an actor's lines. The ability to use the one film in several countries brings down the exposure cost of the campaign very substantially. Consequently the large multinational can produce high quality advertising film, perhaps using very expensive film, stage or television stars, to a degree that is beyond the resources of smaller companies.

- **Some economic consequences of large scale advertising**
  The cost structure of advertising, with its substantial economies of scale and benefits to large firms, tends to reinforce the market power of large, established firms, creating a substantial entry barrier to new competition and, consequently, encourages the trend towards highly concentrated oligopolies. What you believe to be the effects of this depends on how you view the drift towards oligopoly in business markets. This raises important issues concerning the nature of both actual and potential competition and the degree of contestability of markets. These issues are beyond the scope of this course but at this stage you should be starting to reflect on the nature and strength of the competitive forces facing business firms and the way in which they use advertising. By now you will have recognised that advertising can have a double function of being both an aid to marketing - part of the total marketing mix - and a device to reduce the pressure of competition and preserve an established firm's power over the market. We can see this double function at work in washing powder advertisements. This market is dominated by two large multinational companies. Each markets a range of brands with new brands being added from time to time and advertising concentrated on just one or two brands at any particular time. Washing powder is not a technically very advanced product. It can be made at fairly low cost on a small scale. As a product it is not very responsive to price within the range at which it is usually sold. It is generally believed that the two dominating suppliers are able to maintain their market power largely through their marketing strategy with the high place given to large scale advertising. This ensures that any new firm must either develop an entirely new marketing strategy or be willing to incur the costs of heavy advertising. The costs and risks of entry are, therefore, very high. The rewards, unless an entrant were rapidly able to take a major market share, are not very attractive. The manufacturer's profit per packet is not thought to be very high. The two established manufacturers depend on very high turnover and sales volume. Given these market conditions it is not too difficult to see why the structure of this market has not changed materially for many years.

- **Advertising as a product**
  Some economists have pointed out that advertising itself has a degree of consumer utility. This simply recognises that many people enjoy advertisements for their own sake. To some extent advertising is a part of the entertainment industry. Some of the classic advertising campaigns have become part of the cultural history of the Western

market economies. Among these most would probably put the Lever Bros **Bubbles** soap advertisements early this century, the **Bisto Kids** and the **Ovaltinies** of Radio Luxembourg in the 1930s, the Guinness **Toucan Bird** of the 1950s, Esso's **Tiger in the tank**, and perhaps British Telecom's **Busby** of the 1970s. You can, no doubt, suggest your own list of favourite advertisements. There are, however, dangers in this kind of success where the advertisement becomes more memorable and successful than the product it is advertising. Esso's tiger campaign was not believed to have justified its costs in terms of increased sales of Esso petrol, partly because it was quickly countered by Shell with its matching money game imported from the USA. Busby served to irritate people waiting to have a telephone connected to their home or to have a faulty line repaired. Nevertheless the enjoyment derived from inspired advertising should not be overlooked when we encounter criticisms that much large scale advertising represents a waste of scarce resources which would otherwise be used to improve the general human condition. The advertising industry has also done much to raise the level of communication technology. The need to put across a coherent message in a few seconds of television exposure or in a small space on a crowded newspaper journal has led to increased skills of photography, film making and print display. These skills are now available to other industries, including education, though educators in general are not notably swift in learning them.

- **External costs and benefits of advertising**
  An external cost is one that is borne by someone who does not receive any direct benefit from the economic activity concerned. An external benefit is one that is received by someone who has not directly contributed to the cost of the activity. Anyone who has been exposed to the noise of the street microphones in a French city during its commercial week probably feels that a noise pollution cost is being paid without any obvious benefit. However, there are some socially significant externalities associated with advertising in Britain. Most of the national press and much local press operates on the basis that at least half the production cost is paid for from advertising. There is pressure from government to increase the proportion of total television production costs that are met from advertising revenue. This gives very great potential power over important channels of communications to large scale business advertisers. The public receives the benefit of relatively low cost press and television services but with the danger that important areas of legitimate public interest may be ignored for fear of upsetting powerful controllers of advertising spending. Any journal that fails to obtain its share of advertising revenues is virtually doomed. There is a similar element of subsidy to the performing arts. Actors and actresses who can earn substantial fees from work in advertising can afford to take low paid stage work or to 'rest' from time to time. On the other hand it is the best known and most successful actors who can gain most from working in advertising so that little encouragement is given to other, lesser-known people. Whether this kind of financial support from the advertising industry is in the best long term interests of the arts is a matter of some debate. On the whole, economists tend to prefer the people who obtain benefits from an activity to pay the full costs of producing that activity unless there is a strong social or ethical case to the contrary, e.g. the undoubted public goods of sanitation, general health, defence and law and order preservation. Any attempt to apply the principles and concepts of economics and business practice to the arts tends to invite charges of Philistinism from those who regard themselves as custodians of genuine culture, holding firm to a conviction that their own subjective, value judgements are automatically superior to any held by those not belonging to their own particular clique.

There are many aspects to advertising and the growth of the advertising industry and this unit has only touched on those of most relevance to the business organisation. For most marketing managers decisions of how to advertise, which media and methods to use and how much to spend on advertising as opposed to other elements in the marketing mix, have to be taken against a background of practices within the industry, the actions of competitors and past attitudes and strategies adopted by the firm itself. It is often very difficult to judge the success or return achieved from any given amount of advertising expenditure. Nevertheless, in the long run advertising has to play its part in the total product and marketing strategy of the company and must support its objectives. There is constant pressure to improve the effectiveness of spending on advertising. For the people who work in the industry success can be very rewarding but it can be very short-lived.

TEST YOUR UNDERSTANDING

11 To what extent do you think advertising a service requires different techniques from those needed for advertising a physical product?
12 Examine the advantages and disadvantages of sport sponsorship as a method of advertising, from the point of view of the advertiser.
13 For the most part British advertising for consumer products has been manufacturer rather than retailer led. Suggest possible reasons for this. What evidence is there that this tradition may be changing?

Channels of distribution and sales management

The choice of distribution channel is a matter of marketing strategy. Making the most effective use of whatever method or methods have been selected is a matter of sales management. The two are, of course, closely linked. If the marketing manager believes that developments influencing the market are tending to favour a change in strategy it is the manager's function to ensure that such changes are made. The salesperson in the field may be too personally involved with the existing connections to recognise the need for or benefits likely to arise from basic changes.

Distribution choices

The choice facing a producer often lies between communicating directly with the customer, controlling the physical distribution of the product, and reliance on specialist distributors, communicating with them rather than with the ultimate buyer.

Through much of the 1960s and 1970s the trend appeared to be for producers to move closer to the final buyer, particularly in consumer goods markets. There were two sets of pressures for this. On the one hand it was the producer who was making the largest financial stake and taking the biggest risks in setting up large scale production. Firms could not afford to invest millions of pounds in a new product and then leave its actual selling to smaller firms taking very few risks in the distribution system. Moreover, before taking the decision to make the large scale investment, the producers had usually spent large sums on market research and consequently felt that they had a better knowledge of the market than distributors who frequently had only a partial knowledge of their own local market.

There was also pressure resulting from the condition of the distributive trades in the 1960s. Technical and managerial changes came first to manufacturing and spread relatively slowly to distribution. When senior managers in manufacturing examined both the structure of distribution and the managerial structures within distribution organisations they were often less than impressed. To the new breed of professional managers in the large manufacturing companies distribution firms often seemed far too small, far too amateur in their management and grossly under-financed.

There were some manufacturers who were content with the traditional patterns of distribution. They preferred to be the large suppliers dominating a market for a product which was sold to the public through a network of small distributors and corner shops. The dominance of firms such as Cadbury Bros over this type of structure constituted a powerful entry barrier against potential competition. Modern firms seeking entry to the Japanese consumer markets find very similar barriers.

In most markets, however, there was a tendency for manufacturing groups to seek to gain more control over distribution, usually by taking over or gaining a financial interest in distribution organisations. At the same time the structure of the distribution trades changed. Most of the old, small, independent wholesale firms disappeared or were taken over by larger groups. High streets became shopping precincts and local retail firms retreated before the march of the national multiples. Supermarkets replaced corner shops and were in turn largely replaced by superstores. Out of town shopping areas appeared and these are now developing into shopping parks containing a wide range of large stores and small, specialist shops.

By the 1980s it was becoming clear that combinations of manufacturing and distribution groups were not always very successful. The most efficient size for manufacturing organisations was rarely the most efficient size for distributors. Management of distribution was found to require different specialised skills from management of manufacturing. Vertical integration, the term given to mergers of firms at different stages of the production and distribution process within the same industrial sector, was found to lead to some troublesome inefficiencies. Business managers and their financial advisers began to rediscover the virtues of one of the oldest of economic concepts - specialisation - now termed 'concentration on core activities'. The tendency for some manufacturing to be re-located overseas has further reinforced pressures to separate the functions of production and distribution between different specialist groups.

Manufacturers are still deeply involved in marketing, especially in market research, advertising and product promotion but the actual distribution appears to be returning to specialist distribution organisations which control the actual sale to the final consumer. This does not prevent a considerable degree of cooperation between producers (manufacturers and importers) and retail stores. Manufacturers' representatives are often allowed into stores to assist in setting up displays, maintaining shelf stocks and promoting the product at the point of sale. In some stores manufacturers rent space to establish, in effect, their own shops under the roof of the store and using the store's administrative services.

It is not necessary for producers to rely on one channel of distribution only. They may sell to wholesalers, to large retail stores and direct to the public, provided they can do so without directly competing with their own distributors. If they feel it to be in their best interests to sell through a range of different outlets they will do so as long they feel the benefits to be greater than the costs and problems generated.

Sales management

Sales management has the function of ensuring that whatever channels of distribution are chosen these are efficiently managed. Communications with distribution organisations are extremely important and the maintenance of effective communications, together with maintaining and encouraging increased support for the supplier, normally requires the influence of sales staff. Successful selling usually depends on a combination of technical competence, e.g. knowledge of the product, its capabilities, strengths and weaknesses, with the kind of personality that engenders liking, respect and, above all, trust. Sales staff have to build up a relationship with their customers. The salesperson is the supplier as far as the customer is concerned and the customer relies on the personal link with the salesperson to represent the buyer's interests within the supply organisation.

Managing a sales department normally involves selecting, training, supervising and monitoring the work of the sales staff, often in co-operation with the personnel department. It also involves ensuring that orders are handled efficiently and that any queries or complaints from customers are handled effectively. Sales departments will seek new outlets within the company's marketing policies and strategies and close any outlets which are no longer contributing to profits and are believed to be incapable of being restored to profitability. If sales are declining from identifiable sources the reasons for the decline will be investigated and corrective measures taken where possible. Sales staff are also expected to contribute to the marketing department's awareness of changing trends within the market and, of course knowledge of competitors' strategies, their perceived successes and failures.

As sales methods and channels change so too must sales personnel, who are likely to require re-training as much as technical staff. A training manager for a leading life assurance company has pointed out that different sales methods were required on the part of staff servicing 'tied' agents from those needed by staff selling to independent financial agents. Sales people are among the first of those who have to adapt to the changing market environment, but the one thing that never changes is the need for a salesperson to have the ability to build the essential bridge of trust between supplier and buyer. Without this trust there can be no lasting market relationship and the trust must extend to both the technical competence and the personal integrity of the seller.

By now you should have a fuller understanding of the difference between marketing and selling. The marketing manager is concerned with the broad sweep of developments within the market and seeks to find out how the company can profit from these developments and what changes it has to make to extend its influence within the changing market. The sales manager is concerned with the people who interact with and depend on each other in the market and is closely involved with the interplay of personal relationships and the effectiveness of individuals in their work. Both are necessary to successful distribution.

TEST YOUR UNDERSTANDING

14 The qualities required for selling do not necessarily make a good marketing person. Explain and discuss this statement.
15 Hoover has been one of many companies which, when it was a new company launching a new product, sold direct to the public. When, however, its product had become established, it sold through the established distributive trade organisations. Suggest reasons for this tendency.

NOTES TO QUESTIONS

Question 1
A supporter of the view that consumer demand is manipulated to satisfy the profit aspirations of large companies would argue that canned pet food is a largely unnecessary product and is probably intrinsically inferior to the earlier diet of cheap fresh food and household scraps. Demand for branded, canned foods has been built up by advertising, much of it implying that a regular diet of the brand will produce a healthy animal, comparable to the prize show animals that are frequently used in the advertisements. The industry that has been created by these means is dominated by two firms, Dalgety-Spillers and Mars, the owner of Pedigree Pet Foods. These two firms account for over 80 per cent of sales of canned cat food and dog food. Another company, the American Quaker Oats, supplies a significant proportion of the remainder. The two major

suppliers maintain their dominance by large scale advertising and by promoting a range of brands, offered at a range of difference prices covering the cheap to the 'luxury' ends of consumer demand. It would be extremely difficult and costly for a completely new firm to challenge this dominance with any hope of success.

This analysis could be challenged on the grounds that no consumer market can ever be created without substantial customer support. Canned pet food has grown up on the back of two important social trends. These are the growth in pet ownership arising out of rising living standards, improvements in housing provision for the mass of the population and the growth in numbers of older people living longer lives after their children have set up their own homes. The other trend is the increased reliance on convenience foods for humans and this naturally has a parallel in the desire to have convenience foods for pets. Fewer people cook meals for themselves or for their pets. They have less time than in the past for cooking and the modern home does not lend itself to harbouring the kind of cooking smells that used to be associated with, say, boiling fish for cats or cheap meat for dogs. It might be said, therefore, that the latent demand for canned pet foods was already strong when it was stimulated by advertising and the marketing techniques developed by the large multinational food producers. A market can only develop if it is in tune with fundamental social trends. Suppliers simply encourage and speed up these trends. They do not create them in the first place.

Suppliers would also argue that they are competition with other foods and other methods of preparing and marketing canned pet foods so that they can only continue to sell their products as long as these meet a genuine consumer need.

Question 2

This statement reflects an attitude which was very common at one time and can still sometimes be found in a few firms. It shows almost total ignorance of the concept of marketing and assumes that a 'good' salesperson can and should be prepared to sell anything that the firm chooses to produce. A firm which adopts this attitude is unlikely to survive very long in the modern business environment.

This is not to deny the importance of efficient selling to the marketing process. The salesperson is as essential to marketing as the machine is to manufacturing production. Like production where the appropriate machine has to be fitted to the job in hand, the salesperson has to be chosen and trained for the particular task allotted within the marketing and distribution process. Many companies have had to recognise that a person good at servicing one kind of marketing is not always successful at a completely different kind.

Marketing, therefore, involves not only identifying a gap or opportunity in the market place which the company has the resources to fill or seize but also devising and implementing a selling and distribution strategy to assist this achievement. Marketing and production are in partnership to help the company to meet its objectives successfully. Nothing sells itself but on the other hand no one can continue indefinitely selling a product that serves no useful function in the market place.

It must also be admitted that there is an implication of dishonest selling in the statement. Life assurance selling in the past has been guilty of many errors, including making false claims for future returns, suppressing the fact that much better products were available, putting victims under intense pressure to take up policies they did not need or which did not adequately meet their needs. Not only did very few of the rogue companies and personnel prosper in the long run but their activities have given the product a bad name which still lingers in the public mind. This continues to add to the difficulties faced by a more reputable business today.

Question 3

'Random' does not mean 'casual'. Far from it. The idea of a random sample is that there should be no bias in the selection of individuals for 'examination'. The sample should be as closely representative as possible of the total population from which it has been selected, so that information gained from the sample will accurately reflect the characteristics of the target population as a whole. This usually means that great care has to be taken to ensure that the sample is representative. Once the sample has been selected interviewers are required to make every effort to interview the people selected. If, for example, a person is not at home when the interviewer calls it is not admissible to interview the person next door.

An apparently 'random' selection could, in practice, effectively eliminate a high proportion of the target population and produce a very false impression. Simply to go into the street on a Monday morning would rule out large numbers of people who are working and whose incomes would enable them to buy the product. Those likely to be interviewed would probably include a high proportion of people who did not work for one reason or another and who, therefore, were less likely to be potential buyers of family cars. The choice of a single time and place would thus introduce considerable bias into the sample and make it unrepresentative of the desired target population of car buyers. There is also an arbitrary choice of the number of people to be interviewed. In fact the number needed to give a statistically significant representation of the target population depends on the size of that population and on certain other factors. The sample size has to be calculated with some accuracy and once chosen should not be changed during the survey.

Sample selection and the administration of interviews are specialised skills to assist those who need information. Further information about samples and the collection of data can be found in any good book on statistical method.

Question 4

The reason is again related to the question of bias. The response rate to postal questionnaires is always low as many people take no notice of requests to fill in forms, or put the form on one side intending to deal with it 'later' - and then forget about it. There is no means of knowing the motivation or seriousness of those who do return the forms. Some are likely to be filled in carelessly. Some will contain intentional misinformation, or inaccuracies, because of failure to understand the questions. A high proportion of those which are completed carefully and seriously will be from people who have an interest in the result of the survey, perhaps because they have strong views about the topic.

As a result, the findings of postal questionnaires are notoriously unreliable and postal surveys are only worthwhile under special circumstances. For ordinary market research purposes they are a waste of resources.

This does not mean that personal interview methods are always successful but they do have a better chance of success, especially if interviewers are well trained, are aware of the dangers of introducing bias into findings, understand the reason for the survey and are subject to work checks and supervision. Worthwhile surveys are not, therefore, cheap but the more care devoted to any survey, the more likely that its findings are reasonably accurate.

Question 5

Economists suggest that the demand for any product is a function of: the product's own price, other prices, spendable income of potential buyers, market size, the marketing effort of the seller, the availability and cost of money and credit, taste (buyer attitudes), expectations of future changes in any of these influences and any special influences relating to the particular product.

We can use this list to examine the demand conditions for personal computers. One immediate problem is that the term 'personal computer' is used in two senses, the home computer used mainly for pleasure and the individual computer used for business purposes. There are, therefore, two separate markets, each subject to rather different influences.

The home computer market has generally proved disappointing to manufacturers.

After the first novelty and enthusiasm sales have dropped away. People have discovered that a computer needs software and the price and availability of software has to be taken into account, as well as the price of the computer itself. Moreover much software requires some degree of knowledge and skill before it becomes useful. It is probable, therefore, that the normal influences of price, prices of other products (other than software) and income are not very powerful in the case of home computers. More important is the size of the market in the sense of the number of people who have some experience of computers, know their capabilities and limitations and who want them to fulfil definite purposes. This market is likely to grow steadily as computers become commonplace in business and education. On the other hand people are also aware that computer technology is still developing quite rapidly and they do not wish to buy something that will shortly be out-of-date. When computer technology settles and price changes become less frequent, with less expectation of future price reductions, then the demand for home computers is likely to behave more like the demand for other household durables. The business market is likely to be even less price sensitive than the home market. Business owners are more interested in the capabilities of machines and their software and their potential for earning revenue and reducing costs, than with relatively small differences in price. The size of the market is steadily growing as more people become 'computer literate' and as its benefits for the very small business are becoming more widely realised. Marketing the personal computer for business use involves a combination of producing software to meet real business needs, of traditional business advertising and of education through organising courses where managers and staff can learn how to use software for practical business purposes.

The business market also faces the problem of advancing technology, expectations that models will rapidly become out-of-date and that prices tomorrow may be more favourable than they are today. On the other hand inland revenue authorities are becoming conscious that computers have relatively short lives at present and suppliers are seeking to make models that can be updated in order to bring the computer's life closer to the timespan of other business equipment.

The market for personal computers is at an interesting stage where the product is still relatively new and constantly developing, and where demand conditions have not yet settled to a pattern that we might recognise as normal. This account of the market is not based on specific market research and you may wish to discuss a number of elements in the light of your own observation and experience.

Question 6

A product can continue to exist as long as there is sufficient demand for it. This demand will exist if the product meets contemporary wants in the community. Breakfast cereals found a mass market in the 1930s and continued to expand that market in the post war period of the 1950s and 60s. This was a period of very great social change during which family living patterns were largely transformed. The great mass of the working population inhabited the suburbs and had to travel to work. Increasing numbers of married women pursued careers and were cutting to the minimum time spent on traditional household duties, including meal preparation. Breakfast cereals were among the first convenience foods - they represented a satisfying meal that could be poured from a packet without any cooking or preparation.

Breakfast cereals also fitted another social and economic trend. Throughout the postwar period there has been a decline in the proportion of heavy manual work and an increase in office, clerical and similar work. Workers have not needed the heavy breakfasts that were traditional in farming families and which were carried into early urban life styles when families still remembered their old links with farming. For all these reasons, by the 1970s, the 'traditional English breakfast' had become little more than a tourist attraction for foreign visitors.

Most of the main brands of breakfast cereals which were common in the 1950s were still surviving in the 1980s. Manufacturers had also protected themselves by adding fresh brands to appeal to a range of tastes and incomes and to make entry to the market more difficult. Some of these have been deliberately geared or modified to fit modern healthfood fashions. The word 'sugar', for instance has been dropped in favour of 'honey'.

Nevertheless there are signs that a challenge has been made to the dominance of the main breakfast cereal manufacturers. There is clearly little immediate possibility of moving to a totally different style of breakfast but there is every possibility that the old type cereals may be replaced or seriously challenged by an equally convenient and simply but more interesting and varied kind of food. Muesli, for example, has fitted the trend towards contemporary health fashions but these can change quickly. However, the inroads made by the muesli brands suggest that consumers are now ready to consider a replacement for the old style breakfast cereals which could be approaching the stage where sales start a long term decline in North America and the UK. In contrast, sales appear to be rising in a number of countries and this suggests a marketing strategy based on looking for new geographical markets as well as on making further product modifications.

Question 7

Products do not simply arrive on the market. New products are the result of a period of research, both technical and marketing. A full product life cycle shows a pre-sales stage of Product Research and Development. Showing this emphasises the fact that firms have to make a conscious effort to bring products to the market and that during this period the firm will be incurring substantial expenditure with no revenue from the sales of products. It could also be argued that there is a direct link between the resources devoted to research and development and the future success of the product. The more thorough the research and development the greater the likelihood of developing a product that will fit the mood of the market and gain consumer acceptance. From a revenue point of view it has to be remembered that the cost of this period of research and development has to be set against the revenue received from sales. In practice, the profits from the successful products have to support the development of new products and not all of these are going to be successful. This, of course, has been the argument of drug companies when accused of making excessive profits from their major drugs. The costs of research and testing new medical drug development is very great and some are going to fail the tests. However, there has to be a reasonable relationship between these costs and profit levels. Research costs cannot become an excuse for exploitation of monopoly power.

Question 8

The following notes apply to the British market but are also likely to be relevant to other countries. The main line rail passenger services can be divided into two main market segments, inter-city services and commuter services between urban centres and suburban or satellite living areas. The inter-city services contain two segments, business travel and leisure travel. The London underground is a separate system providing commuter services and cross-city travel services for leisure and main line rail travellers.

These different market segments can be distinguished partly by time of travel, attitudes to price and freedom to use substitutes for travelling by rail, especially private car and coach services.

For the inter-city business traveller time and reliability are the most important qualities required. Separate facilities are desirable for the more senior business people and, within limits, demand is likely to be price inelastic as travel costs are a business expense. For longer inter-city routes the main competitor will be inland air services.

The inter-city leisure traveller has freedom to choose the time of travel and is more price conscious although, as income levels rise price concerns may give way to a desire for greater comfort as well as convenience, reliability and safety.

Demand for commuter services is price inelastic. Travellers have little choice and for many there will be little competition from public or private road transport because of lack of reliability, expense and the congested and dangerous state of inner city roads at the present time.

Cross-city leisure travellers, many of them overseas tourists, are also unlikely to be too price conscious. They will be concerned with convenience, comfort and safety.

Rail companies are likely to adapt their marketing mix to the different characteristics of the various segments and this is clear in their pricing policies, based on price differences according to the time of travel. The two class standard of travel has a long history in public transport. Stage coaches charged more for travel inside the coach than for travel outside, the latter being extremely uncomfortable and often dangerous, especially in bad weather. Early rail companies offered three classes of travel, third class being extremely rough. The two class system caters mainly for business travellers but also recognises that some leisure travellers are prepared to pay for a higher standard of comfort. In fact the difference in quality between first and second class travel no longer seems to justify the price differential. British Rail appears to be benefitting from very low price elasticity of demand and lack of effective competition for the business traveller over the main, medium distance, inter-city routes.

Commuter and London underground services offer little evidence that British Rail has yet felt it necessary to pay serious attention to marketing. Reliance is still in a high degree of demand price inelasticity and lack of effective competition. Demand for rail travel has increased as urban roads and motorways have become increasingly congested and dangerous.

If more competition could be developed and if British Rail were to become more market orientated greater attention would have to be paid to the characteristics of the different market segments.

Question 9

Again the following notes apply to the British market. In Britain the demand for wine has increased considerably and has spread to most income groups. In the 1950s demand was largely confined to the higher income groups and there was a great deal of snobbery and mystery associated with wine drinking. Wine was mostly sold in specialist shops which catered for a small, specialist group of local consumers. At that time it was considered that a good wine shop was denoted by the dust on the bottles - indicating that the wine was mature and had not been disturbed by recent handling.

The market has been transformed by both demand and supply changes. Demand has grown because of:

- Rising real incomes combined with falling real prices. In the early 1950s the price of a bottle of reasonable quality wine was around 20 per cent of the average national weekly wage. Today it is around 3 per cent and often less.
- Foreign travel, including cheap package tours to the Mediterranean, wine-growing countries has created a taste for ordinary table wines and shown British people that wine is a drink suitable for the average person.
- The economic and social emancipation of women has made the female taste a major influence on demand and many women prefer wine to the traditional English 'male' drink of beer.

At the same time supply has been influenced by:

- Changes in production technology enabling the wine growers to produce large quantities of wine of reasonably consistent quality, capable of being stored and transported for a reasonable period without damaging its quality.
- Changes in distribution channels, particularly the political decision to permit super-markets to have licences to sell alcohol during normal opening hours so that a bottle of wine could become just another item in the weekly shopping basket.
- Changes in the structure of the market so that supply has become dominated by the major brewery and retail groups which can make large scale contracts with growers,

maintain a degree of control over quality and keep distribution and storage costs to a minimum.

Marketing methods have been and continue to be transformed, along with the characteristics of the market. Wine is being marketed in much the same way as other grocery items which stand on superstore shelves. Considerable attention is being paid to packaging, especially bottle labels, as most wine is chosen on impulse at the time of purchase. The suppliers are researching market characteristics and gaining a clearer idea of the characteristics and identities of the various segments so that they can adapt the marketing mix to these. The distinction between supermarket 'plonk' and 'real wine' is growing less pronounced while much of the snobbery and deliberate mystery surrounding wine is fading. There are indications that some generally understood brand images are being developed, e.g. some of the main retail groups are marketing their own brands of 'claret'. Marketing of wine is at an interesting stage of development and you should watch how the major suppliers stress the various elements of the general marketing mix.

Question 10
Demand for product A is price inelastic because the proportional change in quantity (15 per cent) is less than the proportional change in price (20 per cent).

Demand for product B is price elastic because the proportional change in quantity demanded (25 per cent) is more than the proportional change in price (10 per cent).

Demand for product C has unit price elasticity because there is no change in total sales revenue. This indicates that the proportional change in quantity sold is the same as the proportional change in price.

On this information alone a price reduction would only be a serious possibility as a means of gaining marketing advantage in the case of product B. For products A and C a price reduction would reduce revenue and, almost certainly, profit.

For product B more needs to be known about the product and the position it has reached in the product life cycle, and more information about the structure of market supply would be needed. If the market is dominated by a few large firms which have already segmented the market and have a range of brands and prices to cover all the segments, there is unlikely to be any advantage in featuring a significant price reduction, as the other firms would follow and all would suffer reduced revenue and probably reduced profit. If, however, the market is more genuinely competitive, facing competition from new kinds of products, and if the supplier has technical or cost advantages denied to most other competitors, then stress could be placed on price reductions to gain increased market share or to frighten away less secure competition. Price reductions would also be part of a revised marketing mix following a decision to bring a product which has been successful at the top end of the market into mass production and distribution.

The main lesson to remember is that price is by no means the only consideration in marketing. It is just one element in the marketing mix and pricing decisions must form a part of the total marketing strategy.

Question 11
There are very many ways of advertising a physical product. In most cases these involve showing how a product can be used to make life more enjoyable or rewarding for the buyer. Advertisements can make the product easily recognisable and attractive. The advertising message can be linked with point of sale displays and people can usually be persuaded to come and see something working or being used.

It is rather more difficult to see a service actually being performed. There is no physical product to display and often the service involves protecting the consumer from something unpleasant that most people prefer not to have to think about. Examples include: death (life assurance); old age (pensions); paying taxes (accountancy); facing a legal charge (law services); illness (health insurance). The actual performance of the service is usually just a matter of office routine that hardly lends itself to dramatic photography and the 30 second action packed TV commercial.

If products can be readily compared then the advertising can stress price advantages - or show that quality may be more attractive than a small saving in price. A service such as insurance involves fulfilling a promise and it is not easy to show that one company's way of fulfilling a promise is superior to another's. At the same time the quality of any service depends almost entirely on the quality and training of the people giving that service. The personal qualities really required are integrity and administrative efficiency but these do not lend themselves readily to attractive advertising.

Because the actual service and its fulfilment do not lend themselves readily to advertising considerable attention is generally made to symbols so that the service can become identified with a concrete image, such as the Legal and General's umbrella. Sometimes the symbol becomes a person showing in a humorous way a characteristic which the advertiser wishes to attach to the service or the company giving that service. The bank manager in the cupboard was stressing the approachability of modern banking which had been suffering from its reputation for unfriendliness and inaccessibility, legacies of marble halls, massive counters and restricted banking hours, all found to repel the people who were turning to the more accessible building societies for their everyday financial services.

It is clear that services such as insurance and banking have been seeking to identify those aspects of their current, popular image that have tended to repel potential customers and in their advertising they have tried to reverse the image. Many still regard a bank as having little to offer the ordinary working person. To overcome this image a leading bank has sponsored a major football competition, football being the sport of the ordinary working person. Advertising a service, therefore, appears to be very much involved with attitude changing and image creation. Association with a physical object such as an umbrella or a black horse helps to overcome the abstract complexity of the product that is really being sold. If the image conveys an impression of something attractive and useful then this may well help to alter popular attitudes towards the service and the people providing that service.

Question 12

Association with a popular sport has many attractions for business organisations. If the sport is one that attracts media attention, and it these sports that tend to attract the most business advertising, there will be considerable exposure to the buying public. The name of the business firm is likely to become familiar to a mass audience. Few people outside the insurance industry had heard of the Cornhill until it sponsored a cricket series of test matches. Constant repetition of the phrase 'Cornhill test' was bound to increase awareness of the organisation's existence, as, of course, was the appearance of the name when matches were being televised.

Advertisers clearly hope that some of the qualities of the sport and sportspeople, will rub off on to the people providing the service. Companies employing most of their staff in offices are likely to be employing large numbers of unfit people. If a more attractive image of fitness seems desirable this may be achieved in some degree by association with the fit young sportspeople who practise the sport.

Another attraction of sport sponsorship may be that providing financial support to one of the popular sports is likely to be seen by the public as 'a good thing'. The company gains a reputation for performing a social duty when in fact it has simply re-directed part of its advertising budget. A further benefit has developed from some kinds of sponsorship. The company gains privileged access to some of the most sought after sporting events and is thus able to entertain clients, especially overseas clients, and impress them with impressions of the company's standing and influence.

There are, however, disadvantages and problems. Any disagreeable public image arising out of sporting activity is likely to attach itself to the senior management responsible for the company. When football started to attract adverse publicity because of crowd violence, business sponsors started to reduce the level of their commitments. At the same time there is no guarantee that people will pay much attention to the presence of the sponsoring company's senior staff at a sporting event when their attention is being held by the sport itself. The sport may fade in popularity and lose the attention of the media. This decline will transmit itself to the sponsoring company. Shareholders and customers who do not fully grasp the nature of marketing may resent the public display of company wealth at, say, a football match and seek to undermine the pricing structure of the organisation.

For marketing purposes sponsoring is really only worthwhile from the company's point of view where there is likely to be extensive media coverage to place the company's name before a wide public. In such cases costs are high and there is no satisfactory method of measuring the benefits achieved. Companies which have sponsored major sporting competitions and events are sometimes disappointed with the result and have felt that the cost was not justified. The rather hypocritical way in which some sections of sport management in the UK regard commercial sponsorship has led to some disillusionment. The reluctance to recognise that sport has become a major industry and the clinging remains of amateurism related to an outdated social class structure have too often meant that managers have tried to obtain finance from business while denying to firms the marketing opportunities that would justify expenditure to company shareholders.

In local markets it is common for small firms to sponsor local sporting and other events. Most business owners regard this cost as a contribution to the social life of the community without any significant marketing benefit. As the cost is borne by the owner-managers and benefits often directly received by employees and customers this activity does not involve any significant distortion in the use of resources. Few business owners object too strongly to making a small financial contribution to the community which has enabled them to build up and maintain a profitable business.

Question 13

Until at least the 1970s the structure of the British economy was such that manufacturing was dominated by large firms while distribution was still largely in the hands of smaller organisations. Until 1964 competition in the distributive trades was severely curtailed by the practice of resale price maintenance whereby manufacturers could determine the prices at which their products could be sold to the final customer. This practice was deliberately used to enable small retailers to survive, thereby checking the growth of the large stores which could afford to be more flexible in their pricing and other marketing strategies. Under these circumstances it was difficult for distributors to establish their own market identities and most of the nationally known brand labels were established and kept in force by manufacturer advertising. One exception to this general situation was the market in clothing - the 'rag trade' - which was traditionally supplied by large numbers of small, back street manufacturing firms. In this market, retailers such as Marks and Spencer with its St Michael brand label, were able to establish national identities. Some grocery chains such as Liptons and Maypole were also able to become household names in high streets which still contained large numbers of local family shops. Most national retailers advertised but Marks and Spencer did not and the achievement of this firm in building up such a major position in retailing with very little advertising is quite remarkable; few other organisations are able to boast a comparable success.

During the 1970s and 1980s, after the end of resale price maintenance, and aided by the marketing opportunities provided by commercial television, the social changes resulting from mass ownership of the motor car, the replacement of the high street with the central shopping precinct and the introduction of electronic equipment and professional management into the distributive trades, the structure of distribution underwent a profound change. Supermarket chains developed and entered a period of fierce competition based more on price and site location than on any serious attempt to establish national brand images. However, the war came to an end leaving only a small group of survivors, which started to change its marketing strategies. Competition has now moved to the capital market and it seems likely that a number of the survivors from earlier market competition will become the prey of the major multinational food and store groups. In this new market situation it seems probable that there will be increased influence from the North American experience where retailer own brands have been successful and are now well established. In most of the major stores own brands are now gaining shelf space from the manufacturer brands. Initially it is the smaller manufacturers that lose ground, unless they can secure contracts to produce for a major store. The retailer brands also make progress in those sectors such as wines, where few producers have been able to establish national or international names. The next stage is likely to involve attempts by some of the leading stores to challenge the manufacturers more vigorously and openly in those sectors where they still dominate. This is an area of considerable marketing interest and you should be alert for any developments as they emerge.

Question 14

Marketing covers a very wide area involving investigation of market trends and conditions, co-operating in product development and modification, formulating an appropriate marketing mix and monitoring the performance of the firm in the market. Consequently it embraces policy decisions and the selection of production, marketing and distribution strategy. In contrast, selling concerns the tactical measures taken to assist in achieving the firm's policy and strategic objectives.

Because the functions of marketing and selling are different the qualities required of the people performing those functions are also different. The salesperson has to accept the existing product and distribution systems and to work within the constraints these impose. To a great extent successful selling involves the projection of personality to influence the people who make up the distribution organisations from which the seller must obtain support. To the buyer the salesperson represents the supplier and in competitive markets buyers tend to support the people they like and feel they can trust. Where products are roughly similar, with no great difference in price or quality of service, the deciding factor is almost always the personality of the salesperson, who also represents the buyer within the organisation and seek to obtain the best available terms and conditions on behalf of the buyer.

The effective salesperson, therefore, does not question the product or the selling firm but puts both in the most favourable light possible to potential buyers. The sales manager's world is a very immediate one, dominated by this month's sales figures. The manager will, of course, act as an important channel of communication reporting buyers' views, competitors' actions and the general state of the market, but these can never be accepted as a reason for poor performance now.

A salesperson always has a contribution to make to the quality of service provided by the firm but for the most part has to accept the conditions that exist. It is not helpful to wish they were different. The marketing person does not accept these limitations. That person's concern is with the future, with ensuring that the firm is able to cope with change as it takes place and is ready for the future, without getting too far ahead. The marketing manager deals with market forces and trends rather than with individuals and cannot allow the overall view of a changing market structure to be clouded by considerations of individual personalities. For these reasons it can often be very difficult for any one person to move between the functions of selling and marketing, though clearly the two must be in very close touch with each other.

Question 15

New companies launching new products sometimes have no alternative to selling direct to the final consumer. This is because the established distribution organisations refuse to deal with them. The new product and company are seen as threats to the current market which is providing satisfactory profits to the established organisations it contains. This was roughly the position in which Hoover found itself when it brought the vacuum cleaner to the United Kingdom. Lacking support and facing hostility from established wholesalers and retailers Hoover took the classic route to by-pass the contemporary distribution system. It hired salesmen (women would then have been unthinkable) remunerated chiefly with commission and sent them knocking on doors to demonstrate the product in the place where the product was to be used - the home.

The Hoover cleaner was, of course, extremely successful, so much so that it is one of those products whose brand name was, for a long time, used to describe the product as a class. Biro is another example. Direct selling, however, while useful for entirely new products, becomes increasingly expensive and frustrating as the product becomes established on the market. It would be difficult now to find a household that did not possess a vacuum cleaner. Moreover as a product gets older a direct salesperson is likely to meet a rising proportion of complaints and requests to arrange repairs. Direct selling where the seller calls on the buyer and is thus at a psychological and physical disadvantage to the buyer, can never enjoy the status of a supplier whose premises are visited by the buyer and where the supplier can control the environment and conditions under which selling takes place. Consequently there will always be a tendency for a firm, which starts to introduce a product by direct selling, to move towards the established distribution channels when the product has established itself as a market success. A much more recent example of this process is double glazing and a similar movement seems likely with holiday time share schemes. The Hoover story also illustrates a further tendency for the one time product and marketing revolutionary to become ultra conservative and resistant to change when, in the course, of time, more new firms and products appear and start to threaten its established supremacy. When new designs of vacuum cleaners started to appear in the 1960s, Hoover, for many years, stuck firmly to its traditional upright models and sought to use its market power to discourage the entry of new firms and designs to the distribution networks which it was able to influence.

8
The changing business organisation

Information technology and business organisations

In this final unit we return to some of the ideas introduced at the beginning of this book and, in the light of the knowledge you have now gained, we develop them a little further.

The development of organisations in the past

The structure of business organisations is very much a product of the economic and technological conditions of the time. Early commercial ventures were organised as partnerships, often formed by small groups of people, each of whom contributed skill, knowledge or money. Frequently they involved long sea voyages for the purpose of trade. A great deal depended on the skill and integrity of the ship's master who was normally, therefore, one of the partners. The master, and frequently the first mate, were often allowed to do a certain amount of trading on their own account. The profits on this private trading were additional to any share as a partner. Often one of the financial partners would travel on the ship to accompany the master and share in making the business decisions that had to be made during the voyage. People could, and did, have shares in more than one voyage. This was a simple matter of financial prudence. To risk all one's wealth on a single voyage would be a foolhardy action - the equivalent today would be to use all one's savings to buy shares in just one company. Nevertheless each voyage was an entirely separate business venture. When the voyage was complete, the crew paid off, the cargo sold the ship returned to her owners, or sold, and the profits distributed as agreed, the partnership came to an end. If the same partners wished to engage in a new venture they would make a completely new agreement.

As industry began to develop, the partnership structure was adapted to a more long-lasting and continuous process but much early industry was fragmented with a merchant providing the main source of finance, continuity and organisation. If we ignore agriculture with its very different social and economic structure the earliest large scale industry, catering chiefly for a growing urban population, was the manufacture of woollen goods. However, the actual manufacturing processes were all carried out by individual families working in their own homes, using their own equipment and employing any additional labour needed occasionally from outside their own families. The role of the merchant was to link the processes together, to purchase the product of one and pass it to the next, finally purchasing the completed product and getting it into a condition fit for marketing. The merchant also found the market and arranged for the manufacture of products of the types and quantities that the market required. The merchant could also exercise a degree of managerial discretion, selecting people with suitable skills and known reliability to produce the more important and valuable products and setting prices for work in accordance with the state of the market and the value placed on the product of the worker and his family. The merchant might be financed solely from his own family's resources or, more often as trade developed, from a financial partnership made up of those with money they wished to put to work under the enterprise and skill of a trusted merchant. This is still the way much commerce and industry is organised in the Middle East.

Clearly the purely financial partners were taking risks when they trusted their money to the merchant but, provided the merchant was honest, the risk, in practice, was limited. If the venture fell on difficult economic times, or the organising merchant fell ill, died or lost his skills, most of the money was invested in materials - in wool products in various stages of manufacture. All these could be collected and sold if the venture had to come to an end. There was little risk of a total financial collapse in normal times. Incidentally the use of the masculine to describe this early stage of industrial development is deliberate - business was almost wholly a male preserve!

It was the coming of the factory, or in the woollen and cotton industries, the mill, that changed the nature of business, its financial risks and eventually its organisational structure. The development of factory based manufacturing was associated with the use of power driven machinery in large scale production, but even before this development there was a tendency in some trades to bring workers to a central manufacturing base because of the need to make products guaranteed to be of standard sizes and quality. Standardisation and guaranteed production levels and standards can only be achieved by effective supervision, and supervised work requires a place where workers come to work. When these requirements were combined with the use of expensive, power driven equipment there could no longer be any significant place for home based manufacturing. The actual manufacturing process now required both finance and managerial skill and both were needed in quantities beyond the resources of a single family or small group of partners. At first large partnerships were formed but the risks of financial loss were now much greater. If a firm failed there was no longer sufficient saleable stock to cushion the losses. The partners' money had been mostly used to buy equipment with little re-sale value and to pay workers' wages that could not be recovered. Large scale production brought with it much larger scale risks of losing money and a way had to be found of limiting this risk. It is not difficult to see the forces that led to factory based production financed and controlled by joint stock, limited liability companies.

This became the pattern for business organisation, in the industrial market economies, for most of the twentieth century.

Current trends of organisational change

However, by the 1980s there were signs that changes were already starting to take place. Two trends were beginning to appear. Both concern the location of business activity and both have important implications for the organisational structure of the firm

Location by function

Large firms have been accustomed to operating from many different sites for a long period. The basis for these different establishments tended to be partly historical - merged or taken over firms remained in their current sites unless and until there was good reason to re-locate - and partly to take advantage of locational advantages for production where these existed. The general pattern has been for each distinct subsidiary or division to retain its administrative functions at its main production site, with central administrative work carried out at a separate head office, usually located in London or another major commercial city. The significant change that has been taking place has been to locate as much as possible of the administrative work, with or without central managerial staffs at a single site, in an area with good communications to London and the major cities but sufficiently distant from these for the company to gain reduced land and labour costs. With computer based administration, linked by computer and modern telecommunications such as fax, the administrative centre of the organisation can be located anywhere where costs are relatively low and where there is access to the main national transport networks of rail, motorway and, increasingly, air.

Once the significance of this kind of development becomes more widely recognised we can expect to see further relocation of other functions such as production and marketing, influenced more by contemporary locational advantages and less by accidents of historical development.

Home based work

If groups of workers can be linked by telecommunications so too can individuals and their place of work, or, more accurately their work centre or centres. A growing number of people are now working from home doing work arranged and paid for by one or more firms. This process is now often termed **telecommuting**. It is at its most advanced in computer software production, where software houses can operate an international marketing service, arranging **what** to produce and then organising the production of the software by commissioning individuals or teams of software writers. The writers organise the actual production themselves within the time constraints established by their commissioning organisation.

This kind of organisation, made possible by modern information technology, is remarkably similar to the organisational structure on which the first emerging modern industry - the woollen industry - was based. The software house is the equivalent of the eighteenth century merchant who linked the producers to the market and organised the production chain. The software writers are the equivalent of the spinners and weavers who actually made the woollen cloth. Notice that the actual maker of the product under this latest version of the outwork system has regained control over the actual production process. The writer can choose when and how much to work, provided, of course there is sufficient demand for the writer's work. As in the eighteenth century, those reputed to produce the best work and able to meet contract times are generally offered more work than they can cope with while those with less favourable reputations tend to struggle to earn a steady living.

No other industry appears to have gone as far along this organisational cycle as software production but others are making some moves in this direction. Book production relies heavily on editors and designers and fewer of these now 'go to work' in the publisher's offices. More appear to be working at home, often for several publishers. It is difficult to think of any industry where at least some of its production could not be performed by people working at home.

Notice that the latest technology revolution is having a two-fold effect on the production process. On the one hand it makes it possible for many specialised, non-routine activities to be carried out by individuals in their own homes. At the same time it also makes it possible for much large scale, repetitive work to be carried out by automated machinery, cared for by very few workers. Most of these will effectively be dial watchers trained to spot anything not operating correctly and to take action to take to limit the damage caused by malfunction and breakdown. They will also contact those able to repair and replace failed equipment. These emergency service engineers are most likely to be operating from home but with communication equipment enabling them to keep in constant touch with a base which has the task of co-ordinating their work and ensuring that firms with service contracts are provided for efficiently.

The employing organisation in this kind of production system becomes essentially a co-ordinating body. Management in such a body is still concerned with taking decisions under conditions of uncertainty but the nature of the decisions is changing. In the factory based system production is largely concerned with control and discipline. There is a stock of equipment and labour which have to be adapted to the production requirements that senior management has opted for in co-operation with the marketing and purchasing functions. Adaptation, modification and, from time to time, changes in both equipment and labour are often difficult, time consuming and costly processes. Labour is frequently more troublesome and costly to change than capital (equipment). The new style organisation is likely to have fewer constraints imposed by a fixed stock of equipment and labour. Managerial success is more likely to depend on knowledge, e.g. knowing what and where equipment and labour are available, what their capabilities are and what the cost of various operations is likely to be. The knowledge must, of course, be applied and this involves co-ordination and, in many cases, persuasion. Many different operations, taking place in many different locations, will have to be brought together to satisfy the requirements of the ultimate consumer. Computer packages will, of course, help in storing, sifting and co-ordinating the information needed by managers but a great deal of human judgement will also be required, not least because decisions will still have to be made **now** to meet conditions which the manager believes will be applying in **the future**. One of the constant features of management throughout the ages remains the element of uncertainty about the future.

TEST YOUR UNDERSTANDING

1   If a significant part of future work is carried out by telecommuters what effect do you think this will have on the size and structure of the typical business organisation?
2   What do you think are likely to be the implications of a growth in telecommunicating for industrial labour relations?
3   What do you think are the implications of current business trends for education and training?

Change and the managerial functions

The unchanging elements of management

We have already noted that certain features of management do not change materially whatever happens to the structure of the organisation. It is still necessary for management to organise production, to co-ordinate purchasing and production, to engage in marketing and distribution, to organise and inspire people, to arrange and account for finance and identify those activities which are profitable and those that are not.

Moreover, management will always involve making decisions now to enable the organisation to cope with the future. Management success will still be related to success in predicting and preparing for the future and in the last resort management must always involve some form of control over people. Managerial plans can only come to fruition if managers are able to persuade people to carry out the activities envisaged in these plans. Management is the art of getting people to do the things that the manager wants them to do. Persuading a worker to work overtime or persuading a financier to provide an additional £1m finance are just two different aspects of influencing the actions of people. Influencing people is at the heart of management.

Purchasing and production

In a period of changing technology and production method it is more and more important to co-ordinate production with purchasing. Materials, design and production method are all related. New materials make possible new design which in turn makes new demands on production method. All are interrelated and the overriding need is flexibility. The factory where equipment, lay out and production method were unchanged from year to year, sometimes from decade to decade, belongs to the past and is unlikely to have a big role in the future.

There will be a premium on knowledge but not a fixed stock of knowledge. Awareness of trends and of the direction of change are becoming increasingly important. Production in a changing environment will require a flexible approach to production methods. Managers may have to avoid commitment to a fixed production system that determines what can be done for years ahead in favour perhaps of more contracting to outside firms. The tendency for large firms to contract out their support services such as cleaning, catering, machine maintenance, even arranging conferences, seems likely to spread to parts of the basic production process, all contributing to the increased emphasis, already noted, on co-ordination in place of direct control.

Marketing

The marketing function is certain to become even more important than it is today. The penalties for misreading or ignoring the future and the rewards for reading it correctly are steadily becoming greater. Remember the marketing manager must not only look into the future but interpret its implications for the organisation and assist in translating these into production plans.

Modern marketing will not be successful if it neglects the more mundane but essential work of distribution and sales. Although it is fatal to be so engrossed in the future that present distribution outlets and the people currently selling are neglected or made to feel unwanted, future distribution trends must also be examined and flexibility retained wherever possible.

Few would deny that markets are becoming more and more international. Very few products are now confined to one country only. The firm that ignores foreign markets is likely to find foreign producers eating away at its own territory. British marketing people enjoy a tremendous advantage in that English is the first language of large areas of the developed world and the second language of much of the rest. This, however, is also a disadvantage in that it encourages people to ignore foreign languages and cultures and so to miss or destroy far too many foreign marketing opportunities. The assumption that someone who can speak near perfect English must, therefore, share English attitudes, customs and priorities is a dangerous one and can lead to lost marketing opportunities.

Finance

Financial management has and always will be important. The basic objective of the business organisation is financial. If the organisation in the private sector does not meet the financial objectives of its owners it has little reason to exist. Financial markets are constantly changing and growing in complexity. Although this increases the firms need for the services of skilled specialists it also means that management cannot rely solely on outside services. The firm's own finance managers must understand the developing finance market, its opportunities and its limitations. Lack of financial skills can nullify the best efforts of marketing and production. Skilful management of finance can give the firm greater scope for development.

The major firms are still likely to retain a dominant role in financing private sector production even when more of the production process is contracted out to individuals or small firms. The eighteenth century merchant was the financier as well as the organiser of production and the modern large company is continuing this tradition. In some cases this may mean providing the equipment for use by contractors, often it means making equipment or finance available on terms that only large organisations can achieve. Very often the large firm will exercise a degree of financial supervision and management over its contractors. The dominant firm cannot afford to have its integrated production chain disrupted by the financial failure of one its links.

Personnel

Firms and their financial advisers are not always good at planning for the future. Many personnel managers are prepared to admit that their companies are not doing much planning for the effects of demographic change but are relying on their ability to 'buy themselves out of trouble'. You may think this a somewhat short-sighted attitude. Not all firms can solve a labour shortage by raising wages without doing anything to raise the total stock of trained labour. The shortage is simply re-arranged at a higher general wage and price level. To some extent it is easy to sympathise with the reluctance of firms to plan for future staffing needs. If the future is misread it is not just a machine that has to be scrapped but people whose lives and families are disrupted. Nevertheless failure to plan may put into jeopardy the careers of all the employees of the company. In this area as in others, inaction can be at least as risky and often more risky, than taking the wrong action.

In a period of rapidly developing technology and changing world patterns of production training and re-training are essential personnel functions. Here again training has two aspects. There is the traditional aspect of ensuring that workers have the skills and knowledge they need to operate as efficient employees. Perhaps even more important, however, is the need to develop positive attitudes to learning and acquiring new skills, even when this involves forgetting past knowledge and abandoning old skills. Readiness to give up a skill that may have taken some years of sacrifice and effort to acquire is one of the most difficult qualities to achieve but is just as necessary as the willingness to make new sacrifices to acquire new knowledge and skills. A readiness to absorb new ideas and learn new ways is more valuable to the modern worker than the acquisition of a stock of facts, most of which become increasingly inaccurate and irrelevant as time passes. If a work force is adaptable and flexible it is perhaps less important to make precise provision for future needs because changes can be made from existing personnel as imminent change becomes clear. On the other hand it is more probable that a personnel manager that can achieve this flexible approach will, in fact, be better than most at preparing for future change.

Managerial functions in the public sector

Although most of this unit has been directed towards organisations operating for profit in the private sector much the same developments are taking place in the public sector. We have seen earlier that there are strong pressures to force public sector managers to achieve greater benefits for the public from the scarce economic resources which they employ. Moreover, as managerial standards rise in private sector organisations, people become less tolerant of managerial inadequacies in the public sector. Workers who are employed by firms which employ modern managerial techniques to achieve a high degree of operational efficiency are not likely to accept that a hospital cannot organise an appointments system to prevent people being kept waiting for hours for routine treatment. As most of the former nationalised industries start to develop the customer service attitudes of the competitive private sector, the contrast with attitudes in the rest of the public sector becomes greater.

One of the great problems with the public sector is that procedures established to prevent abuse of public money become so restricting that they become a fruitful source of mismanagement and waste of resources. The budget system whereby finance is carefully allocated to specific purposes frequently leads to wasteful expenditure designed to use up a budget to prevent someone else taking it or to make sure that it is not reduced next year. These administrative rigidities and attitudes spread throughout the organisation and kill any attempt at flexibility and initiative.

How then can public sector management develop flexibility and foster enterprise in the sense of planning *now* to take advantage of *tomorrow's* opportunities without abandoning its attempts to protect taxpayers' money? This is probably the most important challenge facing the public sector and it involves all sectors of management, not just finance. This requires a further change of attitude. The tradition of both central and local government that financial control is an outside discipline imposed on departments by specialist financial officials has led to a kind of gamekeeper versus poacher game with some of the poachers succeeding all of the time - and all the taxpayers losing all of the time.

TEST YOUR UNDERSTANDING

4   What is meant by the statement, 'Knowledge is a flow not a stock'? What is its relevance to business management?

The social obligations of business

Comments are often made about the apparent conflict between business attitudes and social worth. Business activity is sometimes portrayed as anti-social. At one time it was fashionable to suggest that business companies should be subjected to a 'social audit' as well as a financial audit, although no one seemed very clear on the nature of the 'social objectives' to be pursued by companies or how conflicts between objectives should be resolved, e.g. if existing workers were to be guaranteed total job security and profits discouraged how were new jobs to be created?

This attitude has a long history. In the Middle Ages Christians were forbidden to trade in money and the payment of interest was condemned as the sin of usury. Churches could conduct holy wars in which warriors could amass wealth through ransom, kidnap, pillage, piracy and murder but merchants who traded goods for money were despised for their social inferiority. The belief that commerce is somehow anti-social dies hard. Many still believe it to be wrong that one person should profit from providing a service or product needed by another.

Economists are also sometimes attacked for pursuing gross national product at the expense of 'socially worthy' activities such as health and education. This criticism is a clear misunderstanding of both the national product and economists' attempts to measure the value of all activities which contribute to the living standards of the community. It also assumes that the critic's own personal judgements as to the social worth of various social benefits are shared by the rest of the community.

Fundamentally there is no basic conflict between the tenets of economists, business managers and those genuinely concerned with improvements to the social well being of the community as a whole. All are capable of errors and economists have made their fair share. One serious error has been to take a short term view of wealth creation, seeing this in terms of current benefits of goods and services without taking sufficient account of the value of the stock of physical resources available for use in the world. Unlike the earlier economic systems of hunting/gathering and agriculture, the modern industrial system so far has been based on sources of power and materials that are mostly destroyed in the process of use. Consequently the world's stock of reserve sources of future wealth are being used up at a rate which threatens the well being of future generations. In fact there is nothing really new in this. The pressure to develop coal became intense when Britain had virtually destroyed its stocks of timber. Deserts and waste lands have been created in Africa by so called subsistence economies, based on 'slash and burn' methods of clearing the land and overpopulating it with goats. The destruction of the rain forests today are the culmination of processes started many thousands of years ago and, of course the chain saw destroys more quickly than the axe.

The major concern that these processes now raise is the possibility that in burning fuel and destroying trees people may be destroying the delicate balance of their environment, setting in motion irreversible climatic changes likely to destroy the civilisations created by these processes. The creation of some forms of wealth has led to the destruction of other forms. This is indeed a challenge for the physical and the social sciences. The fact that the challenge now has to be faced cannot really be blamed on business. The blindness and greed that have led to this situation is much more deep seated in the human condition.

It is also true that some business activities are undoubtedly harmful. Rogues, tricksters, frauds and criminals of all kinds operate in business, as they do in every other occupation, including politics, the Churches, the law, academic life and farming. Reputable business people seek to cleanse their trades of these people as do the disciplinary bodies in other sectors of the community. It was once believed that public ownership would somehow remove any temptation to profit from a monopoly position. We now know that publicly owned monopolies behave pretty much in the same way as privately owned monopolies but with less efficiency. Large organisations tend to act in ways that are harmful to the public or to individual good because within them it is extremely difficult to establish any single individual who takes responsibility for any action. Everyone acts according to rules and no one admits to having the power to make or break the rules when injustice is being done. This is a problem of size rather than an inevitable consequence of business activity. Individual business people, owners, managers or workers, are kind, thoughtful, generous or cruel, thoughtless, and mean depending on their characters. The small business reflects the character of its owners for good or ill. The large organisation whether organised for business or any other purpose, has no human feelings and consequently behaves in ways that appear heartless precisely because it has no heart. There is no simple solution to this dilemma.

Nevertheless organisations, like individuals, have social obligations. There are ethical and moral codes which are as important for business managers as they are for politicians, lawyers, teachers and other members of human society. Perhaps the best safeguard is to remind all those who aspire to a successful career in business management that however high they climb on the ladder of success they remain human beings. If they betray their own humanity then they undermine the values that distinguish human civilisation from the jungle. The pursuit of profit, indeed of wealth, through the provision of goods and services that others desire is not in itself ignoble and can contribute much to the sum of human well being, but the pursuit of personal gain at the price of another's suffering is a crime against our common humanity and, if allowed to remain unchecked, threatens the existence of humanity itself.

NOTES TO QUESTIONS

Question 1

A significant movement towards work at home is likely to change our concept of the size of the firm. If the people working at home are full-time employees of a single company then the only change is one of location and the firm is able to grow larger without having to increase its investment in buildings and office equipment. The ratio of labour to capital moves in favour of labour. If, however, the practice develops along the lines of many of the home-workers working part-time, perhaps for several organisations, then these workers are forming small, owner-managed enterprises. Some may even contract others to do specific tasks or to share work if they find themselves overloaded at certain times. At this stage the firm organising the work may have very few full-time employees of its own but be supplying work to large numbers of people. By normal methods of measuring size on the basis of number of employees or amount of capital employed firms may appear to be getting smaller but the volume and value of work controlled by the organising group of firms is actually getting larger.

The structure of such firms must also change. The organising firm cannot direct and supervise work as it can when work takes place at a single site. Greater emphasis is placed on allocation and co-ordination. Payment systems are likely to be devised to encourage and reward reliability in relation both to quality and ability to meet agreed completion dates. In many ways this process simply represents a natural development of what is already normal practice for such firms as advertising agencies, correspondence colleges and book publishers. All these have to co-ordinate a range of specialised activities in order to supply the market with a completed product.

Question 2

Some of the problems that appear to be endemic in factory systems are likely to disappear. The closely supervised worker tied to a particular operation on a particular machine carrying out a process remote from the finished product could be forgiven for developing feelings of alienation against the employer and the production system of which he or she often felt more of a victim than a part. The worker who has lost control over almost the whole of the work process may feel little interest in the work performed beyond seeking the maximum possible return for the least possible sacrifice of time and effort. The individual worker at home has regained control and, within the constraints of having to achieve a desired income level, can choose how much, when and, to a great extent, how to work. Such a worker co-operates with, rather than takes orders from, the organising company. The company provides the opportunity to work and the essential entry to a product market but in turn cannot supply that market without the individual worker's or contractor's skill and co-operation. Any economic and social gulf between the two has narrowed considerably.

Nevertheless the home worker is by no means freed from all problems and frustrations. Such work requires far more self-discipline and self-organisation than simply getting up in the morning to report to office or factory. The home worker can also suffer a sense of isolation, deprived of the companionship of fellow workers and the stimulation of being part of a dynamic production system. This kind of deprivation can, in extreme cases, lead to a kind of malaise and inability to work just as crippling as the hostility to the production line, and the desire to do almost anything to stop the line found amongst some car assembly workers in the 1960s.

Telecommuting does not, therefore, solve all labour relations problems though it certainly changes them. A new kind of personnel management is required together with a greater understanding of human psychology. Some software producers have found it necessary to build in regular conferences of home based programmers in order to bring them together away from their home-working environment and provide the human communication and stimulation of which they have been starved. Other organisations developing home based production systems are likely to face similar problems and may need to incorporate a degree of work in the central base or office in order to relieve the psychological pressures on the home-workers. People do seem to need to feel part of a working community. In the eighteenth century most of the spinners and weavers lived in villages or street communities in small towns. These provided a community of people doing similar work, usually for the same merchant. Home based manufacturing was also intermingled at various stages in the year with work for local farmers. Human communication and variety were built into the system. In time, if home-working continues to develop, similar local communities may grow up and people may develop work patterns that do more to satisfy their social needs.

Trade unions will also have to adapt to changing conditions. It is much harder to bring isolated individuals into union organisations than it is to organise a factory based work force. On the other hand the isolated workers may have the greater need to make good their economic weakness as individuals by forming associations capable of concerted action in the face of exploitation.

The fundamental differences in interest between the provider of work and the worker remain in spite of a changing work structure. Each side wishes to maximise the benefits gained from work while resisting any abnormal sacrifice. Rarely are the two sides equal in economic power. The fundamental labour relations conflict or potentiality for conflict remains.

Question 3

Most observers agree that education and training are becoming increasingly important. The distinction between the two may also be getting narrower. We tend to think of education as a preparation for life and for taking our part as a full member of society. Training on the other hand was a matter of learning a set of specific skills and/or absorbing a given stock of knowledge necessary for performing certain work tasks. The more complex the work the longer and more complex the period of training likely to be necessary.

Today, however, both education and training tend to be concerned with developing personal attitudes and qualities as much as with acquiring knowledge. The stock of knowledge required for life and work is constantly changing and often too large to be within the capacity of a single individual. Modern information technology makes it possible for a great mass of information to be readily accessible for those with access to the necessary equipment and the skills to use that equipment. However, as equipment changes skills constantly have to be modified and people have to be prepared to be constantly learning. Adaptability and flexibility are essential attributes to modern work and life. These changing skills are more easily absorbed by those with a sound foundation of basic literacy and numeracy, to which many would now add, computer literacy, i.e. familiarity with and confidence in using computer keyboards and equipment and the generally accepted usages, commands etc which are now becoming standard with most software packages. As electronic equipment takes over the home this new form of literacy is becoming essential for coping with domestic equipment such as videos, disk players and so on.

Interpersonal communications are also becoming increasingly important. The old distinction between the confident, self assertive, articulate leader and the silent, acquiescent and inarticulate led is fast disappearing. As our interdependence increases, as no one can possibly master all the skills and knowledge necessary for life, most of us spend part of our time as experts in some fields and complete novices in others. Consequently there are times when we are the leaders and other times when we have to be led. At all stages we have to communicate. The better we communicate the better able we are to cope with life.

Consequently it is now commonplace to say that both education and training are becoming skill based rather than knowledge based. Without the skills we cannot gain access to and make use of the enormous stock of knowledge available to us.

Question 4

This question is a continuation of question 3 with an application to the managerial functions. Knowledge in general must always be a stock which is constantly growing but the knowledge we need as individuals at work and in life is constantly changing. There is nothing very new in this. Most of us, as children, learned how to ride a bicycle. Many of us later learned how to ride a motorcycle. A high proportion of us learned how to drive a car. As we acquired these new bits of knowledge and developed our skills we did not forget the old but, for the most part we put these on one side and concentrated on the new. So it is with much of the knowledge and skill we need at work. We may become skilled in the use of one word processing package but computer and software technology develop further and we find we have to acquire competence in a new system. Our knowledge and skills flow on. You may contrast this with an older attitude when, having learned, say, Pitman shorthand at the age of 18 some office workers based their entire working lives on the use of this skill.

The functions and techniques of business management are also constantly changing and to fulfil these new functions adequately the manager has to learn new techniques and attitudes. In their present forms financial and marketing management are developments of roughly the last quarter century. Bookkeepers became accountants who became finance directors. The changed descriptions reflect vastly changed functions from simply recording the financial operations of others to managing the financial operations of the firm and influencing a wide range of activities to promote the achievement of the firm's financial objectives. You can reflect for yourself on the functional changes represented by the transformation of the Commercial Travellers Association to the Institute of Marketing, or indeed by the evolution of the office stenographer to become the personal assistant.

You may have noticed that in the notes to questions 3 and 4 the terms 'skill' and 'knowledge' have been used almost interchangeably. This is not entirely accidental. To an increasing extent knowledge has involved the skill of gaining access to knowledge or the skill of using particular techniques to solve a problem. Is the ability to use a computer spreadsheet package to appraise an investment project skill or knowledge? Is there really any difference?

Now that you are coming to the end of this book you may be reflecting on what you yourself have gained from it. I hope you have learned something about the nature of the modern business organisation and about the changes currently taking place. I hope too that you have developed an increased interest in the functions of organisations and the people who work in them. Above all I hope you have gained a willingness to learn and to adapt and a recognition that your own need to go on learning will not cease as long as you wish to remain an active member of the human race.

Index